RICHARD PACE

BY THE SAME AUTHOR

RICHARD PACE

A TUDOR DIPLOMATIST

BY

JERVIS WEGG

BARNES & NOBLE, Inc.
New York
METHUEN & CO. Ltd
London

First published, 1932

This edition reprinted, 1971
by Barnes & Noble, Inc.
and Methuen & Co. Ltd.

Barnes & Noble ISBN 389 04150 5

Methuen ISBN 416 60730 6

Printed in the United States of America

PREFACE

MY thanks are due to the Hon. Seddon Cripps, M.A., Fellow and Bursar of Queen's College, and to Mr. Stephen Wright, B.A., Assistant Librarian of the Bodleian Library, for trying to throw more light on Richard Pace's connexion with Oxford University ; and to my friend Mr. E. C. L. Parker, of Salisbury, for sending me a useful note about Pace. Mr. St. Clair Baddeley amplified the information about Cardinal Bainbridge and his suite already in his editions of Hare's *Walks in Rome*. The Rev. Albert Tomei, of the Venerable English College at Rome, did all he could to find that Pace was more closely associated with the old English Hospice in Via Monserrato than Cardinal Gasquet disclosed in his History of the College. I have discussed points with several friends to my advantage. To all these my thanks, and to Mr. P. S. Allen for his edition of Erasmus' Letters, to which every one turns, who is interested in Erasmus' friends. My book is based on the usual authorities, and on printed records of the period.

J. W.

v

CONTENTS

LIST OF ABBREVIATIONS
IN THE FOOTNOTES

L. and P. . . . *Letters and Papers, Foreign and Domestic, Henry VIII* (the first issue of vol. i. is referred to unless otherwise stated), edited by Brewer and Gairdner, and the reissue of vol. i. by Brodie.

Cal. Ven. St. Paps. . *Calendar of State Papers and Manuscripts*, relating to English affairs, existing in the Archives and Collections of Venice, etc., edited by Rawdon Brown.

Cal. Span. St. Paps. . *Calendar of Letters, Despatches and State Papers*, etc., preserved in the Archives at Simancas and elsewhere, edited by Bergenroth.

Cal. Milan St. Paps. . *Calendar of State Papers and Manuscripts* existing in the Archives and Collections of Milan, edited by Hinds.

Ellis, *Letters* . . Henry Ellis, *Original Letters*, Illustrative of English History.

Sanuto . . . *Diarii* di Marino Sanuto, Venice, 1879.

Allen, *Opus Epist.* . P. S. Allen, *Opus Epistolarum Des. Erasmi Roterodami.*

RICHARD PACE

CHAPTER I

SCHOOL AND ITALY

BATTLES in Italy, and the deaths of emperors and popes, affected the life of Richard Pace suddenly and unexpectedly: the battles of Agnadello, Marignano, and Pavia; the deaths of Maximilian, Leo, and Adrian. Professor A. F. Pollard has pointed out that Pace's name was a two-syllable word; [1] it was written Pacey by Thomas Cromwell, Pacy by John Foxe, Pacie by Sir Richard Wingfield, Passe in one of Wolsey's instructions and by a Spanish ambassador, Paxe by Wolsey when he knew little of him, and Pacee in the French translation of a sermon printed in Paris soon after he had delivered it. He was Paseo to Margaret of Austria, and the Venetians usually called him Il Pazeo or Richardo Pazeo, or even Panzeo. Erasmus latinized his name into Pacœus, but his own translation was Paceus. Sebastian Giustinian, the Venetian ambassador, though he knew him well, turned him into Rizardo Pazoto. The scansion does not show what Shakespeare thought about the pronunciation of his name, and *King Henry VIII* was written some seventy years after his death.

Campeius : My Lord of York, was not one Doctor Pace
    In this man's place before him ? [i.e. Gardiner's]
Wolsey :   Yes, he was.
Campeius : Was he not held a learned man ?
Wolsey :   Yes, surely.
Campeius : Believe me, there's an ill opinion spread then,
    Even of yourself, lord cardinal.

---

[1] *Wolsey*, p. 21, footnote.

I

Wolsey :   How ! of me ?
Campeius : They will not stick to say you envied him,
   And fearing he would rise, he was so virtuous,
   Kept him a foreign man still ; which so griev'd him,
   That he ran mad and died.
Wolsey :   Heaven's peace be with him !
   That's Christian care enough : for living murmurers
   There's places of rebuke. He was a fool ;
   For he would needs be virtuous : that good fellow,
   If I command him, follows my appointment :
   I will have none so near else. Learn this, brother,
   We live not to be grip'd by meaner persons.[1]

    Pace was of good family, studious habits; high principles, good nature, and more than usual intelligence. He was a remarkable linguist, and a man of tremendous tenacity and great industry. To these good qualities he added a love of letters and music ; but his health was always poor, and he easily became over-excited. He turned to the service of prelates and the crown, to fill his empty pockets ; and almost the only way to success lay through the church, so by that way he had to go. Erasmus thought him born to serve the Muses rather than the state, and though a pious man he certainly had little of the priest in him.

    There seems to be no portrait of him, and no description of his appearance ; but once a Venetian ambassador came before the pope wearing a black gown trimmed with black satin ' made in the style adopted by Pace, the English ambassador ' ; and he himself came before the doge, wearing a long gown of black satin trimmed with sables. When news came to Venice, of what must have seemed to him the final humiliation of his enemy the French King at Pavia, he sported a doublet of cloth of gold, and a gold chain, like the other ambassadors. But even such dim visions of him are very rare. So we cannot visualize the man in whom the imperialists saw a possible successor to Wolsey in the King's favour, and who had such a spirit beneath his black robe of peculiar fashion that he once wrote to the emperor, Charles V,

[1] *King Henry VIII*, ii. sc. 2, line 122.

that he had come to the conclusion he had been sent into the world to be the cause of the ruin of France.[1] Francis I himself was so interested in him that he asked for a description of his person and stature. The Venetian diarist thought it worth recording when he looked pleased at some fresh news, a more common entry being that he was ill again.

It has been supposed that Pace was born in Hampshire, because it is there that he is first found, and it was to the New Forest that he retired at the end of life. He was born about 1483, the year in which Richard III came to the throne, and made his Christian name popular. *The Victoria History of Hampshire* (1908) shows that the manor of Mainsbridge *alias* Swaythling, near Southampton Water, was the subject of an action brought by a John Pace in 1501, on behalf of the Dudley family, and that it became the property of Edmund Dudley, Henry's VII notorious minister. Richard Pace's brother was named John. In November 1509, which was just when Richard Pace was for the first time engaged on public business, there was a John Pace, groom of the King's chamber.[2] The manor of Holbury, in Hampshire, was in the possession of the abbots of Beaulieu until the dissolution of the abbey, when it passed to a Thomas Pace, who was then steward to Peter Compton, the son of Sir William Compton, at Ashley and Arnewood. Thomas Pace was then possessed jointly with his wife of the manor of Cadlands or Cadland, which stretched down the shore of the Southampton Water, on the Beaulieu side, near Fawley, and of the manor of Langley. In Richard Pace's time Cadlands was in possession of the abbots of Titchfield. So there were Paces in Hampshire ; and during his madness at the end of his life Richard Pace was put in the care of the Abbot of Beaulieu, in whose diocese he held two livings, for the abbot was also Bishop of Bangor. The abbot asked Wolsey to reward a young relation of his own, who had tended Pace in his illness, by giving him the Stewardship of the estates of Sir William Compton, of which Thomas Pace is found to be Steward.[3] So we may conclude that the young relation of the abbot's was Thomas Pace, for this

[1] *Cal. Span. St. Paps.*, ii. 581. [2] *L. and P.*, i. (Reissue), 228.
[3] See p. 284.

abbot and bishop, Thomas Skevington, was himself born with the surname of Pace, apparently in Leicestershire, the son of a John Pace, but changed his name on becoming a monk. We may guess the abbot was uncle to Richard Pace, who was perhaps uncle to the young man who nursed him. One of the Leicestershire Paces, Thomas, married a girl from Southbourne, in Hampshire ; [1] he may have been Richard's brother. It is not much help to find, in Cooper's *Athenae Cantabrigienses*, that a certain John Pace of Stepney, Middlesex, was admitted to King's College, Cambridge, in 1539, at the age of seventeen, coming up from Eton, to be made a fellow in 1542, and to become the King's jester later on ; but Richard Pace was Vicar of Stepney, and very likely lived in the parish for some time just before his death, for he was buried near the high altar in the parish church in 1536. This John Pace, who became a jester, was born while Pace was in Italy, and the *D.N.B.* suggests he was the son of John Pace, Richard's brother, who was appointed customer at Lynn, Norfolk, in 1522. Such relationships seem to matter little to Pace's history.

We get some biographical details from his book *De Fructu qui ex Doctrina Percipitur*. He owed his education to Thomas Langton, Bishop of Winchester, whose secretary he became. Langton was bishop from 1493 to 1501 ; so we can roughly fix the date of Pace's pupilage, and say he went to Langton as a boy of about ten in 1493. But let us translate a page of *De Fructu* to see exactly what he wrote about his boyhood.

' And the science of music also demands her place, particularly from me, whom she distinguished when a boy, among other boys. For Thomas Langton, whose *manu-minister* I was, noticing my advance in music, far beyond my years, would pronounce and assert (being perhaps biased in my favour by his love) " This boy's talents are born for higher things." And soon afterwards (*paucos post dies*) he sent me to Italy, to Padua university, then at the top of its fame, to study Letters, and generously provided for the annual expenses, for he befriended all learned men exceedingly, and in his time was another Mœcenas, rightly remembering (as he often said), that it was for

---

[1] J. Nichols, *Hist. of the County of Leicestershire*, i. 548.

learning that he had been promoted to the rank of bishop. . . .
And he valued the Literary Humanities so highly that he provided for the teaching of them to boys and youths in his own
private school (*domestica schola*). And most of all he delighted
in hearing the boys repeat to him in the evening what they had
learned that day from the schoolmaster. And in this examination he who did well was nicely complimented, and given something he wanted. For that best of masters had always on his
lips the saying that worth thrives on praise. And if a boy seemed
dull, but willing, he did not treat it as a fault, but with kindness
urged him on, that diligence might strive with nature, quoting
the example of others who had succeeded under similar circumstances.'

It seems reasonable to suppose that this ' *domestica schola* '
of the bishop's was in Wolvesey, the bishop's castle, or palace,
at Winchester, which, Leland says, ' hemmed in ' the town walls
from the close-wall almost to the High Street. It was well
towered, and for the most part watered by an arm of the Alres-
ford river. It is less likely that the bishop's school was at
Bishops Waltham, or any other of his houses not so much a
centre as Winchester was. The King, Henry VII, had just then
revived interest in Arthurian legends concerning Winchester,
and in the city itself ; for he wished to be thought descended
from that King, after whom his eldest son was christened in the
cathedral.

It has been supposed that, after leaving Langton, Pace went
to Queen's College, Oxford ; [1] but, if he did, it could not have
been ' *paucos post dies* ' that his benefactor sent him to Padua ;
and, as Langton died in January 1501, Pace's expenses in Italy
were likely to have begun about 1498.[2] Most likely he stayed
with the bishop till then, and went straight to Padua ; for at
that moment there seemed a chance of peace in north Italy.
But it is to be remembered that students went very young to
Oxford, and he may have gone there in 1496, when he was about
thirteen years old, and then to Italy. If he did so he would have
found Langton's nephew, Christopher Bainbridge, provost of the

---

[1] J. R. Magrath, *The Queen's College*, i. 154.
[2] *English Historical Review*, xviii. 516, 1903.

college.   Bainbridge succeeded Langton himself in that position
in 1496, and later on gave Pace his first great opening to public
life.   The activities of Padua university had been almost stifled,
during the fourteen-nineties, by the wars ; but lectures were
delivered in 1498, and then it would have been worth an English
student's while to go there.   But tranquillity was not restored
till 1500, when a lull came in the wars, with the capture
of Milan by the French.

Pace's future was to be concerned with matters of world-wide
importance, and it is well to note events, which he must have
heard of, as happening during the ten years which covered his
stay at Winchester, and brought him to Italy.   The New World
was discovered, Ferdinand and Isabella crushed the Moors in
Spain, the Portuguese crept round the Cape of Good Hope, and
—most important of all to him—Charles VIII of France burst
into Italy, and overran it as far as Naples.   Less important, but
nearer home, was the rising of Perkin Warbeck, who took sanctu-
ary at Beaulieu, whose abbot received Pace, when, at the end of
life, he sought refuge, broken in health and miserable.

Pace was not rich enough to travel to Padua in anything but
the greatest discomfort.   The usual way was to cross the channel
to Calais, or a Flemish port, and go through Flanders and Liège,
up the Rhine, over the Alps by the Brenner pass, through Trent
to Verona.   Scores of penniless Flemish painters went that
route during the coming century, and on to Rome, walking all
the way, unless a lift was offered on road or river.

Italy was suffering from pestilence and famine, almost continuously at that time, as well as war.   The position there,
either at the time of Pace's arrival, or soon after it, according
to its date, was this.   The Spaniards had got possession of
Naples, the French were in Milan, and the pope had begun to
feel the difficulty of a position between the two.   So whether
to side with the Spaniards or the French was the pope's greatest
doubt during Pace's life, and Pace had at certain times to help
his holiness to make up his mind.   The other great power in
Italy was Venice, which was becoming too great, and was, therefore, to be broken or weakened.   Florence had become of little
importance politically, Ferrara was likely to fall to the pope, or to

Venice, and the lesser tyrants and towns would group themselves as might be convenient to them. The Spanish power, in
the south, came to mean the emperor, when Charles Quint came
to his own, twenty years afterwards ; and the French power,
in the north, came to mean François Premier. Besides these
two foreign foes Italy was threatened by the Turk, and there
should have been a great crusade by Christian princes ; but
there was nothing but a great deal of talk of one. Soon after
Pace arrived in Padua the French, secure in Milan, were in
alliance with Venice, which meant peace for Padua, which lay
between the two in Venetian territory. At Padua Pace learnt
to look on the Signory of Venice as a great and beautiful protector of the university, and of all that was best in the world,
and as the defence of Christendom against the Turk. He learnt
to look on the emperor Maximilian as a needy adventurer, who
might at any moment come down from the mountains on Verona
and Padua, and upset all the north of Italy for his own profit.
He learnt to fear the French King, as one who had done enough
to suggest that he had the power to lead an army, not only to
Naples, but to Constantinople, or Amsterdam for that matter,
or Scotland. He was to see the French King form the iniquitous
League of Cambrai to destroy Venice. This student learnt to
love Venice, to fear France, to dislike Maximilian. These
opinions remained with him throughout his life, and all the time
he loved England fervently, and the King of England—his
prince. It was a religion to him. He would speak of ' his
natural country,' and he loved it as a man loves his
mother.

The only authority to hand shows no English students at
Padua university between 1480 and 1500, and Pace's name is
not among those of the following years, but such lists are probably incomplete.[1] Most people remember the town of Padua
for the frescoes by Giotto and Mantegna, for Donatello's high
altar with the angel-musicians, in Il Santo, and his Gattamelata.
They were there for Pace to see, but he does not seem to have
taken this opportunity of learning to appreciate early Italian

[1] J. A. Andrich, *De Natione Anglica et Scota Juristarum Universitatis Patavinæ.*

painting and sculpture. He seems, like Erasmus, to have cared
little for any of the arts but music. Once, when on a campaign
in Provence, he wrote of the Roman remains there ; but it is
his only reference to antiquities which comes to mind, beyond
a statement that he studied ancient inscriptions in Rome.
Erasmus could appreciate painting, when the work in hand
was his own portrait.

When Padua university is mentioned, English readers think
of Lucentio's arrival there. Even the *D.N.B.*, in the article on
Pace, calls Padua a ' nursery of arts ' as he does—and we recall
the jolly jests played off in Baptista's house, but few behaved
in Padua with such freedom.   It was not a rich man's university,
and even by exercising great care it was hard for a poor student
to live there, or at Bologna—too expensive for Erasmus. As
lecturers in his time Pace mentions Leonicus, Aquila, and
Leonicenus.   Leonicus had been teaching Greek and philosophy
since 1497. He dedicated a book to Pace twenty years afterwards. For two hundred years young Englishmen had been
going to Italian universities. In *De Fructu* Pace tells us that,
when he began to apply himself to the study of literary humanities at Padua, he learnt from Cuthbert Tunstal and William
Latimer ; which suggests that they were there when he arrived,
and with them, as with Leonicus, he formed life-long friendship.
He does not tell much more about the men of his time, but a few
close to him afterwards were Padua men.   Francesco Guicciardini and Paulus Jovius, the historians, who were about his
age, studied at Padua.   Probably Gasparo Contarini, who went
to Padua in 1501, at the age of eighteen, and studied Greek
under Musurus, and philosophy under Pietro Pomponazzo, just
missed him, but they knew each other when they met.   Twenty-
five years afterwards, Leonicus had become tutor to Reginald
Pole, and was still living at Padua. He wrote to William
Latimer, that Pace, after a trying embassy at Rome, had come
back to rest his brain. He was staying with Pole, and they all
three spent their time discussing literary subjects, and those
early days, when Latimer, Tunstal, and Pace were students, and
Leonicus was lecturing.[1] In a dedication to Tunstal, of his

---

[1] Gasquet, *Cardinal Pole and his Early Friends*, p. 57.

translation of Plutarch made many years afterwards, Pace referred to their common master Nicolas Leonicus.

The university had lived for some two hundred and eighty years, and had flourished splendidly, between the wars, since the town had fallen to Venice, who sheltered and cherished it. Venice's long association with the East and Greece brought the Greek language to Venice, and it went on to Padua. In 1493 the signory had taken the lease of a great house in the centre of the town, to be the university building, and take the place of scattered lecture rooms. It had been the Ox Inn, Osteria del Bo', and from it the university got its name of ' The Bo'.' [1]

Thomas Langton died in January 1501, and, by his will made just before his death, bequeathed the sum of £10 a year for seven years to Richard Pace. He described him as his scholar studying at Bologna,[2] which shows that Pace did not stay long at Padua. Langton may have written Bologna in mistake for Padua, but Pace certainly went to Bologna ; most likely straight from Padua. Twenty years afterwards William Latimer told Erasmus, that he had had to spend six or seven years in the study of Greek ; and that Tunstal and Pace were kept longer at it than might have been expected, considering their abilities, through the ignorance and negligence of their teachers.[3] Perhaps Pace was dissatisfied with the teaching of Greek at Padua, and went on to Bologna before the autumn of 1500. In De Fructu he refers with enthusiasm to his old friend John Clerk, and says they were together once, as students in Italy, and lived in the greatest friendship, sharing everything and working together. This Clerk might have been the future Bishop of Bath and Wells, or a man of the same name, who was known as an author. The former took his M.A. degree at Cambridge in 1502, and then went to Bologna, and was back in England in 1508. Pace may not mean that John Clerk had been his boon-companion at this university, but in Italy at some other time ; and he may refer to a John Clerk, who was afterwards in Cardinal Bainbridge's service with him in Rome ; who may not

[1] C. Foligno, Padua, p. 172.
[2] Tanner, Bibl. Brit., p. 568, quoting Wharton's MS. in Lambeth library.
[3] Allen, Opus Epist., ii. 442.

have been either of the other Clerks. At Bologna Pace sat under Paulus Bombasius, reader in rhetoric, poetry, and Greek, who, in the great university hall, discussed not only books, but good manners. Pace describes an argument between them about Greek diphthongs. They met again after the university days.

In January 1504 Pace, then about twenty-one years old, delivered at Venice an oration on the study of Greek—a strange opportunity for so young a scholar—and it was printed afterwards, in Basel, by Froben. This was the unbroken Venice of Leonardo Loredano, [1]which Aldus Manutius knew, and she glowed with all that was beautiful just then. The Bellini, Carpaccio, Giorgione, Titian, Palma Vecchio, and Cima were all at work. Her builders were setting up fairy palaces, her books were bound in beauty, and even her drinking vessels brought dreams. A crowd of Venetians was a subject to inspire a great colourist, and no man who visited S. Marco came out of it unchanged. But the European powers were preparing for their tiger's spring at her.

If Pace spent all Langton's legacy in acquiring what Bologna had to offer him in the way of learning, he would have made it his headquarters till Erasmus got there in 1506, to be surprised by the approach of an army with a pope, Julius II, and his cardinals at its head. Preferring peace, Erasmus went to Florence, and stayed there, until he found he could safely return, when the pope entered the city in the middle of November. He spent a whole year there studying Greek, working on a new edition of *Adages*, on *Antibarbari*, and on other books ; and becoming great friends with Bombasius. The pope had Michelangelo over from Florence to settle a dispute between them, and to make a statue of him. Even if Pace was not still in Bologna to see Julius, the whole series of this fine old man's doings was of such importance to Italy and Europe that he must have sought a daily account of them. Alexander VI had died miserably in 1503, and after the short reign of Pius III, had been succeeded by Julius. Julius soon set about making war on the Venetians, who were supporting the tyrants in Romagna, who

[1] His portrait, by Giovanni Bellini, is in the National Gallery.

had been driven out by Cesare Borgia, but had scrambled back on Alexander's death. Julius was determined to establish the church as the greatest power in Italy, and took the field to capture Perugia and Bologna, as an earnest of an energetic policy. The people of Bologna were pleased to see him ; for they hated their tyrants, the Bentivogli, who should have been papal vicars. After Christmas Julius returned to Rome, well pleased with his expedition, as a first step against Venice, and in the re-conquest of the Romagna ; but he determined to form a league to help him to carry out the whole matter—a decision of importance to Pace's future.

In *De Fructu* Pace tells of his meeting at Ferrara with Erasmus, who had gone from Bologna to Venice, to see *Adages* through the press, and on to Padua. The emperor Maximilian had invaded Venetian territory from Tyrol, and frightened him to Ferrara. Their meeting in December 1508 is the first of which a record remains. Erasmus, writing in the previous September to Lord Mountjoy about *Adages*, which he meant to dedicate to his lordship, said he had thought of undertaking a work on the Greek authors. However, he understood that something very similar had already been begun by Richard Pace, ' a young man so well equipped with knowledge of the two literatures, as to be able by his genius alone to bring honour to England, and of such purity and modesty of character as to be worthy of your favour.' [1] This indicates a previous meeting between the two, but in a letter to Aldus, 28th October in the previous year, Erasmus did not mention Pace among the English scholars he then knew—Linacre, Grocyn, William Latimer, Tunstal [2]—which suggests that he did not know him, when he reached Bologna. Perhaps he regarded him only as ' a coming man,' a little younger than Latimer and Tunstal. The young man had evidently read diligently, wherever he had been, and was keen to become an author. Pace tells a story of Erasmus, who seems to have been his guest at Ferrara, which the latter thought to his discredit, as showing him to be something of a snob. They were talking of the interest taken by the English royal family in Learning, and Erasmus produced with pride a

[1] Allen, *Opus Epist.*, i. 445.   [2] *Ibid.* i. 438.

letter written to him in Latin by young Prince Henry, a treasure he was still carrying about with him. But it concerned the death of Philip, the young King of Castile, which only occurred in 1506 ; so Erasmus had not carried it for what should be considered a long time, in days when letters were rarer than they are now, and therefore curiosities—especially when written in Latin by princes. Erasmus was still giving copies of it twenty years afterwards. Erasmus in turn made the disclosure that at Ferrara he had entrusted to Pace the manuscript of two books of *Antibarbari*, and the draft of two others, and some other papers. Mr. P. S. Allen says that Pace entrusted these treasures to William Thale, who, when he left Ferrara, sold what he could, and gave away the rest.[1] Erasmus never recovered the bulk of them, and was continually asking if anything had been heard of them.

Seventeen years later Erasmus wrote to Celius Calcagninus, the Hebrew scholar of Ferrara, reminding him of their meeting in Pace's lodging, and asking after Leonicenus and Paniceatus, whom he met there in December 1508.[2] Calcagninus spent most of his life at Ferrara, holding a canonry in the cathedral, and a readership in the university. The Duke of Ferrara and the other members of the d'Este family were his patrons, especially Cardinal Hippolito. There is, in Calcagninus' answer to Erasmus, a reference to their conversation in Pace's lodging at Ferrara, about Aspendius the lute-player, and the use of certain terms of music, in the course of which Erasmus had whipped out from his saddle-bags his *Adages*, just printed at Venice. Erasmus referred once more in after years to meeting Pace at Ferrara, in a letter dated 1524, in which he told Richard Bere, Abbot of Glastonbury, that Pace had often mentioned him as a lover of Letters, and as one who had assisted him with money for his studies.[3] Bere went through Italy to Rome in 1503, as Henry VII's ambassador, to congratulate Pius III on his election, and he may have met Pace at Bologna. If Pace was at Ferrara for the purpose of studying at the university in 1508, this would

[1] Allen, *Opus Epist.*, i. 121.   [2] *Ibid.* vi. 77.

[3] *Desiderii Erasmi Roterodami Opera Omnia*, Leiden. P. Vander Aa. 1703, No. 700.

have been the last of the seven years, for which Langton's legacy provided. But it is possible that he had already found a patron, perhaps in one of the d'Este family. Mr. F. M. Nichols speaks of him as being there as English minister ; [1] Mr. P. S. Allen, as working under Leonicenus.[2]

This year was a rather interesting one for Ferrara ; for a son was born to the duke, Alfonso, the duchess being Lucrezia Borgia. Carnival had been very joyous ; for the duke was home from the wars, and Lucrezia, and the duke's brother, Cardinal Hippolito, were at court. It was this cardinal who had blinded his bastard brother, because a woman he lusted for had praised his eyes. Ariosto was still making poetry, but Ferrara's other poet, Ercole Strozzi, had ceased to sing. He had married a beautiful young widow, Barbara Torelli, who went to court and patronized poets. Unfortunately some mighty person, perhaps the duke, loved her, and one morning Ercole's dead body was found stabbed in many places. Some thought he had been on terms of intimacy with Lucrezia. He received the consolation of a magnificent funeral, and Calcagninus delivered a funeral oration. Pace could learn something at this court : it was unwise to fall in love with a woman without inquiring about her other lovers, and punishments were severe. Above his head as he walked by the Torre dei Leoni, lay imprisoned two of the duke's brothers, who had completed but two years of their long imprisonment, for conspiring against him and their other brother, the cardinal. Alfonso was not so great a patron of scholars and artists as his father had been, and was more intent on casting cannon ; but we have heard a good deal about his sisters, Isabella and Beatrice d'Este, who married the Marquis of Mantua and the Duke of Milan. Beatrice was dead, but Isabella visited Ferrara in this year ; and she found Pace many years afterwards, as English ambassador at Venice. Ariosto and Calcagninus were considered the jewels of the court, and there were other scholars, jurists, and medicos, but no painters of great importance.

While Erasmus and Pace were with the learned men and poets of Ferrara, the war clouds had been gathering. The

[1] *Epistles of Erasmus*, i. 100.   [2] *Opus Epist.*, i. 445, footnote.

League of Cambrai was being formed, and took shape just
before Christmas. The Venetians had driven the emperor out
of their territory ; but Louis, King of France, and the Habsburgs
were making their plans, and rather suddenly a league sprang
into existence. It consisted of the pope ; the emperor ; Louis ;
Ferdinand, King of Spain ; the archduke Charles, lord of the
Netherlands ; the Duke of Ferrara ; the Marquis of Mantua, and
smaller states, and had as its object the destruction of Venice.
It was unusual for the great Christian states to combine against
one of themselves. If they had waited they would have found
that Venice might have been left alone to decay ; for the
discovery of the sea-route to India was cutting her out of the
trade in spices, and Indian produce, and her commercial decline
was only a matter of time. This was not yet evident, and if
the Turks seemed to be ousting her from the Levant, she was
still rich and powerful. What she lost to the Turk she would
have liked to have taken in Italy on *terra firma* behind her.
She would have gone down the coast of the Adriatic, all round
the Italian seaboard, and across Italy as far as possible, past
Bologna towards Florence.

The pope might have good right to stop Venice, and the
emperor more than a little excuse for doing so, but France
always seemed an intruder in Italy, disturbing students and
quiet universities and courts. She was hated ever since Charles
VIII's expedition to Naples, as great military powers are always
feared and hated ; and Pace had heard everything said against
her and her king that could be. She was the enemy of Europe ;
she was trying to put the world in her pocket ; her soldiers
behaved brutally, and were braggarts ; she had brought back to
north Italy and France a foul disease which had hitherto been
confined to Naples, and the students of Padua hated her for it.
Sixteen years afterwards Pace was pleased with a rumour, which
said that the King of France was suffering from his own disease.
It was said that these invaders of Italy were themselves dirty,
immoral, and cruel ; they had stripped modest women naked in
the streets of Milan, and they had violated nuns. The English
hated the French as hereditary foes. They were inclined to
call every one who came from the continent a Frenchman,

meaning that they noticed in him defects somewhat similar to those which they saw in Frenchmen, but not in Englishmen. They showed some favour to the Flemings, as it was easier to understand their language, and they seemed more like Englishmen than other foreigners did, and they bought English wool, which made a great difference ; so did the Venetians, and the English favoured Venice.   They knew nothing about Venice, but saw her embodied in the three galleys she could send to England. Other foreigners thought that the English, at this time, rather overdid this hatred of France.

Hostilities began in April 1509 ; the pope excommunicated the Republic, and Louis rushed to overwhelm her. On 14th May the Venetians were routed by the French at Agnadello, and chased through the vineyards on the bank of the Adda.   Venice seemed on the brink of ruin.   Julius recovered his cities in the Romagna, and Maximilian got part of what he wanted in Venetia ; but France was the conqueror.   Pace's old university —Padua—had a bad time, for the town was taken by Maximilian, retaken by Venice, and besieged by Maximilian.   Ferrara was with the allies.

England had taken little interest in the League of Cambrai ; but between its formation, and the battle, Henry VIII had come to the throne, and his anti-French policy flung English diplomacy further than it had ever gone before.   There had been no war between England and France for quite a long time—seventeen years.   Old Henry, and some of his council, who lived on into young Henry's reign, rather favoured the policy of letting France amuse herself in Italy.   It would keep her away from England, Scotland, and Flanders, and she would find Italy difficult to rule.[1] But young Englishmen could not sleep while the King of France appeared to be a great and aggressive military power, as he did after Agnadello.   When the battle of Bosworth had put an end to civil war, England had begun to foster friendly relations with Spain ; for an alliance against France might become necessary.   Henry VII had married his eldest son to Catherine of Aragon, and, on the accession of Louis, her father had suggested to Henry VII an alliance of Spain, the emperor,

[1] *Cal. Milan St. Paps.*, i. 601.

and England against France ; [1] but Louis paid money to keep England quiet. The rumour in London after the battle was that when parliament met money would be demanded for a war against France. There was much talk of an old friendship between England and Venice, which must not be broken ; the Venetian galleys had lately been sailing to England almost annually. Such interference by England on the Continent had hitherto been confined to the affairs of France and Flanders, but now she began to play a part on the Italian stage, which had become the chief theatre of Europe. In order to get her into the part, accounts of French atrocities during the advance on Venice were circulated in England, and it was said Louis hoped to make himself supreme in Europe.

Every English adventure, every military expedition on the continent, launched by Henry VIII during Pace's active life, was aimed at France. Henry might ally himself with the pope, the emperor, or Venice ; he might enlist Swiss mercenaries ; he might try to get himself elected emperor, and Wolsey elected pope ; but it was always to check the King of France, and he had reason good enough. The ducal families of Burgundy and Austria had become united in the little Archduke Charles, at Malines ; and this new great Habsburg power was, as we know now, to become equal to the French monarchy, but it was impossible then to see what was in store. France had outgrown England ; she stretched from the Atlantic to the Mincio ; Ferrara, Mantua, and Florence followed her counsel, and she held Milan and Genoa. The English were alarmed ; France had ships, and they knew she could go down to Naples, and could hire a great fleet from Genoa. Readers of Shakespeare's plays can catch the anti-French spirit, which even survived the Spanish Armada. Englishmen talked of a renewal of the old struggle. The little Habsburg at Malines would have to defeat the French King very decisively, before they could feel sure that France would not become master of the world. When they knew so much as that, England would turn her strength in other directions ; but until then her sons would regard the French King as their natural and hereditary foe. The Wars of the Roses, and the

---

[1] *Cal. Span. St. Paps.*, i. 167, 188, 357.

prudence of Henry VII, had kept the English armies very much at home. For a time Italy being the scene of every prince's adventure, the pope and Venice became important in every contest ; for the one was powerful in south Italy, and the other in the north. Neither bred men to fight on land ; and Spain was more powerful in the south than the pope was ; and whoever held Milan was more powerful on land in the north than Venice was. Even before Agnadello was fought Venice had gone to Henry VII for help and sympathy ; and his son was glad to enter European politics.

Christopher Bainbridge had been created cardinal in 1508, but his creation had not been published,[1] and he had been elected Archbishop of York. So he had planned to wait in England for the coronation and marriage of the King to Catherine of Aragon, and then to go to Rome, to procure the publication of the creation, and receive the confirmation of the election. He seemed just the man to represent the King in Rome, his chief duty being to assist in forming a league round the pope, which would drive the French out of Italy—a holy league for the protection of the church. He was to begin by reconciling the pope and Venice. He seemed extraordinary well-chosen for this embassy ; for he had a great affection for Venice, and was imbued with a deadly hatred of the King of France. The importance of the mission demanded that he should be supported by an efficient staff, and a fine train of servants ; so Richard Pace, who had spent some eight or ten years in Italy, was made his secretary. The chance for which the young man had been hoping had come, thanks to Agnadello.

[1] Raynaldus, *Annales Ecclesiastici*, xi. 523 and 593.

2

CHAPTER II

JULIUS AND BAINBRIDGE

BAINBRIDGE'S party encountered bad weather on their journey through Italy, and found fighting between the armies of Venice and Ferrara. The state of war had become sufficiently bad to drive Pace from Ferrara, if he had not gone earlier in the year. He may have joined the Archbishop at Ferrara, or on the road to Rome, or at Rome. Mr. P. S. Allen makes him go to study under Bombasius at Bologna, after being at Ferrara ; but Langton's will seems to prove an earlier residence there. Anthony à Wood and other authorities suggest that he returned to England after his studies were completed in Italy, and proceeded to Oxford (perhaps for the second time), to Queen's College, and the *D.N.B.* follows them in this. His name is found among Oxford men,[1] and there is evidence that he was at Queen's ;[2] but there is no trace of a journey to England between December 1508 and September 1509. He had, perhaps, planned a return to England, and Erasmus had hoped he would carry *Antibarbari*, and the other books, to some place of safety this side the Alps, when he himself was going to Rome. Then, perhaps, being suddenly called to Rome, Pace changed his plans, and left the books with Thale.

Bainbridge was Langton's nephew, and he was born at Hilton, near Appleby, in Westmorland, which was his uncle's birthplace. He had been prebendary of Salisbury while Langton was bishop, and had succeeded him as provost of Queen's. Perhaps Pace had been at Queen's while he was provost ; at

---

[1] Joseph Foster, *Alumni Oxonienses* (1892).
[2] J. R. Magrath, *The Queen's College*, i. 286.

any rate Bainbridge must have heard well of his uncle's protégé, and have seen him if he came home. Bainbridge had been his uncle's executor, and later on he was to ask Pace to discharge this office for him.

Bainbridge entered Rome with a regular cavalcade on 24th November (1509), and was received, according to custom, by the cardinals, the officers of the papal court, and the ambassadors—orators, as they were called in Rome—of the several powers. The Romans had been expecting him for some days, and were glad to see him. The Venetian ambassadors, who had come to Rome to conciliate the pope, were not with the others, as they would have liked to have been, to honour the King of England's representative ; because the papal ex-communication hung heavily over them, and they were anxious not to displease his holiness.[1] They had been in Rome for four months, six of them, until one died ; for the most part confined to their lodging, and treated as if they were lepers. The pope absolved one to make him clean enough to enter his holy presence, and carry his orders to the rest. They sent a secretary to explain their position to Bainbridge, who received him with great favour, and assured him of his King's goodwill towards Venice.

Bainbridge was now about forty-five years old, and a rich man. The chronicler, Hall, says : ' This was a wise man and of a joly courage.' Perhaps he was ambitious, but the most apparent trait in his character was an undying opposition to French schemes of aggrandizement ; the chief defect in him being his inability to hide or control his anger. Some of the compilers of the older biographical dictionaries have confused this Christopher with Christopher Urswick, who was a henchman of Henry VII in the time of his troubles. His commission, dated 24th September, made him ambassador, proctor, agent, etc., in the court of Rome, for all business of the King, and his subjects, and all other proxies were revoked by it.[2] He was chosen partly for his great wealth, for it would cost a fortune to cut a good figure in Rome for long, among the cardinals and archbishops, and partly because he had planned to go to Rome

[1] *Cal. Ven. St. Paps.*, ii. 21. [2] *L. and P.*, i. (Reissue), 96.

in any case, on private business. If he conducted the young King's business skilfully, he might succeed Richard Fox as chief counsellor when he came home : he was not too old for that, but Wolsey seemed to be rising. It all depended on his coming back a cardinal, and perhaps legate *a latere* ; for one empowered by Rome was still great in England. The emperor thought he would return to England as soon as he was made a cardinal.[1] Young Pace was lucky to be in his service.

John Clerk had been appointed Bainbridge's chaplain, and William Burbank his steward. The latter seems to have met Erasmus in Rome in 1509, and, if so, he must have been there before Bainbridge arrived. Perhaps he went on ahead to prepare his house for him. Cardinal Adrian, who had been English ambassador at Rome at one time, had given the King his magnificent new house, the Palazzo Giraud (now Torlonia), on the Piazza Scossacavalli, in the Borgo, built in Renaissance style, within a bowshot of St. Peter's. It is possible that the new ambassador and his suite lived there ;[2] but it is more likely that they went to the English hospital of St. Thomas, on the site where the English college now stands, in Via Monserrato, or to one of the houses belonging to it, and near it. That neighbourhood was recognized as an English quarter, and the hospital was frequently, if not generally, the residence of the English ambassadors to the pope.[3] Close by were the Campo dei Fiore, and the new Via Giula, then the finest street in Rome. Anyway, Bainbridge was made custos or guardian of the Brotherhood of the hospital soon after his arrival—an appointment which had fallen into the King of England's hands. Being too busy to see to them himself, he handed over the duties of the office to a deputy. Probably Bainbridge moved house more than once during his stay, and he would always try to be close to St. Peter's, the Vatican, the hospital of St. Thomas, and Sta. Maria del Popolo, a church much used during the rebuilding of St. Peter's. Bainbridge's mission was to be a long one ; as it turned out, it ended only with his death, five years later ; and

[1] *L. and P.*, i. (Reissue), No. 669.   [2] Hare, *Walks in Rome.*
[3] Gasquet, *The History of the Venerable English College, Rome*, p. 46.

he was to cut a good figure in honour of his King. Rome was to be taught that Henry was now a great power in Europe.

At once he began to negotiate between the pope and the Venetians, who, on their part, pointed out how splendid it would be if young Henry joined a league with them, the pope, the emperor, and the King of Spain ; and conquered France, as the fifth English King of his name had done. It would have been a glorious deed, but France was not as she had been. The Signory sent injunctions to their ambassadors to impress on Bainbridge the love and goodwill Venice bore his King ; and his holiness at once treated the new ambassador as a man of importance, apart from his representative character. He added him to a court he had made—of Cardinal Caraffa and Cardinal Riario—to hear what the Venetians had to say. So successful was Bainbridge that, on Sunday 24th February (1510), the papal censures on Venice were removed, with impressive ceremony, in the presence of the cardinals, and a great number of prelates, and of the English, French, and Spanish ambassadors, in the porch of St. Peter's Church. Paris de Grassis, the master of ceremonies in the papal court, had searched the records for the proper procedure in such cases, and found it varied. It sometimes went to the extent of tapping, with rods, on the shoulders of the penitents—sometimes stripped—in which the cardinals joined. He submitted that a few strokes by the pope himself would on this occasion serve a useful purpose ; but his holiness preferred to modify this part of the ceremony, if the emissaries first begged for forgiveness, and kissed the toe. The pope imposed a visit to the seven basilicas, as a penance, and then pronounced absolution.[1] So the League of Cambrai was broken up. It was considered that Bainbridge had done much to further this matter, and afterwards he, and Pace, his secretary, were always spoken of by the Venetians as their friends. Pace had done some useful work, and on 1st May this young man, who has not hitherto appeared to be an ecclesiastic, was made prebendary of North Muskham, in Southwell ; a mark of favour for his share in a difficult piece of negotiation.[2] Julius had been influenced to take Venice back into favour,

[1] Raynaldus, *Annales Ecclesiastici*, xi. 547.   [2] Le Neve, *Fasti*, iii.

more by his desire to enrol her against the French, whom he had begun to fear and wish out of Italy, than by Bainbridge's arguments, but the Venetians felt he had assisted in turning the scale in their favour, and they thanked him. The pope had received a letter from Henry in favour of the Venetians, two days before the absolution took place, and, although the details of the ceremony were already arranged, the Signory could scarcely deny that the King had done what he could for them. Their ambassadors in Rome had it from the pope himself, that Henry had assured him that he would not league himself with any one, Christian or infidel, if the Venetians were not included in the treaty. The pope determined to reward Henry for his share in the negotiations, and at Easter sent him the golden rose, the emblem he presented to the King he most relied on. It was borne through the streets to Bainbridge's house by a train of the papal guard, the ambassadors of France, Venice, Florence, and Ferrara, and was taken to England by Christopher Fisher, clerk to the sacred college. Paris de Grassis says, in his *Diary*, that Bainbridge had to return thanks to the pope, and sacred college, for this honour done to his King, and that he broke down in his speech, and had to quit the consistory in confusion. This is the first hint that all Rome did not think this priest a tower of strength.

By this time Pace had got through his first winter in Rome, and should have acquired some knowledge of the city. Along the Borgo he would have come to what was left of old St. Peter's, and the first portion of the new basilica. The Vatican beside it was being rebuilt in part, and decorated by great painters. There was to be seen painting by Perugino, Botticelli, Ghirlandaio, Cosimo Rosselli, Melozzo da Forli, Filippino Lippi, Signorelli, and Piero di Cosimo, but connoisseurs were talking more of young Raphael, new come from Florence, and Michelangelo. *The Laocoön* and other groups, and inscribed tablets, had been unearthed ; and Pace could see them arranged in rows in the Belvedere. To live in Rome—even to visit Rome— was the desire of every cultured Christian. Erasmus, who had recently left it, said a river of Lethe alone could quench his regret, when he thought of the climate, the landscape, the libraries, the walks, and the conversations he had left behind. Pace should have met some old friends, and made new ones among scholars. Ariosto and Calcagninus came as the Duke of Ferrara's ambassadors to the pope. Baldassare Castiglione came from the Marquis of Mantua, and Alberto Pio from the emperor.[1] The musician in him must have loved to listen to the choirs and organs in the basilicas, and the hundred churches and monasteries. He tells us that during this sojourn in Rome he read much in the Vatican library, partly in books on music ; and that it was William Latimer who suggested the study to him. It had not reached the point he desired when he was called away.[2] He knew Stokesley in Rome, a keen student of Greek, who was afterwards Bishop of London, when he was still Dean of St. Paul's, but a dying man. The spring of 1510 seems to have been a merry one, preluding war. Francesco Maria, Duke of Urbino, had married Leonora, Isabella d'Este's daughter, and they were the centre of festivities at carnival. Young Federico, of Mantua, Leonora's brother, was riding through the streets, in white and gold brocade, and a cap of purple velvet. He was being held by the pope, on behalf of Venice, as a hostage for his father, the Marquis of Mantua. Luther was in Rome in 1510 and said : ' If there is a Hell, then is Rome built upon it.'

The French ambassadors had done their best to prevent any reconciliation between the pope and the Venetians, knowing that it would be the first step towards hostilities against their King ; for Julius' fear of the French was increasing, and the English ambassador missed no opportunity to keep him in such a frame of mind. The pope's plans were bound to mature slowly, and be made secretly ; for there were no less than five French cardinals, and he was reluctant to take any steps which might lead to an open breach. By the time of the raising of the excommunication, he and Venice could be counted firm friends, and it seemed as if it was he who was the most keen

---

[1] We seem to have a portrait of Alberto Pio in the National Gallery, painted at this time, and perhaps one of Ariosto. Castiglione's is in the Louvre.
[2] *De Fructu*, p. 34.

of any on forming an alliance against France. There was great suspicion as to Henry's attitude with regard to France, in spite of the old enmity between the two nations, and Bainbridge was in a difficult position. Many in Italy foresaw Henry would suddenly enter an alliance with Louis to get over some temporary difficulty. The French in Italy knew what was coming, their only doubt was how far Henry would go in defence of the church, as he was pleased to describe any adventure on which he might embark. Such was his excuse for preparing for war. His choice of a churchman as his negotiator in Rome was therefore a wise one—indeed, Sir Thomas More was perhaps the only layman who could have been sent. England had made an alliance with the Scots, and Bainbridge, in an interview with the pope at which the Spanish ambassador was present, suggested that the pope and Venice should come into it against the French. The pope seemed agreeable. Bainbridge was always hostile to France, even when his King was not. There had been a rumour in Rome, at the end of February, that England and France had made peace. Bainbridge declared he had no news of it, and suggested it was spread by the French. The news was premature ; but in the middle of April more news reached Rome to the like effect. This time it was true, but Bainbridge said he had no knowledge of it—so the Venetian ambassador reported to the doge ; he went out hunting to escape questions, and as if he was ashamed. The French could now invade Italy. Bainbridge was being kept in the dark about what was going on between England and France ; as happened to him again later on. In truth, the pope, Venice, and Henry were all equally anxious to turn the French out of Italy, but Bainbridge was too ready to commit Henry prematurely. One of the Venetian ambassadors dined with the pope, and talked things over with Bainbridge, who said he thought Louis would not come into Italy that year (1510), and there would be neither peace nor war between England and France. He was getting impatient with Henry. Up to 12th April he had heard nothing from his government about the treaty with France, which had been signed on 23rd March, but letters reached Rome from France with the news that it was being proclaimed there. On this the French cardinals in Rome went to the pope, and asked for rejoicings and bonfires, and wanted Mass at the altar of S. Louis. The pope gave consent, but they had the temerity to invite Bainbridge to officiate. Bainbridge, like Julius, like Henry, and Wolsey, was apt to fly into a passion, and this was one of the occasions on which he did so. He declined even to attend the Mass, declaring he had heard nothing from home about this league. The French cardinals made their bonfires, and the Romans were much impressed. Julius and Bainbridge must have been shaking with rage as they looked through their windows at the glowing sky ; and the firework displays, which the latter made before his house, could not have been an expression of his delight at the news. Somewhat unfairly the pope blamed Bainbridge for what Henry had done, and when he protested that he knew nothing about it, cried : ' You [the English] are all villains.' Even the official confirmation of the news, that the treaty had been signed, did not shake Bainbridge's faith, that, if Louis invaded Italy, Henry would side with the pope. It was only in September that he was ordered to obtain the pope's confirmation of the treaty. The French regarded Bainbridge's influence at the Vatican as a menace to their peace with England, and watched the roads for his dispatches ; so he had to resort to devices, such as hiding them in the covers of books. The warlike Julius would have liked support from Henry, but his zeal for his kingdom made that of Venice seem sufficient, and he was sure to be in the field before long.

Hostilities in Italy began over the affairs of Ferrara, which Julius was so anxious to capture, that its duke was forced to keep in league with France, lying as he did between the pope and Venice. Papal diplomacy had a way of leaving one of the Italian states out of a league, and so driving it into alliance with a foreign enemy ! Ferrara became an outpost of France. Julius ordered the duke to relinquish hostilities against his ally, Venice, and on his refusal excommunicated him, according to his custom. The five French cardinals fled from Rome to the French camp, in Lombardy, as might have been expected. Then, in the middle of August, this vigorous old man started with his court to Bologna, while the army commanded by the Duke of Urbino, Francesco Maria, made for the Po, to co-operate with Venice against Ferrara. Just then appeared a comet in the northern sky, in the direction of Bologna ; human limbs fell from nowhere ; Tiber rose and, towards Ferrara, armed hosts were seen in the sky ; guns were heard, and trumpets, and shouts of men, which caused much surprise in Rome. According to plans, the Venetians and the Swiss were to attack Milan, and there was to be a rising against the French in Genoa. It was quite likely that Ferrara would be crushed, and the French driven from Italy, before succour reached them ; for they were not very strong. Genoa did not rise, but Julius reached Bologna, where he found intense dissatisfaction, among the inhabitants, with the rule of his legate, Cardinal Alidosi. He became very ill, and it was then that he grew the beard we see in Raphael's portraits of him.[1] Down to the city came the French army under Chaumont, and the disgust with Alidosi made it unlikely that the pope would be able to hold the town. Alidosi was known to be pro-French ; so the presence of Bainbridge, famous for his hostility to France, was a great comfort to old Julius. Guicciardini tells us that the ambassadors of the emperor, the King of Spain, and the King of England pointed out to the pope how great Alidosi's tyranny and oppression had been. On the advice of the cardinals and of the ambassadors, Julius opened negotiations with the French commander, who withdrew three miles from Bologna. Next morning the secretaries of the ambassadors went out to him quite unexpectedly —Pace, as we may suppose, being the English ambassador's secretary. A little later, after this preliminary discussion, the ambassadors themselves went out to the enemy, and they went backwards and forwards for some time ; but reinforcements suddenly arrived to the pope from Venice and the French withdrew. The French commander said he withdrew at the entreaty of the ambassadors, and to give the pope time to think over the offers he had made, and to give himself time to consult his King. Some said [2] he withdrew not at the en-

[1] There is one in the National Gallery.
[2] See footnote, p. 126, Guicciardini, vol. v. of 1763 (English) edition.

treaties, but at the menaces of the English ambassador, who
protested, in a haughty manner, that if the French did not
depart out of the dominions of the church, the peace between
France and England would be considered as violated. The
Venetian senate received letters showing that Bainbridge had
been to the pope, and suggested a league between him, Henry,
and the Signory, by which the pope and Venice were to bring
2000 men-at-arms and 10,000 infantry into the field. Henry
would attack France, and suggested that James of Scotland
(with whom he had made a treaty) would make a good commander for Venice, who always hired a general. The pope
told Bainbridge, so say the letters, that he could not do his
share, and Bainbridge spoke to the Venetian ambassador about
it, adding other very secret clauses.[1] Plans for such an alliance
against France were always in Bainbridge's head ; and he
brought them out in conversations with the pope and his
cardinals, and the Venetian, Spanish, and German ambassadors,
whenever he saw a favourable opportunity. He was constantly
tempering them to suit the situation. Just before Christmas
the small town of Concordia fell to the pope, and in the new
year he had himself carried in a litter, over the snow to the
army, while he was in a condition in which even a younger
man might have been thought to be nearing death. He joined
the Duke of Urbino before Mirandola, an outpost of Ferrara,
and took it on 20th January. He wanted to go at once against
Ferrara, and part of the army went on to Finale, under the Duke
of Urbino ; but there was great want of everything, and he
went back to Bologna for reinforcements and supplies. A
peace conference was held at Mantua at the suggestion of
Isabella d'Este, at which were the ambassadors of France,
England, Spain, and the emperor, but nothing came of it.
Margaret of Austria, the regent of the Netherlands, had complained to Henry that Bainbridge had favoured the Venetians,
contrary to the League of Cambrai, when the other ambassadors
were trying to bring about peace between the pope and France.
She asked Henry to order him to attend the peace conference
at Mantua, to bring such a thing about. Her interest in the

[1] *Cal. Ven. St. Paps.*, ii. 90.

matter was that her father, the emperor, wanted towns round Verona, which the Venetians claimed, and she wrote to Henry at his command.[1] This Englishman, whose King was at peace with France, was taking an active part in Julius' army. His secretary and pupil, Pace, was to find himself in a similar position later on.

From Bologna the pope went to Ravenna (10th March), where he created eight cardinals, none of whom were French, to restore his authority in the *curia*. One was an Englishman, one a Swiss, and the other six Italians. The Englishman was Bainbridge, and the Swiss was Mathew Schiner, Bishop of Sion, or Zitten. Bainbridge took his title from the church of S. Prassede, but he was usually called the English Cardinal, or the Cardinal of York. His creation had really been in 1508, publication being delayed.[2] His title was originally to have been from SS. Pietro e Marcellino, and it was sometimes used for him. These anti-French creations were much disliked by the other cardinals. It was supposed that Bainbridge was created to induce Henry to enter the league against France, or to reward the recipient for his efforts already made for the league ; but it is possible the pope felt he had a strong man devoted to him in the irascible Englishman. As senior cardinal made on this occasion, he had to thank the dean of the sacred college for their congratulations ; but he broke down, as once before, and, what was worse, spoke directly contrary to instructions given him by the master of ceremonies. Such a failure is worth noting, because an unreliable public speaker needs a scholarly secretary to help him prepare his speeches. Julius after this, in consistory (8th April), made Bainbridge legate with the army against Ferrara, and something more than legate, for he was to command. The report to the Signory, concerning this appointment, said that it was ' a big thing that an Englishman should hold this post, and he is very Italian.' The other cardinals escorted him according to custom to the gates of Ravenna, when he set out to join the troops.

When Louis was satisfied that he had nothing to fear from England, he sent reinforcements to his army in Italy ; and Trivulzio,

---

[1] *L. and P.*, i. (Reissue), 681.   [2] Raynaldus, xi. 523.

who had succeeded to the command, was able to help the Duke of Ferrara. The papal army was suffering from lack of everything, and wanted to fight and get it over. Bainbridge found it lying round La Bastia, a strong fortress on the Po, Finale, Bondeno, and Massa. A legate was a remarkable figure in a camp, and his position was not always a happy one. Giovanni de' Medici was afterwards legate in the army defeated at Ravenna, and he was among the prisoners taken by the French. The Venetian ambassador reported that the pope and the English cardinal had great hopes of taking La Bastia. The latter, in armour, was seen by Venetians on several roads round Ferrara, but he found the enemy too strong for him, and raised the siege, and withdrew to Cento.[1]

From Ravenna Julius went back to Bologna for Easter, entering it on horseback like a young soldier, but with a long beard ; and the people cheered. In May the successes of the French in the Romagna, which the exertions of the English cardinal could not stop, caused the pope to retire again to Ravenna, leaving the unpopular Cardinal Alidosi in charge of Bologna. When the French approached the town the people rose, nor would the Duke of Urbino, whose army was close by, do much for the town's deliverance, and it fell to the French (23rd May)—a terrible blow to Julius. This was said to have been due to Alidosi's treachery, but he tried to throw the blame on the Duke of Urbino.

Bainbridge had emulated the old pope's conduct ; he had led an attack on a bastion in full armour, and this, too, at a time when it was said that the cardinals, and all the papal court, were enervated and demoralized by their luxurious life in Rome. No wonder he was in the favour of a pope who, when half dead, would exhibit more energy than any of his court ; and at Mirandola had planted artillery and caused himself to be carried through the breach at the head of his troops. A cannon-ball hit his lodging, and he changed it, but returned when the same thing happened to the new one ; he had the cannon-ball sent to Loretto as a votive offering. A terrible scene was enacted almost under the pope's window, near

---

[1] Sanuto, xii. cols. 125-6.

S. Vitali, in Ravenna. The Duke of Urbino struck Cardinal
Alidosi dead for his treachery at Bologna. This so upset the
pope that he set out next day to Rome, and on the way heard
that Louis was summoning a general council at Pisa for September ; a threat to his spiritual authority. The French King
seemed to grasp at all power. Julius reached Rome 27th June,
and his answer to the council of Pisa was the council assembled
at the Lateran in the spring 1512.

After the French had taken Bologna, they went from one
success to another in Romagna. The papal army fell back, and
Bainbridge returned to Rome, to make fresh plans for a holy
league. For a year he had stuck to his object ; he had resorted
to every expedient to stir up trouble for the French. A Greek
statue had been found near Cardinal Caraffa's house, and Caraffa
had set it up, not far from the English hospital, and had dressed
it on feast days, as the people of Brussels dressed up their
menneken. It came to be called Pasquino, and wits affixed
verses, lampoons, epigrams, and jibes to it ; and there was much
food for jests in Rome at the time. Pasquino could say in safety
what would have broken a man. Caraffa died in 1511, and, on
his return to Rome, Bainbridge became Pasquino's patron, and
the statue began to indulge in jests against the French. Some
thought the new cardinal abused the licence accorded to Pasquino, and a Frenchman hung to the statue :

> Je suis Pasquin le malhereux
>   Dextra tombe es mains dangloys
> Yaymesse mieulx extre forieux
>   Et tomber en mains des franczoys.[1]

Perhaps Bainbridge's witty secretary wrote some of Pasquino's lines. He called him Master Pasquyll. Bainbridge
ceased to be guardian of the English Hospice on becoming a
cardinal, and Pace was appointed in his stead,[2] having perhaps
come back to Rome in the spring to attend to business while
the cardinal was in the field. He may have gone to the wars
with Bainbridge, and returned with him when the papal army
broke up. Anyway he was now back again, to associate with

---

[1] E. Rodocanachi, *Rome au temps de Jules II et de Léon*, x. 158.
[2] Gasquet, *History of the Venerable English College, Rome*, p. 50.

scholars and students, after a long course of prelates and soldiers. In February 1512 Erasmus, in writing to Dr. Thomas Halsey, the penitentiary of the English nation at Rome, who was a friend of Bainbridge's, sent his compliments to Pace. He begged him to take care of the books he had entrusted to him at Ferrara. He complained that he had written six letters to Halsey, and had received no answer, beyond one letter from Pace.[1] Very likely Pace and Halsey had been students together at Bologna. It seems as if the English residents met so often in the hospital of St. Thomas that even those who did not live in it had letters addressed to them there.

When the papal court got back to Rome, a consistory was held, and after it the pope wrote letters to Ferdinand of Spain, Henry, and Maximilian protesting against the seizing of Bologna by the French. It was just at this time that Bainbridge was annoyed by the affair of Jerome Bonvisi, whom the pope had sent to England to stir Henry against France. The chroniclers Hall and Polydore Vergil tell us about him. He lived in good style, resorting to court and council there, to deal with the pope's affairs ; but he was a traitor and at night resorted to the lodging of the French ambassadors in London, and revealed to them what was being planned between the pope and Henry against France. Fortunately Henry got to know what was going on, and Bonvisi was surprised in conversation with one of the French ambassadors on London Wall, at midnight, and taken to the Tower. Bonvisi seems to have stated that he was set on to what he had done by Cardinal Alidosi, a known friend of France.

On 2nd August the pope and Bainbridge went with a small retinue to Ostia, and stayed there until 7th, riding back by way of Viterbo ; a jaunt for enjoyment and health, and perhaps to inspect fortifications. At that moment Julius was sending a ship to England for tin, for the roof of St. Peter's, and he sent Henry a present of parmesan cheese, and barrels of wine.[2]

Just after the pope returned from Ostia, he invited Bainbridge to meet the Venetian and Spanish ambassadors at dinner, to talk over plans against France, and Bainbridge held out

[1] *L. and P.*, i. (Reissue), 1053.   [2] Sanuto, xii. col. 362.

hopes that Henry would break his league with France. The pope and the ambassadors were close to an agreement when the old pope became terribly ill, and on 23rd August Cardinal de' Medici announced that he could not live through the night. Preparations were made to hold a conclave, and it was expected in Rome that its choice would rest on one of the French cardinals ; for it seemed impossible to form a strong league, or to drive the French out of Italy without a league, and many thought that under the circumstances it would be well to yield them all power. On 24th the pope received the Holy Viaticum and on 25th he was worse. He had eaten nothing for several days, but now it seemed so certain he would die, that his physicians allowed him to have anything he fancied to eat. He ate some peaches and plums, and drank some Malmsey. He slept and woke up much better, and by 28th was able to attend to business.[1] After his illness he redoubled the energy with which he had set about forming the league.

There was great coming and going at the Vatican ; and at length on 4th October the Holy League was signed by the pope, the Spanish ambassador, and the Venetian ambassador, places being left for Henry and Maximilian. The league was stated to have as its object the abolition of the schismatic council of Pisa, the recapture of Bologna, and the rest of the territory of the church. It seems as if Bainbridge satisfied the contracting parties that Henry was certain to ratify the treaty, and it was published next day in Sta. Maria del Popolo in the presence of his holiness and the cardinals. Henry ratified it on 13th November, thus making his first overt move in European politics ; but his marriage with Catherine of Aragon, and his participation in breaking up the League of Cambrai, had shown his hand to be against France. Julius excommunicated the French armies, and the French cardinals, who were holding the council of Pisa, which was withdrawn to Milan, in French hands. When hostilities began in Italy it was clear it was they which would settle the disputes, and not the schismatic council ; so this challenge to the pope's spiritual authority came to nothing. The plan of the allies was for King Ferdinand to

[1] Pastor, *History of the Popes*, vi. 370.

attack France from the south, and Henry from the north. The Swiss were to enter Lombardy to co-operate with the papal and Spanish army in Italy, under the Viceroy of Naples, Raymond de Cardona. The allies, with Cardinal Giovanni de' Medici as legate, were concentrated round Imola, at Christmas 1511, and began operations at the end of January 1512 by laying siege to Bologna. In February they took Brescia, and were threatening Milan, when Gaston de Foix [1] came by forced marches through the snow to Modena and Finale. He relieved Bologna, re-took Brescia, and at the end of March led his army to join the Duke of Ferrara, and then to Ravenna. He forced battle on the papal and Spanish army on 11th April, Easter Day, and won a glorious and famous victory.

As soon as the news of the disaster reached Rome the cardinals met in great anxiety, expecting the French to march on Rome, and set up a pope of their own choosing. They feared their throats would be cut, and Rome sacked. Even Julius talked of flight, or reconciliation with France.[2] He wanted Gonsalvo de Cordova sent for, and Bainbridge cheered him with assurances that the English invasion of France had already begun ; [3] a co-operation which always drew the French out of Italy. When Julius talked in consistory of peace, it was Ferdinand's ambassador and Bainbridge (according to Guicciardini) who there and then, in the names of their sovereigns, most strongly urged him against France. But this rather dramatic scene was thought by some to have been ' put up ' between the three of them. However, the death of Gaston robbed the French of the advantages their victory should have given them, and the pope's Swiss mercenaries appeared from the alpine passes. The French could not get reinforcements, while their country was likely to be invaded from England and Spain. They never consolidated their successes in Italy, and were liable to be swept across the Alps with the suddenness with which they came down again next time. They simply worried and impoverished the country. It was not until 21st

---

[1] There is supposed to be a portrait of him by Giorgione in the National Gallery.
[2] Pastor, vi. 401.   [3] Sanuto, xiv. col. 185.

3

May that Henry's ratification of the treaty arrived. The pope entered the Lateran Council, and, after Mass and sermon, Henry's letter of 13th November was read, announcing his adhesion to the league, and there were great rejoicings in Rome. In his letter Henry described France as a ' tyrant.' [1] Proclamation was made at S. Marco, at Venice, that the doge had received notice that Henry had joined the league, ' the entire conclusion having been negotiated by the Right Reverend Lord Christopher of York, Cardinal of England.' [2]

The Lateran Council opened in less than a month after Ravenna. Its objects were to settle accounts with Louis, to deal with church reform, and to plan measures against the Turks. A hitch had occurred with regard to Henry's representatives at the council. He had appointed special ambassadors, who were about to depart, when news of Ravenna reached England. He kept them back, and appointed Silvester Giglis, Bishop of Worcester, and Sir Robert Wingfield, his ambassador with the emperor; the former being then in Rome, and the latter half-way there. He wrote to Bainbridge that the disaster to his allies had not turned him from the alliance. He spoke of the French as the foes, not only of the church, but of all Christians, and the slaughter of Ravenna would have to be avenged. He had entered a treaty with the King of Spain, supplementary to that made at Rome, for a joint expedition against Guienne. The hostilities between England and France spread over two years. An English force went to Fontarabia in June 1512—that is to say just about the time the news of Ravenna reached England—to co-operate with Ferdinand against Guienne ; but everything went wrong, and, when Ferdinand had got all he wanted, he made peace with France. The English were so ashamed of the disaster that they were glad to let great power fall into Wolsey's able hands, hoping to do better next time. On 22nd June the pope heard of the defeat of the French by the Swiss, and there was great rejoicing. The French were soon scuttling out of Italy. Genoa and Milan threw off the French yoke, the council of Pisa retired to France, and the Duke of Urbino recovered Bologna. The Holy League had done its work,

[1] *Cal. Ven. St. Paps.*, ii. 165.   [2] *Ibid.* ii. 163.

and Italy was clear of French for the first time since Pace had been in the country. Another peace conference at Mantua put Maximilian Sforza in Milan, and the Medici in Florence, now purged of the French and their influence. It was desirable to get the emperor, Maximilian, into the league, and Mathew Lang, Cardinal of Gurk, came to Rome from him in November. He was received almost like a king by the pope, his cardinals, and the Romans. Maximilian's difficulties were really with Venice, and to get his friendship the pope abandoned her, although she must have been the stronger of the two. It was always difficult to get the emperor and Venice into the same alliance, and of the two the former was at this time the best ally for the pope ; for his friendship facilitated the entry of Swiss into Italy, and they were still under contract to serve him as infantry. On 25th November the entry of Maximilian and Sforza into the league was publicly proclaimed, in Sta. Maria del Popolo, in the presence of the pope and fifteen cardinals. Bainbridge sang Mass,[1] but it was thought on the lagoons that he had opposed an agreement which left out Venice. The doge wrote to tell the Venetian ambassador in England how grateful the Signory was for the prudent and becoming way in which he had so often acted.[2] He could not have been entirely opposed to the admission of Maximilian to the pope's league, but he always thought of the good of Venice, who would now be forced to join the French. By this new treaty the pope was to invade France from Italy, the emperor from Germany and Flanders, and Henry from Calais ; and a large army of Swiss was to be recruited.

When the league against France was formed and hostilities began there was not much for Bainbridge to do in the papal court. The object of his mission was accomplished, and he might have returned home. But he had gone out as much on his own business as on that of Henry, and he wanted to stay in Rome. Henry and Wolsey were employing Silvester Giglis, Bishop of Worcester, in their affairs, and Wolsey did not like Bainbridge, but it was difficult to deprive him of the status of King's ambassador, while he stayed in Rome, and it was difficult to recall him. Wolsey did not want him in England

[1] Sanuto, xv. col. 375.   [2] *Cal. Ven. St. Paps.*, ii. 208.

for several reasons, one being that the pope might send him as legate *a latere*. He was ill, and though he still tried to help Venice his work was less interesting. This change of fortune saw him into the reign of a new pope, who had not Julius' love for him. The new actor on the stage, Dr. Silvester Giglis, although an Italian not resident in England, had been rewarded for services, according to custom, with an English bishopric.

CHAPTER III

LEO AND BAINBRIDGE

A T the end of the year 1512 old Julius could have congratulated himself on the results of his schemes and his warfare; for the temporal power of the church was greatly increased. But Spain had got too strong a hold on the south of Italy; and would get a hold on the north of it, too, when the twelve-year-old Archduke Charles, at Malines, inherited the possessions of both Ferdinand and Maximilian, his grandfathers. Ten years after Julius' death, when Pace was leaving Rome to perfect another league against France, he told a Venetian, Marco Foscari, ' Had pope Julius chosen, he could have expelled the French from Italy, and subsequently steps might have been taken for the expulsion of the Spaniards likewise. Thus should the signory do.' [1] This opinion may be misleading, for Julius did ' choose ' to turn the French out, but could not finally rid Italy of them. It shows, however, that Pace, when a ripe diplomatist, felt that, between Julius' death and 1524, there was no one in Italy who had a better chance of doing so. When Cardinal Grimani referred to the Spanish power in Naples, Julius cried ' If God grants me life I will free the Neopolitans from the yoke which is now on their necks.' [2]

On the eve of Pentecost 1512 the pope had felt so weak that he had told the master of ceremonies he would not again take part in long functions, but on the eve of St. John Baptist he made a pilgrimage to his titular church of S. Pietro in Vincoli, which brought on an attack of fever. He went down to Ostia in November ; came back better, and could attend meetings of

---

[1] *Cal. Ven. St. Paps.*, iii. 809.
[2] Pastor, *History of the Popes*, vi. 430.

the Lateran Council. He was obviously ill at Christmas ; and, after it, was unable to leave his bed, but continued to receive the cardinals. By 4th February it was realized that he was dying, and there was great excitement in the city. Bainbridge was admitted to see him on the 15th and, according to the current report, came out with the story that his holiness' tongue had swollen. On 20th Julius received the Sacrament, and the cardinals were summoned to his bedside. He died that night. His obsequies lasted a week, and unusually large crowds of people came to his lying-in-state in St. Peter's.

Twenty-five cardinals, including Bainbridge, entered the conclave held on the second floor of the Vatican, made famous by Raphael's frescoes. There was some delay about getting to work, because the cardinals were reluctant to hold the first scrutiny on a day on which there was an eclipse of the sun. The French party in the city, led by the Orsini, tried to stir up trouble, and the election of a French pope would have led to a schism, but the absence of the French cardinals, who had held the schismatic council of Pisa, minimized the danger. The most active influence in the conclave was that of the young cardinals, and before dawn on 11th March their candidate, Cardinal Giovanni de' Medici, was elected. They came out of conclave looking very pleased, but a Venetian thought Cardinal St. George and Cardinal Bainbridge looked very much out of temper.[1] De' Medici was certain to be reluctant to continue the wars against France, unless the existence of the papal power was threatened. He took the title of Leo, but Alberto Pio thought there was more of the lamb than the lion in him. He was placed in the pontifical chair and carried into St. Peter's, accompanied by the whole conclave and the ecclesiastics of Rome, and was enthroned before the high altar. He was only thirty-eight, and the Romans were surprised that one so young should be elected. They shouted ' Palle, palle ! ' in allusion to the balls in the Medici coat-of-arms. He was a kindly, gentle person, and very popular everywhere ; but he was not as strong as Julius. He was crowned on the steps of St. Peter's on 19th March. It was customary for the pope, on

[1] Sanuto, xvi. col. 39, 40.

the day of his coronation, to grant all the cardinals demanded ; but Leo was surprised at the multitude and nature of the demands of these cardinals. ' Take my tiara,' he said laughing, ' and then you can, as popes, grant all you think fit.'

On 11th April, the anniversary of Ravenna, at which, when papal legate with the army, he had been captured by the French, he went in procession to St. John Lateran. The streets were gaily decorated and strewn with flowers, and the procession through Rome was said to be the most magnificent since the days of the emperors.[1] The cardinals were ordered to ride, not on white horses as usual, but on mules. Some, however, insisted on riding horses, and those who were poor horsemen were much distressed when a cannon was fired. Leo rode the white horse which had carried him at Ravenna. The procession started from the Vatican, and at the church of St. John Lateran Leo received the insignia of his great office ; in the chapel of S. Silvestro the nobility kissed his toe, and at the hall of Constantine he took possession of the estates of the church. There he remained till the evening, when he returned to the Vatican. The houses were lighted up at night and the people shouted ' Palle, palle, Medici ! ' through the streets. The Duke of Ferrara was present at these ceremonies, no longer fearing the pope, and so was the Duke of Urbino, hoping Leo would not disturb him in his duchy.

While these ceremonies were occupying Rome, Venice made a treaty with France, as her isolated position in Italy was sure to make her do ; and Leo, Maximilian, Henry, and Ferdinand entered a fresh league, at Malines, for an attack on France. But the pope meant to do nothing. Ferdinand made a secret truce with France, and Maximilian served for English pay, with which he was to get help from the Swiss. With his congratulatory letter to Leo on his election, Henry sent Bainbridge an assurance that he looked for great things from his expedition to Picardy. But Leo was a man of peace, and was going to trim to whichever side might suit his turn. He soon wearied of Bainbridge's assertions, that his King was waging war against Francis in defence of the church. Leo loved music—perhaps

[1] Pastor, vii. 26, etc.

understood it better than any other man of his time—and Pace thought he would have rightly been made pope for that alone. He greatly improved the choirs in the Vatican and the churches, but hunting was the only pleasure he shared with Bainbridge, and Bainbridge's hunting was perhaps fiercer than his. When he rode he sought to escape a little from his own holiness, by wearing such boots that none could kiss his toe. He filled the Vatican with poets, writers, and dilettanti. He called Lascaris and Musurus to Rome for their Greek. Any scholar was then welcome at the wealthy Angelo Colocci's villa on the Quirinal, and in John Goritz's wine-garden near Trajan's forum. Amateurs bought pieces of sculpture, and paid for paintings by Raphael. To Rome came Bernardo Dovizi, known as Bibbiena, who had been Leo's tutor.

Leo showed his desire for peace by a *volte face* with regard to France, in the sixth session of the Lateran Council, opened on the 27th April 1513. He suggested that the French cardinals, who had been excommunicated by Julius for their adherence to the council of Pisa, should be allowed to make submission. This was enough to make Julius turn in his grave, and was strongly opposed by Bainbridge, Mathew Schiner, and the ambassadors of Maximilian and Ferdinand. Leo won his point, and they were called to Rome, and made submission before the pope in consistory, in the Vatican ; but Bainbridge and Schiner refused to be present, for Henry was at the moment preparing to invade France, alleging that he did so in the church's service. Louis invaded Italy again in May, in co-operation with the Venetians ; but was heavily defeated by Maximilian Sforza, and the Swiss, at Novara on 6th June, and again driven out. Leo had told his master of ceremonies that he had no wish to be in opposition to the King of France, and so the political situation in Italy had been entirely reversed by Julius' death.[1] When on the evening of 10th news came of this victory, Leo did not dare do otherwise than rejoice, in the presence of Bainbridge, and have guns fired at S. Angelo ; but he did not seem full of the joy which would have animated Julius. Yet this defeat of the French put an end to the schism

[1] M. de Bréquiny, *Notice du Journal de Paris de Grassis*, p. 580.

they had created, and about that he, as pope, was sure to care. When news came in September of the English victories in Picardy, Bainbridge and Alberto Pio, Maximilian's ambassador, caused High Mass to be sung at Sta. Maria del Popolo, at which were four other cardinals, and the ambassadors of Spain and Milan ; and they made bonfires. The pope said the news was very likely untrue, for he had found both English and French news unreliable.

The first letter to Pace, which has been noted with the State Papers, is from Brian Tuke, clerk to the signet, from Tournai ; and tells him about Flodden and the victories in Picardy. It is dated 22nd September,[1] and soon afterwards begins a series of his own letters to Henry and Wolsey, covering the whole of his life in the King's service. They are in Latin or English, and nearly always partly or wholly in cipher. His writing is described as the usual English court-hand of the period. It is at this time also that his name begins to appear often in Erasmus' letters. Ammonius, Henry's secretary for the Latin correspondence, received letters from him, addressed to Erasmus, and forwarded them with a covering letter. Erasmus wrote to Ammonius, 21st December : ' You are philosophical in your letter about the Muses and riches, and our friend Pace seems to me to forget his scholarship, and to assume a style more agreeable to Midas than the Muses. . . . I learn from Pace's letter that you have written an account of the Scottish battle [Flodden]. . . . I am very glad Pace likes you. He is made up of affection and honesty. . . . Please, in your next letter to Pace, ask him to let you know what has happened about my books, which I left at Ferrara. I am suspicious of his silence ; not that I have any doubt of his good faith, but I fear something may have happened to my commentaries, which neither of us would like.'[2] His manuscript might have been stolen and published by the thief.

When news of Flodden reached Rome, Bainbridge wanted a Mass of thanksgiving, but the master of ceremonies ruled that such a ceremony was not usual in the event of a victory by one Christian state over another. Bainbridge went off in a huff to the pope, who, on hearing what de Grassis had said, replied,

[1] *L. and P.*, i. (Reissue), 2290.　　[2] Allen, *Opus Epist.*, i. 543, seq.

laughing, that he wondered as much as Bainbridge did at his objections.[1] So the service was held in Sta. Maria del Popolo, and five cardinals friendly to Henry and many people attended, and Bainbridge sang Mass. Julius had issued a bull of excommunication against James, who believed it to be Bainbridge's doing, and Leo had actually found it in his heart to confirm it ; but he tried to keep James quiet. Bainbridge got the blame or credit for most moves made against the French and England's other enemies. Leo wrote a letter of congratulation to Henry, and urged him to a crusade. Meanwhile his desire for peace with Louis had been growing. It arose from his reluctance to be at war, and was increased by his fear of the growing power of the Spaniards in Naples. The result was a reconciliation on 6th November, that is to say, about the time that Henry's campaign in France was finished. The treaty was read in the Lateran Council on 17th December.

Negotiations for peace between England and France had been begun in Rome by the pope and Giglis, but were soon withdrawn to England. Bainbridge's position in Rome had suffered something of an eclipse in 1513, for two reasons. The artistic, lazy, Medici pope did not like the vigorous English cardinal—hunter and fighter—as Julius had done ; and, in the second place, Wolsey was relying on Giglis to represent him, not only in the Lateran Council, but in many matters in Rome. On 10th May we find Giglis writing to Wolsey, that he had presented the King's letter to the pope, and had spoken to the datary about Wolsey's wish for a dispensation to hold three benefices at once. They were unwilling to grant it, but he had pressed it, and Wolsey would hear the latest news by the letters of Cardinal Bainbridge, who had been very ill. The illness of Bainbridge, which continued until his death, though he was soon a little better, accounts to some extent for the employment of Giglis in English affairs ; but he seems to have been employed by the King, Wolsey, and even the Queen, behind Bainbridge's back, on private matters, as in the case just mentioned. On 13th May Giglis wrote to Queen Catherine about six chaplains for

[1] Raynaldus, xii. 27.

whom she wanted favour from the pope. Leo had much of the dilettante's indolence, but a great deal of business was done at the Vatican. It was difficult to get past the Swiss guards. Even important prelates had to wait four or five hours to see cardinal Giulio de' Medici, who was his cousin's prime minister, and perhaps six more to see his holiness.

As long before this as 20th March 1512, in Julius' time, during the war against France, the consistory had approved and sealed a papal brief, depriving the excommunicated King of France of that title, and of the title of Most Christian King, and conferring them both on Henry and his heirs.[1] The brief was not meant to be published until Henry had conquered France ; and not then if Louis had become reconciled to the pope. At the beginning of 1513, in spite of the fact that the expedition to Guienne had been a disaster, Bainbridge had pressed the pope to issue this bull ; and, after much discussion, consistory decided to entrust it to the cardinal of Sinigaglia. After Henry's successes in Picardy, Sinigaglia handed it to Bainbridge, but Leo, on his accession, delayed confirming it, to see which way the wind was blowing. After he had become reconciled with France no more was heard of it. In June 1513 Leo put Bainbridge and Schiner, with six other cardinals, on a committee of the Lateran Council, to plan the reform of the *curiae*. This shows that he wanted to keep these two pugnacious fellows quiet, or else there was less for them to do. At that time they were waylaying his holiness, to warn him that they were opposed to, and would have nothing to do with, the reinstatement of the schismatic pro-French cardinals. All this was very worrying for this pope of peace, who reminded Bainbridge that he was bound by an oath to promote the peace of Christendom. Bainbridge shows his feelings, in a letter written to Henry, 12th September, with regard to his new position in Rome. He complained that Cardinal Adrian, who was very active in bringing about the reconciliation of the pro-French schismatic cardinals, managed to get his news through first, by bribing secretaries. The first news of Henry's victories, over the so-called enemies of the church, had actually reached the pope and Bainbridge, through

[1] *Archivio della Reale Società Romana di Storia Patria*, xix. 427.

the Florentine ambassador, which was very humiliating for
Henry's representative in Rome, but he still bubbled over with
patriotism.   He wished he had been with the English army in
France, he wrote to Wolsey.   A conclave and the Lateran
Council decided on a war against the Turk, which was a project
after Leo's heart—peace between Christians and a crusade.   He
suggested sending Bainbridge as legate *a latere* to England to
plan it,[1] but Henry wanted no legate in England, or rather we
may suppose, in the light of subsequent events, Wolsey did not
want one.   The pope would rather have sent Bainbridge than
any one else—anything to get rid of him from Rome.   It was
Giglis who got the pope to send Henry the sword and cap, which
he had blessed on Christmas eve.   The pope handed them
formally to Giglis on St. John's day, in the presence of cardinals
and ambassadors ; and caused them to be carried in procession
to the sound of trumpets to his house, which was more than the
usual custom.[2]   The letters of the next few months suggest there
was little of national importance for the King's emissaries to do
in Rome.   It seems as if Giglis could have done it all, but he
joined in several letters with Bainbridge and Cardinal Adrian,
whose position in Rome in relation to Henry at this moment is
obscure.   We find Giglis, Bainbridge, and Adrian trying in vain
to get the annates on Lincoln diminished for Wolsey's benefit.
Bainbridge did friendly service between Henry and the Marquis
of Mantua, who thereupon wished to send the King some of the
best of his famous horses.   The marquis, like the Duke of Milan,
and the signory, was turning towards Henry, on account of his
victories in Picardy, in the expectation that he would make war
again in the spring.   Giglis was very industrious, and was
evidently doing all he could to win Wolsey's favour.   Then
comes a curious letter, dated 20th May 1514, in which Bainbridge
told Henry that some people in Rome, who ought to be devoted
to him, were not so.   Giglis' secretary had been encountered on
a dark night, coming from the French ambassador's house, with
a torch borne behind him.   The shortest way to Giglis' house
lay past that of Bainbridge, but this night-walker went ' by a
secret back lane.'   This naturally aroused Bainbridge's sus-

[1] *L. and P.*, i. (Reissue), 2353, 2512, 2517.   [2] *Ibid.* 2530.

picions, especially as Giglis was frequently in the French ambassador's company, in ' vynes and garthynges ' (vineyards and gardens) outside Rome, by day and night—Bainbridge's friends had told him this. Giglis saw more of the French ambassador than of any one else in Rome. Bainbridge felt Giglis had tried to discount the news of the English victories, and Julius had warned him against him.[1] Peace negotiations were going on between England and France, and Bainbridge did not like them ; much preferring that the Cardinal of Sion should work the Swiss up against France. Henry was not answering his letters, and the matter of the new title for Henry had petered out without his hearing about it.

But there is something which does not appear in this letter that had an important bearing on his ability to transact business. He was for a time without the services of his secretary, Richard Pace. At some time in the spring of 1514, if not before, Pace left Italy and returned to England ; probably sent by Bainbridge, to transact some business, having the isolation of France as its object. The pope, the Duke of Milan, the Swiss, Maximilian, and Henry were all anxious as to what the French were planning. The best thing, from the English point of view, would be the formation of a fresh league ; Henry's part being to pay Swiss mercenaries, and perhaps the emperor, to do the fighting necessary to stop the French coming down through the passes to attack Milan. The French had been defeated in Italy by the Swiss, and in France by the English. The fear in England was that Louis might get hold of the Swiss first. It was usually impossible to enlist them without getting their diet to enter a treaty to provide an army *en bloc*, but sometimes a few cantons would break away from the decision, or the indecision, of the diet. The pope was sending the cap and sword to Henry by Leonardo Spinelli. It had been handed to Giglis on St. John's day, but so inclement had been the weather afterwards, that Spinelli waited in Rome till March, and arrived in London in the middle of May. We may surmise that Pace for the same reasons did not arrive much earlier, unless he had

[1] Ellis, *Letters*, Series II, i. 226.

started in the autumn.[1] Perhaps he came home with Spinelli. That he was usually resident in Rome at that time, and came to England some time after Christmas, seems probable from the fact that, in the middle of the following June, there were letters from Erasmus following him about, as if he had come from Rome to some unknown address in England, and the only way to find him was to send them to Ammonius, the King's secretary for Italian affairs. In 1513 he was succeeded as Guardian of the English Hospice by Dr. Thomas Halsey, which looks as if he was in Rome, but planning to depart.[2] Mr. P. S. Allen suggests that a letter of Erasmus may show that he was in England by 21st December 1513.[3] On the 6th April 1514 he was given the prebend of Bugthorpe, in succession to Wolsey. He wrote De Fructu in 1516–17, and, in the dedication, spoke of an incident which occurred in England ' some two years ' previously. This seems to place the incident in his 1514 visit, rather than in his 1515 one, for his recollection would have been clear that it did not take place during his last stay there. ' When about two years ago I had come home from Rome, being at a feast, when the wine was in, one of the party, I don't know who he was . . . began to talk of his children,' and emphasized the importance of a good education. To him made answer one of those who were described as well born, and who always carried a horn hanging on their backs ; as if they expected to hunt even at meals, says Pace. This sportsman poured contempt on the study of Letters, for the little reward it brought. All the learned men were poor, even Erasmus, as he had heard. He said he would rather his son hanged himself than studied Letters. ' It better becomes the sons of gentlemen to blow the horn properly, to hunt with skill, to teach and manage the falcon. Truly the study of Letters should be left to the sons of yokels.' Pace could hold himself in no longer, and broke out in defence of Letters. ' You do not perceive that, if there came to our King from abroad such a man as princes make ambassadors, and an answer had to be

---

[1] L. and P., i. (Reissue), 2530, 2688, 2929.
[2] Gasquet, History of the Venerable English College, Rome, p. 50.
[3] Opus. Epist., i. 546, footnote.

given him, your son, educated as you propose, would only blow his horn, and the peasant's son would read the answer. Your son should be a huntsman or a falconer.' The squire looked round in surprise, and asked who it was who spoke thus. When they whispered Pace's name, he tried to hide his confusion in the wine-cup, and changed the subject.[1] So Bacchus saved Pace from a talker, not Apollo who had saved Horace. This anecdote reveals to us that Pace was devoting himself to the service of the State ; looking at everything from the point of view of a civil servant, and that, although so rarely in England, he had a reputation for learning and good sayings. In Castiglione's *Courtier* we find ' They think the worst reproach you can address to any one is to call him a clerk.' Judging from his later disapproval of hostility offered to clerks, we may suppose Pace thought no laymen should interfere in ecclesiastical affairs. He thought it the duty of the nobility and gentry to serve the King, and saw that an ignorant laity might drop out of the affairs of State, which were properly their concern.

We seem to get another hint about this visit of Pace's to England, in a letter written by Sir Thomas More,[2] who says that Erasmus, when in England, lived with Colet, Warham, Mountjoy, Tunstal, Pace, and Grocyn. Erasmus left England on 8th July of this year, after a long visit, and did not return. But these scholars were apt to write down lists of names a visit to England or Rome suggested—the names of scholars at the moment associated in their minds with the place—and they did not always mean they had actually seen them. It seems that Pace got to know More at this time, for he certainly knew him well on his next return to England. He found that Wolsey's influence was getting greater every day, and that he was getting the credit for having organized the last successful military expedition in France. He should have realized that Bainbridge was the only other Englishman, who was a cardinal, or within sight of becoming legate *a latere*.

Among the Swiss at the moment was Mathew Schiner, Cardinal of Sion, recently from Rome, influencing them to an

---

[1] *De Fructu*, 15. [2] Froude's *Erasmus* (1894), 136.

alliance against France. While Pace was in England, ambassadors arrived from Zurich,[1] to confer with the King's council. Ultimately William Ringt, doctor of law, and Pace, who is now described as secretary for the Latin and Greek tongues to the King—which he was not—and sometimes as protonotary at the apostolic court, returned with them to Switzerland to negotiate.[2] Ringt was probably Ryng, and connected with the merchant firm who were to find the money needed. Henry's letters commissioning these two are dated 10th May 1514.[3] It was on 20th that Pace was made Archdeacon of Dorset.

The Swiss had made an enormous reputation at the battles of Morat and Nancy, forty years before this, and had maintained it in spite of some desertions. At this time they were at the service of the highest bidder. They had been persuaded by Schiner to enter a five years' treaty with Julius in March 1510. A treaty with the Swiss was always one to supply footsoldiers for pay, and was likely to get all of them or none. The Helvetic diet had wisely come to the conclusion that it was wasteful for such good soldiers to fight on opposite sides. Schiner had well earned his red hat, for, when the Swiss came down, they, with the Venetians, had cleared Italy of French. There were no better infantry. A decision of the diet would send the whole nation to fight for a prince ; it was a matter of persuading—buying—the magistrates of the towns, the deputies to the diet, and the military leaders. Nearly up to this time Cardinal Schiner had wielded an enormous influence over them, and he still had their ear. He spent his life struggling against French predominance. He was known as 'the great priest' of the Swiss. He had been with them in battle on a Spanish jennet. He was Bainbridge's friend, who had received the red hat on the same day as he had, and who had several times stood with him against the French influence in consistory. Not even

---

[1] *Die Eidgenossischen Abschiede*, iii. 807 : and Gisi. *Der Antheil der Eidgenossen an der Europäischen Politik*, 1512–16 : and Büchi, *Korr von Schiner*, i. 318.

[2] *Die Berner-Chronik* des Valerius Anshelm, published by Historischen Verein des Kantons Bern, iv. 12.

[3] *Die Berner-Chronik. Ibid.*, p. 14.

Bainbridge hated the French more than he did ; he hated the French and he hated friars, but apart from this unreason in him he was a fine man, virile and honourable, devout and conducting himself well in all things, but passionate—again like Bainbridge. He must have known Pace well in Rome. Now any prince who wanted to hold Italy knew he must hold Milan, which he could not do without the Swiss. They had invaded France in conjunction with Maximilian and Henry, in the autumn of 1513, and reached Dijon, where they made peace for a promise of money, because Maximilian had not sent their pay. In the year we have now reached, 1514, the prize was again Milan ; and the treaty between Julius and the Swiss had been put to an end by the former's death. It had not been universally popular ; Schiner was sometimes blamed for it, and all money he had promised had not come punctually from Rome. But this discontent with the pope was outweighed by disgust with Louis, who had not paid the money promised at Dijon. One could never quite tell whom the diet would support, or rather members of the diet bartered their services to raise their price. In March 1514 Schiner had told Wolsey he was trying to keep the Swiss out of an alliance with France ; and he was communicating with Bainbridge in Rome, hoping to form a new treaty between Leo and the Swiss. They should be kept for the pope, or for the King of England, if he would pay them. Leo did not like making war, but he was less reluctant to send money to make the Swiss fight for the church. Henry could not do better, as a soi-disant defender of the church, than enlist the Swiss in her service, and he had still a good deal of his father's money.

Ringt and Pace reached Zurich on 12th June. With them were three other ambassadors, and they were shown more honour by the Swiss than had ever been shown to ambassadors ; double the usual quantity of wine was given them. On 20th they met the Diet and mentioned what sums Henry would pay the mercenaries ; and the haggling began. The usual method of the Swiss was to appear to be on the point of serving some one else—on this occasion the King of France. This was Pace's first experience of such dealings, and of the shifty conduct of

4

the impecunious emperor. Wolsey's plan was for English and Swiss to invade France simultaneously, as they had done in the previous year, and it was only for similar usefulness that Maximilian was likely to receive anything from Henry. Therefore the negotiations at Zurich were to be kept secret : indeed such negotiations were usually carried out by secret agents. Again, it might be useful to get the Swiss to serve the emperor in the field against France, even if France and England were at peace. One could never tell what might be wanted. Anyway they could be paid to watch the Alpine passes, without compromising any one. In point of fact negotiations for peace, between Henry and Louis, were going on in London ; and these negotiations at Zurich were only to put England in a safe position in the event of there being war ; or more likely still, to prevent Louis making a treaty with the Swiss, which could keep them quiet while he took Milan. Louis meant to go into Italy again, and the betting in Rome showed he was expected before the summer was out, but at times he found it difficult to raise enough good infantry in France, and he might want some Swiss. Before any decision of the Diet was reached came news for Pace. On 23rd July Dr. William Knight wrote to Wolsey from Berne that, on the previous day, the Cardinal of Sion had received letters from Rome, announcing Bainbridge's death, and he had requested him to recommend him to Henry for the vacant archbishopric of York. Knight thought Wolsey would gain the Swiss if he gained this cardinal. On 29th July Galeazzo Visconti, a Milanese *condottiere*, who was the commander the Swiss soldiers liked to serve under, and who acted as representative of the Sforza interests, wrote Maximilian Sforza, Duke of Milan, from Switzerland, that Ringt and Pace were then expected at Berne. So Pace could not have been with his old master at the time of his death.[1] Articles were at last drawn up at Zurich, and the treaty was signed at Berne on the last day of July, and the English ambassadors were pleased with themselves. While the Swiss were in the field Henry was to pay 40,000 Rhine gulden a month. Into the league were to come the pope and the emperor, who were the

---

[1] Büchi, *Korr, etc., des Kard. Schiner*, Band i. p. 539.

ostensible principals. The ambassadors left Berne on 6th August.

The first sign of Pace in Rome, after Bainbridge's death, is a reference to him in a letter written by Burbank, Bainbridge's steward, at the end of the month. Perhaps he left the Swiss before his colleagues did. During Pace's absence Polydore Vergil was in Rome, working Cardinal Adrian up to get Wolsey made cardinal.[1] Adrian said that, if Wolsey was influential with the King, it would be well to make him cardinal. Bainbridge seems to have been sinking more and more into the background, during Pace's absence, and to have become almost unregarded in Rome. He was very ill in June, and an English bishop was expected to take his place as ambassador, which is strange, as Giglis was already doing his work, but the relative positions of the English representatives in Rome is by no means clear. During his illness—perhaps just before it—a rumour said England and France had come to terms, and this must have distressed him and made him unpopular, for it would have set Louis free to invade Italy again. The treaty was actually signed on 12th August. Just before his death he said, ' This affliction I am suffering for my country, and the honour of my beloved King.' On 14th July Cardinal Giulio de' Medici, who had become Henry's protector at the papal court, announced his death to Henry. When Pace got back he found that in the ambassador's household, and all over Rome, it was being said that Bainbridge had been murdered. He got the idea into his head from what Burbank, the steward, and John Clerk, the chaplain, told him, and as he, with Burbank, was the late cardinal's executor, he took the matter up at great personal risk. The pope ordered the body to be opened, and the doctors found the right side of the heart in an unexpected condition. A priest of little standing, named Rinaldo of Modena, who had been in Bainbridge's household for many years,[2] and was his chamberlain, was suspected of having given poison, mainly because he had been much in the deceased's chamber. It was

---

[1] *L. and P.*, i. (Reissue), 2932.
[2] *Ibid.* i. (Reissue). A number of letters written from Rome at this time.

guessed that there was a powerful person behind him—who but
Dr. Silvester Giglis, Bishop of Worcester ? It was notorious in
Rome that Bainbridge and he had been enemies. Some people
in Rome made a different accusation, saying that the murder
had been committed by Bainbridge's cook, at the instigation
of some prelate in England. It is very pleasing to read that
Pace and Burbank told such people ' that prelates of England
and English-born were never disposed to such acts.' [1] This
statement by these two suspicious executors must clear Wolsey,
who was admitted to be hand-in-glove with Giglis, and who
stepped into Bainbridge's shoes, and certainly profited by his
death at a critical point in his career. But the limitation of
Pace's trust in prelates of England to those who were English-
born was meant to exclude Giglis, and Rinaldo had been in
Giglis' service. There was not a good spirit among the prelates
in Rome. As for the horror of poisoning among the English,
it may be remembered that when the Bishop of Rochester's
cook caused the death of some persons by poison in London,
a special Act of Parliament was passed to make it legal to boil
him alive. The pope ordered the arrest of Rinaldo, and he was
put in the Castle of S. Angelo, and examined in Burbank's
presence, by a court presided over by the auditor of the chamber.
He confessed nothing, beyond acknowledging that he had made
Giglis privy to Bainbridge's secrets. He was evidently told the
nature of the accusation against himself and Giglis. He was
then put to the torture and confessed nothing, and Burbank
started to England with the archbishop's household by way of
Florence. The dead man's house had been closed within three
days of his death, and his retinue sent packing ; but Pace
stayed in Rome to wind up his affairs, and try to find his
murderer. After Burbank had started, Rinaldo, without
torture, confessed to the crime, and Pace sent two letters after
Burbank to Florence, containing the details, evidently thinking
that was the best way of sending the news to England.[2] Rinaldo
confessed that he had put poison in Bainbridge's pottage, soon
after Corpus Christi, at the desire of Giglis, who said, ' If we
do not get rid of the cardinal, we shall never live quietly in

[1] L. and P., i. (Reissue), 3203.   [2] Ellis, Letters, xxxvi. 100, 106.

Rome.' [1] He went on to state that Giglis' chamberlain, Stephen, was privy to the crime, that Giglis had given him fifteen golden ducats, and he had bought poison at Spoleto, and kept it in his chamber under a tile-stone. He said Bainbridge became ill immediately after taking the soup, but was relieved by treatment, and went to supper with Cardinal Finario, but next day had a relapse, lay in bed very ill, and died. But Corpus Christi is in the middle of June, and Bainbridge did not die till 14th July. Rinaldo wrote out his confession himself, and gave it to Cardinal de' Medici, Henry's protector, to whom the pope had entrusted the inquiry, and who reported to the pope. Rinaldo acknowledged other crimes, and asked the pope not to disgrace Giglis by revealing the confession. Hearing next day that he was not to be pardoned, he wounded himself with a small knife, and was on the point of death when, according to Pace, he was induced by his confessors, at Giglis' instigation, to withdraw his confession. For two days he stuck to his recantation, but cursed Giglis, wishing he had never had anything to do with him. Just before his death he confessed again to his surgeon and physician that he had poisoned Bainbridge ; but he did not say at whose instigation.

Pace desired a bloody revenge, and Giglis complained of his ' rage.' The pope promised to do justice, and all documents and evidence were to be sent to Henry. Cardinal de' Medici promised Pace that Rinaldo's body should be either burnt or quartered. Pace wrote to Burbank at Florence that many great men had offered to kill Giglis, and that all Rome was inflamed against him. There was even a rumour that he had been arrested, but, being Henry's ambassador, it did not seem wise, even to the revengeful Pace, to proceed against him, until the King's pleasure should be known. Pace feared that his powerful friends would save him, and that the pope would gladly hush up the matter, because Giglis had done much to further the peace between France and England ; had in fact undone Bainbridge's work. Pace spoke of friends Giglis had made by his money, but Giglis' own correspondence tries to make him out a poor man. Stephen was arrested, but nothing

[1] *L. and P.*, i. (Reissue), 3213.

was got out of him, and he was released. The pope ordered Rinaldo's body to be hung on a gibbet, with his confession attached, then to be beheaded and quartered, the quarters to be exhibited for one day on the gallows. Pace without authority had some labels tied to the feet, casting aspersions on the Bishop of Worcester. He could be a great hater, and would tie placards to a dead body as willingly as he would to Pasquino.

In the sixteenth century, especially in Italy, if any one died suddenly people were too ready to suggest that he had been poisoned ; but such a catastrophe was not at all unlikely to happen. Some cardinals were accused of trying to get rid of Leo in this way, and one was put to death. It was suggested, when Leo died, that he had been poisoned, and the servants who had served his wine were thrown into prison. We have seen the Cardinal of Pavia killed at Ravenna by the Duke of Urbino. Alexander was said to have had some cardinals poisoned. Cardinal Riario had been mixed up in the Pazzi conspiracy, to murder the Medici in Florence, and the pope of the time (Sixtus) had known what was going on. Prosper Colonna was said to have been poisoned, and so was Adrian VI. Bainbridge was just the sort of man to make enemies in Rome, especially at Leo's court. He was an angry man, and fiery— ' of bold speech.' He was arrogant and anti-French, at a time when a reaction in favour of that nation had set in. The Italians said the English hated the very name of France. Cardinal Surrentinus, who was his great friend, told Henry he was very strict, perhaps too ' vehement ' in all that pertained to the King's honour. Pace himself, long afterwards, was described as being too vehement. Bainbridge was said to have beaten Rinaldo, or struck him, and he was killed for it. He could not control himself, and blackguarded, not only his own household, but others. He had a bad name for it in Rome. He was in this like Wolsey, who assaulted a nuncio. Such arrogance was thought to come badly from the purple. Giglis was nicknamed ' *talpa*,' the mole ; but was usually regarded as an able man and a scholar. He was a friend of Baldassare Castiglione. Pace said that, if he had not inquired fully into the cause of his master's death, he might reasonably have been thought in league with a poisoner.[1] He was naturally aroused by Giglis continually speaking evil of the dead man, by his unfair treatment of himself and his master, and by what he was pleased to regard as disloyalty to Henry. ' Such men cannot be loved of any conscience, for the holy law doth not only excommunicate, interdict, curse, and ban men of such demeanour, but also commands the ruin and destruction of all their progeny.' [2]

During his last illness Bainbridge complained to Henry of Wolsey's treatment of his servants at York, and of Giglis' treachery to him and Henry, in Rome. He rightly regarded Giglis as acting for Wolsey in Rome, and he regarded Wolsey as one who had upstarted in England during his absence. Bainbridge died on 14th July, and Wolsey was given the temporalities of his archbishopric of York on 5th August, apparently without having been elected by the chapter ; [3] and he was translated on 6th November. So soon after Bainbridge's death as 26th August [4] Giglis was writing to Wolsey and Fox about tenths, subsidies, and annates, complaining of Bainbridge's handling of the matter in Rome. He calmly said he would have liked to ask for the diocese of Lincoln (which he supposed Wolsey would relinquish on becoming archbishop in Bainbridge's place), but had heard from Ammonius that it demanded residence, which he could not give it. He supposed he might expect the next bishopric, as he needed a more decent support. He had written to Ammonius about the stigma attaching to him through the suspicions of some of Bainbridge's domestics. His contention was that Rinaldo was no one of importance, and, though a priest, had only performed servile offices in the chamber ; that he himself had had to get rid of him from his own service, and that he was insane. He said the confession had been extorted under fear of torture, and that the fellow had himself admitted that he had accused him (Giglis) to save himself from being charged with stealing in Bainbridge's house—though one finds it hard to appreciate such a defence. Giglis complained of the persistence of Pace and Clerk in attributing the crime to him, after Rinaldo's withdrawal ; and he asked Wolsey at the end of August to make

[1] Ellis, *Letters*, Series I, i. 109.   [2] *Ibid*. Series I, i. 111.
[3] A. F. Pollard, *Wolsey*, p. 21.   [4] *L. and P.*, i. (Reissue), 3197.

them drop it. He was interfering with the executors, and trying to get hold of some of the dead man's property for Wolsey, but he found it difficult, ' the persons be so subtle and crafty, that the best remedy we can find shall be little enough.' A few days later he was writing to Ammonius [probably] to say the pope would give Wolsey money (20,000 crowns) if he could make peace between Louis and Maximilian Sforza secretly. Wolsey was again after a cardinal's hat, and Giglis told him Cardinal Adrian, who had been attending to the matter, was his enemy in Rome. He hoped soon to send a bull, declaring his innocence of the murder. Wolsey described the charge as a ' slander of great malice,' and threatened to punish those who thus maliciously had accused the Bishop of Worcester, as if they had accused himself ' in such wise that all the world shall take example how to enfame the King's ambassador and orator.' [1] At the same time Wolsey desired Giglis to get the pope to sequestrate Bainbridge's goods in Pace's custody, and to levy as much as possible on them, and send the proceeds to him. Wolsey said Giglis was quite at liberty to send a citation into England against Clerk, then on his way home, ' one of the most malicious conspirators against you.' He might rely on having the assistance of the King and Wolsey in prosecuting all who maligned him. Pace did not know it, but, at the end of August, Ammonius drew Wolsey's attention to the delay in the arrival of a letter from Giglis. It ought to have come with one from Pace. The delay was owing, he thought, to some trick by one of Giglis' enemies, and he suggested that the surgeon who revealed Rinaldo's final statement of his guilt had been suborned by such persons. One is surprised to find Ammonius writing in this way. Cardinal Adrian recommended Pace and Burbank to Wolsey, and so did Cardinal Surrentinus to Henry, because they had faithfully fulfilled their task as executors, and were without a master. It looked as if Pace was to have an enemy at court just when he was going home to make friends. Unfortunately for Bainbridge's estate in the diocese of York the probate of any will disposing of it was a matter for his successor, Wolsey, to deal with. Pace's position as executor was made more difficult by

---

[1] *L. and P.*, i. (Reissue), 3497.

this. He had served two archbishops of York well, in one year, one in Rome and the other in Switzerland.

Bainbridge had left a considerable sum of ready money and plate in Rome, and it was said his property there amounted to 110,000 ducats. He had bequeathed 20,000 to the building of the new St. Peter's. The residue was to be distributed among his relations and servants. His estate was liable for dilapidations in York, and the whole sum seized from his estate was not spent by Wolsey on these dilapidations, but partly on Hampton Court and Moor Park. With peace between the pope and Louis, the task for which Bainbridge had been sent to Rome had come to an end. He had carried it out well. He had been instrumental in making peace between the pope and Venice, and had combined those two powers with England against France, and kept the pope to it until England's old enemy had been driven out of Italy, and her arms discredited.

After Bainbridge's death Giglis became Wolsey's agent in Rome, and was instrumental in getting him made cardinal and afterwards legate *a latere*. Bainbridge had been a cardinal, and had been within an inch of being made legate to England, and, if he had been, he would on his return to England have been less in offices than Wolsey was, at the height of his fame, only by the chancellorship, and he might have held that too. Professor A. F. Pollard shows that ' no Englishman before Wolsey combined either the chancellorship or an archbishopric with a commission *a latere*.' [1] That is what Bainbridge would have done if he had not been murdered. Just before Bainbridge's death Wolsey protested against his being made legate *a latere*—such a legate was not wanted in England. But Bainbridge was dead, and Wolsey succeeded him as Archbishop of York and as an English cardinal, and then became legate *a latere*, with the help of the Italian, whom he had employed to oppose Bainbridge's appointment to the last dignity, and who had been accused (falsely as it would seem) of Bainbridge's murder. Within a month of Bainbridge's death Henry had asked the pope to make Wolsey cardinal, with all the honours held by the dead man. On 17th August Leo wrote to Henry notifying him officially of Bainbridge's death, and inform-

[1] *Wolsey*, p. 168.

ing him that Richard Pace and William Burbank were appointed
executors ; he recommended them—especially Pace. On 18th
August Antonio Vivaldi agreed to advance the money to pay for
Wolsey's pallium and the expenses of his promotion to the archbishopric of York, to be repaid, £2000 by John Withers, who was
an agent in the diocese of York, and 5704 ducats by Richard Pace
and William Burbank, who gave a bond. These expenses of the
incoming archbishop were to be paid out of the estate of the
deceased one. Certain money does seem to have been due from
Bainbridge's estate to the diocese, but Wolsey was prepared to
take more than Pace thought was due, to the detriment of
legatees. One of the charges against Wolsey at his fall was that
he embezzled the goods of his predecessor in the see of York.[1]
Pace wrote him that there was not enough money in his hands,
in the estate of the deceased, nor in Grimaldi's bank for expedit-
ing his bulls, and Vivaldi had not been entirely repaid at the
time of Wolsey's death. All the clothes and household stuff,
left when Burbank went home, did not amount to more than
4000 golden ducats, and Pace had paid that into Grimaldi's.
Wolsey wanted him to produce more, and Pace agreed to try to
make it up by selling some rich vestments and altar-cloths.
He was ready to make good the dilapidations at York out of
the deceased's estate, to please Wolsey, and for the good of
Bainbridge's soul. Withers had no right to promise Wolsey
money out of the estate. Pace recommended the late cardinal's
brothers and kinsfolk to Wolsey, and hoped for something for
himself for his great labours and little profit. The pope owed
the estate 700 golden ducats for plate, but Pace could not get
the money out of his holiness ; and he wished that those who
asked that the rest of the property should be sequestrated would
sequestrate also the 700 ducats. This led him to think of the
Bishop of Worcester, and the poisoning, and he reverted to it
with the statement that the matter had been in the hands of the
most learned men in Rome. It had been determined by the
majority of them, he wrote, that Bainbridge had been poisoned,
in such manner as was comprised in the commission of him that
did it, that is to say at the instigation of Giglis. Giglis, Pace

[1] A. F. Pollard, *Wolsey*, p. 259.

thought, had ' marvellous great favour ' in hiding the truth, but God appeared to hate such dreadful crimes.[1] There was a personal reason for Pace's hatred of Giglis ; he had tried to get hold of Bainbridge's goods for Wolsey's use, without respecting the testator's intention that Pace should take as much out of the estate for himself as he felt he deserved. He complained to Wolsey that his services were being overlooked, and that Giglis wished to beggar him in revenge for his accusations about the poisoning which—' the dead doer did confess ' and the writings made apparent. He said that if he could write freely he would desire no other judgment than Wolsey's on the point. But Pace had lost his master, and he had soon done all a loyal servant could do at the papal court to call attention to his murder. He wound up the estate in proper fashion in spite of those who tried to prey on it. ' I had rather have no part of his goods, than ever it should be said by any one, that I for mine own private profit would hinder any kinsman or servant to my late master of the value of a halfpenny.' [2] The time had come for him to make friends with Henry and Wolsey, to get further employment, and he had been recommended by cardinals at Rome and by the pope. He urged in his own favour that he had only been acting as a faithful servant would do in the matter of Bainbridge's death. He made to the King loud complaint of Giglis having spoken evilly and falsely of his late master—' which is neither honesty nor good Christianity,' for though he admitted that Bainbridge had certain vices—he did not say which—he was the most faithful man to Henry that ever was born, and most vehement in defence of his causes, when no one else dared open his mouth.[3] Pace was aware untrue reports derogatory to Bainbridge had been sent to Henry by enemies. He complained that Giglis was actuated against him (Pace) by malice without cause, for he had loved him [been his friend] until the murder, and until it became patent that he had no love for Henry and England. It seems as if Pace was as indignant as ever against Giglis, but felt that if Henry and Wolsey were not soon won over to suspect him of the murder he would have to drop the matter

---

[1] *L. and P.*, i. (Reissue), 3261. [2] Ellis, *Letters*, Series III. i. 176.
[3] *Ibid.* i. 110.

against him—indeed he could not push it further at the papal court, without the King's approval. The pope was diplomatically allowing the accusers to find out the weakness of their case. Wolsey offered Pace promotion and to take him into his service in England, or outside it. This secretary to the late archbishop had to be regarded as some one of importance, after his visit to the Swiss. He was acting for Wolsey in Rome. In his letter to Wolsey, 25th September, we find a new Pace, who is doing no more than allude wearily to the murder, but who is fitting into a new position he feels he will be called upon to occupy. He is now keen on getting Wolsey the red hat—he has been talking about it to three great persons, one of whom is in the pope's secrets.[1] He himself would like to see Wolsey a cardinal ' not only for your Grace's private honour, but also for the common, both honour and profit, of the whole realm.' He thinks Henry ought to have one, perhaps two cardinals, resident at the court of Rome, to get knowledge of business to be transacted there, and to take part in the election of popes. This is a matter of great importance to the princes by whose means they are created ' as they might be by our most Christian King.' So Pace, like some of the civil servants at home, confers the King of France's complimentary title on Henry, although Henry himself had no thoughts of it, after he had made peace with Louis. Pace is ' marvelous desirous ' to see his late master's successor no less in dignity than his late master was. This is because he is going to be the new man's secretary. This new Pace is like the old one in breaking off a letter, and then remembering matter to put impetuously into another, or into a postscript. In his new capacity, which he feels himself coming into, of watcher at Rome over Henry's interests, he has been contradicting French rumours, that ten thousand English archers are going to join a French army and go into Lorraine. A letter from Louis has reached Rome saying that Pace is working to get him (Louis), or perhaps Henry, elected emperor—an extraordinary statement for the French King to have made, unless he knew more of Pace's movements in 1514 than we do. Louis was making the most of his new treaty with Henry, and such

[1] Ellis, *Letters*, Series III. i. 178.

rumours spread by the French caused Pace trouble. ' Your grace may know hereby in what case I stand. I have no need of this French trouble, for I have too much besides that, with little bodily health, by reason of most fervent heats which we have now here.' He was a very delicate man and always felt the heat in Italy.

Cardinal Adrian was the most influential among Giglis' accusers. He had been Henry's representative in Rome at one time, and was still collector of Peter's pence in England. At the end of October the pope took the latter office away from him, at Henry's request, and gave it to Andreas Ammonius. His reputation in England had been such that when Julius was thought to be dying Wolsey would have put him forward to succeed him. Polydore Vergil had been Adrian's sub-collector in England, and said the ' prizefighter ' had now got the collectorship by the intervention of the ' mole.'

The pope seems not to have believed the Bishop of Worcester guilty of the murder, and in England the fact that he allowed him to celebrate Mass, in Sta. Maria del Popolo, in September 1514, in honour of the peace between Henry and Louis, was thought to be an indication of his confidence in him. But he refused (1520) to make him a cardinal in spite of Wolsey's request. His accusers were dispersed or discredited: Burbank, and then Clerk, left Rome, and Cardinal Adrian was disgraced by being deprived of his collectorship. So only Pace was left of his accusers. Then he (Giglis) managed to confuse Pace's accusations about the poisoning with private complaints Wolsey had against Pace for being so niggardly about providing money out of the estate committed to his charge. In duty to his deceased master Pace laid charges before Wolsey against the very man who had, without his knowledge, been helping Wolsey to the red robe. When Pace realized his position he had to collapse before Wolsey ; for he had to get employment. Here is a letter written by Giglis to Henry which seems to prove this. It is dated 2nd December. Giglis was anxious to show his gratitude to the King for protecting him from the accusations under which he had suffered, and for the resolution he had expressed to punish their authors. As to the King's command

touching his accusers, especially Pace, although he could not
legally proceed to any execution against them, yet he had commanded Pace to deliver an inventory of the goods of the late
cardinal, and it had proved to be very inadequate.[1]   One would
have thought it not right, for one whom Pace had accused of
murdering his master, to be in a position to point out some
defect, in his administration of the estate of that master, to the
prince of the man who was trying to get part of it into his hands.
On the same day a certain William Shvagger wrote to Wolsey
from Rome that Giglis was doing all he could for him, and that
Bainbridge's goods in Pace's hands were sequestrated with him ;
as the King had ordered.   This Shvagger had brought an action
of some sort in Rome, and to his annoyance Bainbridge had
thrust himself forward, to give evidence, and had compelled
many of his household to do the same.   Shvagger had lost the
case, but the loser adds that anyway Bainbridge is dead, with
the stigma of avarice, pride, and anger resting on him.   He
hoped that Wolsey, who had succeeded him at York, would not
imitate his vices.   Giglis was doing so much in Rome for Wolsey's
pocket that he could expect to be white-washed.   Just before
Christmas the pope in consistory ' absolved ' him,[2] and sent
Henry a copy of the absolution passed unanimously in consistory,
saying he had never credited the charge ; but he had not sent a
complete exculpation earlier, as he wished to allow the matter
to be threshed out.   The excellent character of the Bishop of
Worcester, and the vacillation and frivolity of his accusers, satisfied him—he said—and this had been confirmed by skilled
lawyers employed to investigate the case.[3]   And here one may
leave the matter, for Pace had come round to feeling glad that
Giglis was found not guilty.   Before he left Rome the two must
have shaken hands ; for Giglis wrote Wolsey that they were fully
reconciled, and begged that Pace might have recompense for a
prebend he claimed.   He reported that Pace had acted prudently in the administration of the late cardinal's estate ; and
they were on good terms ever afterwards.   Pace had resigned

[1] *L. and P.*, i. (Reissue), 3511.   [2] Sanuto, xix. col. 336.
[3] *L. and P.*, ii. 13, and see *State Papers King Henry VIII*, vi. Pt.
5, xiv.

the prebend of Bugthorp in September, perhaps because he found himself at odds with Wolsey, the new Archbishop of York.

It is hardly likely that Bainbridge's monument in the church of St. Thomas of Canterbury, which adjoins the English college, was set up before Pace left Rome, but he may have given the order for it. It is a fine sixteenth-century recumbent figure, in mitre and vestments, with a heavy handsome face, shrewd but not ill-tempered, aristocratic, clean shaven, with a prominent nose. Stowe records that he was honourably buried.

Pace had seen something of a very important period in Rome, under Julius and Leo, who made the city a greater art centre than Florence. Bramante had been slowly rebuilding St. Peter's and the Vatican, and the decoration of the latter had been progressing. Restoration, rebuilding, and beautifying of churches had been going on, and masterpieces of classical sculpture, such as the river-god, Tiber, and the She-Wolf, had been dragged one after another from their hiding-places. Pace tells us in *De Fructu* that he studied the inscriptions on the antique marbles. Part of Raphael's work in the Vatican was finished, and part of Michelangelo's frescoes in the vault of the Sistine Chapel. Sodoma, Romano, and Piombo had been decorating Agostino Chigi's new house, the Farnesina, with frescoes. Michelangelo had made some figures for Julius' tomb, —Moses and the slaves. Pace should have known Bembo and Sodeleto.

The records of Pace's early career are not full enough to show clearly his movements, between his setting-out to Padua university and his return to England in 1515. It is probable that his visit to England in 1514 was not the only one. It is not likely that he took the long, dangerous, and expensive journey many times ; perhaps once after he had completed his studies at Bologna, about the end of 1507, and again in the summer of 1510 ; when Julius and Venice had become reconciled, and he was admitted prebend of Southwell. He could have taken this holiday after the completion of the piece of business for which Bainbridge in the first instance went to Rome, and have been back again before Julius took the field against France and

Ferrara. He was likely to have been almost all of these fourteen years in Italy. He came home with the Latin, Greek, and Italian tongues, probably the German, perhaps the French ; and a thorough knowledge of the forces in Italy. He had been brought up under the old policy of war for England against France, and in Henry VIII's new policy—or rather the revived policy—of interference in European affairs, to check the growth of the French King's power. He knew Rome, Venice, Milan, Ferrara, and the cantons of Switzerland. He had perhaps been over-zealous in the defence of his old master's memory and in his desire to find his murderer. He had got into Wolsey's bad books, but he had got out of them again ; and among the Swiss, and with Bainbridge in Rome, he had done so well that Wolsey wanted him in his service, to see if he was good enough for that of the King.

CHAPTER IV

THE SWISS

PARIS was surprised on New Year's Day by the death of old Louis. So much for his invasion of Italy ; and Pace could travel home peacefully through France, past camps of lansquenets in Provence. Young Thomas Lupset travelled at least part of the way with him.[1] Possibly he went by sea from Genoa to Marseilles, but whichever way he took he did not enter France by the Colle de Tenda ; for he says he saw these mountains for the first time in 1524. All France was talking of the handsome King Francis, aged twenty. Henry was twenty-three ; the Archduke Charles, who was in a few months to come into great possessions, had just been declared of age at fifteen ; Leo was thirty-eight. On 29th March Sir Richard Wingfield, who was on an embassy with the Duke of Suffolk, wrote Wolsey from Paris recommending Richard ' Pacye,' the bearer, who had just arrived from Rome.[2] He had travelled on the heels of Sebastian Giustinian, whom the Signory of Venice was sending to England as ambassador. Giustinian wrote to the doge from Paris on 20th March that the French were afraid the Swiss were going to invade them—the Swiss whom Pace had spent the previous summer bringing into the field—and he thought that were it not for this danger, on his frontier, young Francis would begin his reign by invading Italy. Francis, it was felt, wished to prove himself another Gaston de Foix, but treaties he renewed with Charles, Henry, and Venice seemed to promise peace. On the other hand, he set his uncle, the Duke of Savoy, to get round the Swiss, which looked as if he required infantry. The Swiss went on recruiting

[1] L. Delaruelle, *Corr. de G. Budé* (1907), p. 26, footnote.
[2] *L. and P.*, ii. 273.

for the league against him, composed of Leo, Maximilian, Ferdinand, and Maximilian Sforza, their chief care being the defence of Milan.   It seemed to be against a Swiss invasion that Francis was collecting an army.

The coronation was over by the time Pace reached Paris, but he could have seen the Duke of Suffolk riding about with a goodly band of yeomen all in mourning.   He had gone over to bring home the widowed Queen of France, Henry's sister, with whom he had been in love when she was given to old Louis.   During these very days he married her secretly, and they left Paris on 19th April, while Pace was on the road to Calais in front of them.

Pace was now to serve Wolsey, who was rising beyond all precedent, and was to be chancellor, and cardinal in a few weeks ; was already Archbishop of York, and the statesman who had organized the recent brilliant military expedition against France, and wound it all up by a peace, which bound Henry and Louis together by family ties.   But the treaties of peace which England entered into with France, in Wolsey's time, up to the battle of Pavia, were made to keep France quiet while a time of doubt passed by.   Wolsey was the greatest man in England, perhaps in Europe.   England was ruled by the King's council, or rather by its executive—the chancellor, the treasurer, and privy seal—offices filled by Wolsey, the Duke of Norfolk, and Fox—the last soon to be replaced by Ruthal, who was at the moment the King's secretary.   All power was passing into the hands of Wolsey, and of the young men who were his nominees and deputies on the council—such men as Ruthal. Warham, Fox, and the older councillors were on the eve of retiring, and Suffolk had little capacity.   Andreas Ammonius was secretary for letters in Latin and Italian, but the work was done by Wolsey.

Parliament was prorogued in April, and did not meet again until the late autumn.   There was conflict between the two Houses over the liberties of the church, such as the benefit of clergy allowed to criminal clerks of the lower orders.   The doings of Parliament are not important to a knowledge of Pace's career, as it only met once while Wolsey was chancellor, and

Pace was then abroad. His last months in Rome had been passed under the shadow of a murder, and, when he arrived in England, it was to hear every one talking of another. A man accused of heresy, Richard Hunne, who had refused mortuary dues to the clergy, had been imprisoned in the Lollards' tower by the Bishop of London, while awaiting trial. He was found hanged. Either he killed himself, or was murdered by the priests ; the people said he had been murdered. This incident fanned the growing hatred of a certain type of ecclesiastic. The controversy interested Pace, and some time afterwards, when in personal attendance on the King, he did his best to prevent Henry Standish, the greyfriar who had preached against benefit of clergy, being appointed somewhat furtively by Henry to a bishopric,[1] ' whereof I would be right sorry, for the good service he was like to do to the church.'[2] It seems as if his opposition was not put up only to please Wolsey, who proposed another candidate, but out of his dislike, as a church-man, for the anti-clerical views of Standish ; and it is true that, afterwards, Standish took part in the suppression of the monasteries.

A few months after this visit to England Pace wrote a letter to his old colleague Burbank, who had become Wolsey's chaplain, which suggests that these two friends hired chambers close together, and boarded with the cardinal's household at York Place, now Whitehall. Pace settled down to his work with Wolsey. In the summer the treaty between the pope, the emperor, the King of Spain, and the Duke of Milan, and the arrival of Swiss to guard the Alpine passes seemed to secure Italy, even if Francis was preparing to invade her. There seemed little chance of war in the near future. Europe was much more peaceful than usual. To study the King and home affairs was useful, and entertaining. On May Day Henry and Catherine, and many lords and ladies, went Maying from Greenwich to Shooter's Hill. They met yeomen of the King's Guard, masking as Robin Hood and his merry men, who proved that the English still handled the long bow cleverly. There was plague in London, and in the summer Henry went on

[1] H. Ellis, *Letters*, Series III. i. 185. [2] *L. and P.*, ii. 4074.

progress westward to avoid it. Sebastian Giustinian, the newly arrived ambassador from Venice, was drawn towards Pace by his known love of the republic, and became his friend. He liked him, too, for his learning and his possession of every amiable quality. Sir Thomas More was in Flanders with Cuthbert Tunstal, bored at a peace conference, and wrote to Pace to ask if he could persuade Wolsey to let him come home.[1] This is the first sign that Pace knew More. In the middle of September the King reached Woking, and was joined by Wolsey, whom he heartily welcomed. It was there that Henry heard that Leo had made him a cardinal. This news arrived on 20th September, and the courier who brought it reported that, as he came from Rome, he had found all Italy under arms, in expectation of an invasion by the French. Yet it seemed hardly likely that any invasion in force would be attempted before the spring. The Swiss were guarding the passes, and their army in Lombardy seemed able to stem any rush into Italy there was likely to be within the next six months. The English government was very much in the dark as to what military preparations were being made in France, and trusted very much for information to travellers and couriers. Pace knew as much about the chances of war in Italy as any member of the council. Soon came disquieting rumours of a French attack and then, in the first week of October, the almost incredible news that Francis had crossed the Alps, in five days, by a little-known pass, had fought the Swiss at Marignano, nine miles from Milan, on the night following 14th September, and routed them, the best infantry in the world. There was intense excitement, and nobles and gentlemen rode up to London to hear all about it.

Henry's policy had hitherto been anti-French, with a peace following his victories. Now that Francis had begun his reign with such a great victory in the field, fear and jealousy were likely to keep it anti-French. The pope could do little, and was a man of peace, Ferdinand was old and would do little, young Charles had only just come into his Netherland dominions and his councillors were likely to pursue a French policy. Maximilian was too poor to do anything, without help. It

[1] *L. and P.*, ii. 1552.

was out of the question to send an English army to south
Europe, and it was late in the year for another attack in Picardy.
Francis might overrun Italy as far as the Vatican. The pope
must not come under French influence ; but how was it to be
prevented ? The old councillors would have left the French
alone, unless some good alliance could be found against them,
and even the new men thought it madness for England to make
war on France single-handed. Francis soon had all Lombardy
in his power, and Henry and Wolsey might well fear he would
soon rule all Europe. He had sent Albany to Scotland to
engage England's attention, and had shown favour to the de
la Poles, who had a claim to the English throne. If there was
no one to stand against Francis in Italy, it would not be long
before he was overrunning the Netherlands, taking the new
English possession, Tournai, as he went through, and Wolsey
was Bishop of Tournai. Marignano had made a tremendous
difference among the various groups of states in Italy ; the
small tyrants began to plunder the church, as they always did,
when a pope died, or seemed in adversity. The defeated Swiss
were soon flocking home ; Erasmus saw them going through
Basel, still boiling with rage against the French, because, as he
put it, they did not civilly allow themselves to be thrashed, as
they had been by the English.[1] They were ragged and wounded
and their ensigns tattered.

The idea that Henry should again work up, and pay, the
Swiss, to fight the French, originated with Cardinal Schiner
and Francesco Sforza, brother of Maximilian Sforza, Duke of
Milan, who had both gone to the emperor after Marignano.
They sent Maximilian Sforza's secretary, Michael Abbate, to
England with their plan, but they put it forward as one for the
formation of a league, as much with the object of setting Henry
on the throne of France, as of putting Sforza into Milan, or
helping the Swiss to revenge themselves on Francis. They
promised assistance rather than asked for it, but Sforza promised
Wolsey 10,000 ducats a year for himself, if he persuaded Henry
to help him to get Milan. Henry had sent money to the
emperor, for his Swiss in Lombardy, in spite of the peace between

[1] *L. and P.*, ii. 985.

England and France. The allies' army was now dispersed, and Maximilian was not likely to have any money for a new one. It seemed wise to pay the Swiss to march again, under the emperor, to take Milan from the French, and set a Sforza on the ducal throne. For that purpose money must be conveyed to them direct ; for it was believed that the emperor had pocketed most of what had been sent before. Pace had arranged the matter in the previous year, and he was at hand to do it again.

Whatever may be said against the policy of going into continental affairs at all at this moment, it cannot be said the English government were dilatory. In the middle of November the usually well-informed Venetian ambassadors complained they had no advice from the senate about the battle. Pace had been gone to the Swiss three weeks by then. Wolsey negotiated about the money with the firm of Frescobaldi, who were the best merchants trading in London, but quite second-rate people. Jerome Frescobaldi lived at Bruges, and his son Leonard managed the London business. The old King had done business with them, but for some years there had been doubt among the English agents abroad as to their reliability. They had carried on a good business in Flanders, but were now inferior to the great German firms, like Fugger and Welser. Pace had started for Switzerland before any definite agreement with them had been arrived at, for no time could be lost in preventing an alliance between Francis and the cantons, who were by no means certain to let themselves be guided by Schiner. That much must be done even if the Swiss could not be induced to serve against France. Charles once wrote that if one wanted to fight, the secret of secrets was to gain the Swiss at any price ; and it was a saying of Pace's ' to whomsoever the Swiss incline, he is like in time to be lord of all.' They had Milan and perhaps all Italy in their gift, in 1515, although their military reputation had been somewhat dashed at Marignano.

Pace's instructions were to work up all the allies against France, especially the Swiss and the emperor. The others were the pope, the King of Spain, the Duke of Milan, Florence, and Genoa, with most of whom he would not come into close touch.

The original plan was that he should pay 100,000 crowns to 20,000 Swiss, after they had taken the field, to serve wherever Henry wanted them. When he had seen Milan taken he was to inform the pope of his commission, through the English ambassador at Rome ; he was to lay a line of posts to the court of Margaret of Austria (who was usually with young Charles at Brussels or Malines), so that Henry could hear quickly what was going on in Italy. If the Swiss defeated the French they were to be kept in pay, with a view to an invasion of France later on. It is obvious that the government thought Pace had an easy task ; that he would have a Swiss army at his command as soon as he had arranged terms, and that the French would soon be beaten. Wolsey hoped that he himself would be able, through their ambassador in London, to detach the Venetians from France ; so that when Milan was taken, the whole league would invade France. Wolsey told Pace to be guided in all things by Galeazzo Visconti, the old *condottiere*. Pace was informed, and promised, that money would be sent to Augsburg at once, and that more would be waiting for him in Italy.[1] The whole matter was to be kept secret, for England had recently renewed her peace treaty with France, and Pace's commission was not signed by Henry or Wolsey. He hardly knew himself, in what capacity he went—Henry's ambassador or Wolsey's secretary, or neither. He took no proper letters of credence ; he went as a secret agent with the brain of an ambassador. He was not to make clandestine levies, so detested by the Swiss ; but to go before the diet, and try to get a treaty made with Henry. If every canton had refused to assist Henry, that would perhaps alter the case, and excuse secret recruiting ; but all was to be above board as long as possible. Before he started he had an interview with the King, at which Wolsey and Suffolk were present ; and Henry spoke ' most discreet words ' to the effect that he did not wish him to offer empty promises, but ready money to the Swiss.[2] What Henry said made a great impression on Pace, and the King never went back on this instruction and promise ; but things did not go according to his wishes. On 2nd October Sir Robert Wingfield, Henry's

---

[1] *L. and P.*, ii. 1065.   [2] *Ibid*. ii. 1244.

ambassador with Maximilian, wrote Wolsey from Innsbruck, that Maximilian seemed inclined to help Henry against France, and that Schiner thought the Swiss would serve him. Indeed, before Pace had started Maximilian had promised to go into Italy, if the Swiss would fight for him, and they were discussing the matter at each diet.

Pace rode down to Dover with Michael Abbate, crossed to Calais on 24th October, and departed immediately. As he rode out of Calais he met a post, whom he wanted to pump for news ; so a gentleman riding with him pretended to be a servant of the constable of France. A little farther along the road, at Gravelines, they met Thomas More ; Pace asked him to write for him to Wolsey, as he had been in too much of a hurry to do so. More was going home from the peace conference, thinking of a book—*Utopia*—he was planning. Pace hurried on after a very short conversation. He heard talk everywhere of what the Swiss would do to the French when they went down into Italy again. They hurried on as fast as they could,[1] reaching Antwerp on 25th, where they heard the castle of Milan had surrendered to the French, and that Maximilian Sforza, Duke of Milan, was a prisoner in their hands. Pace interviewed the Lady Margaret, and was aided and advised by Thomas Spinelli, Henry's agent, at Brussels or Antwerp, about the money. They left Antwerp on 28th or 29th. They passed through the Ardennes dominions of Robert de la Marck (an ally of Francis, called the devil) ' not without great fear,' for, six days previously, this devil had robbed six or eight merchants of a large sum of money. So they went through byways, as far as possible. They were at Spires on 1st November, thoroughly tired out by the long rides. A special instruction had been given to Pace by Wolsey. He was to thank Francesco Sforza and Schiner for their offers to help Henry to recover his French possessions, and to say that French ambition must be checked, if there was to be universal peace ; and that, if the emperor, the Swiss, and the other allies could be induced to fight the French in Italy, Henry would attack northern

---

[1] *L. and P.*, ii. There are a great number of dated letters which show Pace's movements at this time.

France, perhaps in person. Henry would pay the Swiss gold crowns for as many men as he could get, for a two-months' campaign, to invade France at a point of his own choosing. Pace was specially urged by Wolsey to keep secret who he was and what he was doing. He was not even to let any one know the sort of mission he was on. He was to pretend to have been sent by Wolsey to transact some business, the nature of which he could best invent, when the occasion arose. His messages to Wolsey were to be in cipher, and to come through Thomas Spinelli, in Flanders, and the imperial post-master, at the cost of Francesco Sforza, who on the capture and abdication of his brother claimed investiture as Duke of Milan from the emperor.

Pace reached Innsbruck on 8th November, and found the emperor, Cardinal Schiner, and Sir Robert Wingfield, the English ambassador, and many other important people. Some were from the pope to talk of a crusade, others from the Duke of Ferrara and other princes, to seek an alliance, and there were many noblemen and gentlemen who had fled from Milan. The Cardinal of Gurk, Maximilian's minister, was anti-French, and there was no French ambassador at the court. Pace had been delayed on the road for three days, by Michael Abbate having fallen from his horse and hurt his leg. He went at once to Mathew Schiner, and found that already French agents had persuaded the majority of the cantons to consider favourably a treaty with Francis that would keep them from attempting to capture Milan. Schiner's plan was that Maximilian should support Francesco Sforza's claim to the duchy of Milan, and lead against Milan an army composed of Swiss infantry in Henry's pay ; Maximilian supplying artillery and cavalry. Pace was persuaded by Schiner that, if he had brought money with him, he could have had the Swiss on the move in ten days ; but money was neither easy to get nor to transport. Francis had no money either, and was wandering up and down Lombardy trying to extort it from the Italians. Pace was soon enthusiastic about this enterprise. He felt there never was a man of greater ability and experience than Mathew Schiner ; and he formed, at first, a high opinion of Sir Robert Wingfield, the English ambassador with the emperor. Later on he used to laugh at this older ambassador, and he was certainly a different kind of diplomatist to Bainbridge, though the two had been sent on much the same mission, at about the same time—to pope and emperor—to make enemies for France. On 11th November Pace and Abbate informed the burgomaster and council of Zurich of their coming and powers ;[1] so that they could not be accused of making clandestine levies. The next diet was to meet at Zurich, and Zurich was the canton best inclined towards serving Henry. The common people among the Swiss were thought to be strongly against Francis, wishing to avenge their defeat, and because he had failed to pay the money promised at Dijon. They thought, also, that the French had ill-treated Swiss wounded after Marignano. A close watch had, however, to be kept by the cardinal and Pace lest bribery of leaders should lead to influential pressure by captains, deputies, and councillors. The diet was to give the cantons an opportunity to ratify a treaty with Francis, approved by some of them, even before Marignano had been fought. Eight of the thirteen were known to favour ratification, and five—Schwitz, Uri, Zug, Unterwalden, and Zurich—were likely to favour Henry. Pace wanted to have money by the time the diet met, to show Henry's good faith. Abbate reported that nothing could exceed his diligence.

About 16th November Pace, Abbate, and Schiner left Innsbruck for Switzerland, and stayed at Kempten in Bavaria. On the way Pace seems to have realized that the Swiss were far gone towards a French alliance, or were pretending to be so, to raise their value. Bribes were coming to their leaders from Francis, through his uncle the Duke of Savoy. Pace had made his third request to Wolsey for money by 20th November, and he had not received even a letter, since he left England. He revealed his life-long hatred of the French King : ' It is time to look to the oppression of his intolerable ambition, for he doth now, after his late victory, openly avaunt himself, that he will do more and more excellent acts than ever did Alexander Magnus.'[2] Pace arrived on 22nd at Constance, and there found

[1] *Eidgenossichen Abschiede*, iii. 943.
[2] *State Papers King Henry VIII*, vi. Pt. V. xviii.

Francesco Sforza, now recognized by the emperor, the feudal lord, as Duke of Milan. He got to Zurich on 24th November for that month's diet ; and the magistrates of the town visited him at his lodging and sent him presents. He listened to a lot of gossip : it was really the only way to find out what the people thought of the choice of alliances offered them. The flattering saying among the people in Zurich was, that they had been deceived by all Christian princes, excepting Henry, and that they would side with him, to the point of insurrection, if their rulers tried to get them over to the French. But Pace reported to Wolsey that it was his coming alone that had prevented the leaders making a treaty with France. The French emissaries who were working among the Swiss, tried to make out that he was not an Englishman at all, but a Spaniard, a nation the Swiss hated like dogs. ' And verily this untrue rumour did greatly alienate from me the minds of the council here, . . . in so much that, when I was called into the council before the ambassadors of the cantons, I was put to this exigent, either to show that I was sent from the King's grace, or else to let the French peace be concluded, or else to stand in manifest jeopardy of my life by the unthrifty felons, moved thereunto by those corrupted by Francis. When I was in this perplexity, I desired to speak secretly with one or two of the most wise of the council, and so was committed to the Lord Galiac Vicecount (i.e. Galeazzo Visconti). . . . and the emperor's ambassador.' [1] At the end of November he did not dare go out of the town, for fear that the townspeople would think he had fled, and that Henry's offers to them were withdrawn. Wingfield and Galeazzo Visconti had tried to set the cantons right on this—Pace had been sent by Henry and was Wolsey's secretary. Francis could just then offer the Swiss 200,000 crowns in ready money, which he had extorted from Milan ; whereas ' sola spes ' was what Pace had for them, in spite of all Henry had said. Pace had not yet learnt how difficult it was to convey a very large sum of money to Upper Germany. The Swiss would not move except for money, ready money being the best, since Louis' letting them down after Dijon. They said they would not believe the pope's word, that

[1] J. Planta, *Helvetic Confederacy* (1807), ii. 425.

he was sending money—spoken or written—until they saw it. They would not trust the King of Spain, or any other prince, so often had they been deceived—certainly not the emperor They pretended that a letter from Henry made all the difference, and that they would trust him, and no other. Pace was doing remarkably well for one engaged on such intricate business for only the second time, the first being a very brief and hurried minor experience, in which he was not the leader. He managed to get to see the suggested articles of treaty, between Francis and the Swiss, and learnt what the constable of France said at his dinner table at Milan. He was a staunch Englishman of the old school, who now saw in the Swiss the best weapon for enforcing Henry's right to the French throne. In these negotiations he could rely on the assistance of certain men : Cardinal Schiner; Galeazzo Visconti ; the Cardinal of Gurk ; Francesco Sforza ; Sir Robert Wingfield ; Ennius, Bishop of Veroli, the pope's legate (who put up a doctor of divinity to preach against the French) ; and Maximilian, up to a point. Maximilian had been almost in agreement with Francis when Pace arrived, but hearing Henry's offers he turned in the opposite direction. Galeazzo was very popular with the Swiss ; they honoured him like a saint, but his property lay in Milan, and he had to be well paid while Milan was in French hands. Of course Henry's money was really his best argument with emperor, Galeazzo, and Swiss.

The December diet was to be held at Lucerne, ' and undoubtedly, if I had brought money with me, the King's grace, and none other, had had the Swiss surely.' If the gold crowns arrived, he thought he and Schiner could make the Swiss march in eight days ; ' This custom of taking money is so engendered in them, that they do take them (sic) for a fool, that cometh to treat any matter with them, without such money ; nor wisdom, nor good reason, nor persuasion is here admitted without money.' [1] He carried away with him the conviction ' that money present in that land bringeth every matter to the desired end.' His instructions had been to make no payment to the Swiss, until they had won a battle against the French ; but they

[1] J. Planta, *Helvetic Confederacy*, ii. 427.

would not move without a month's wages in advance, and he had not got any money. The Swiss had learnt wisdom by experience, and, unfortunately, Schiner had made promises of money, on behalf of the pope, which his holiness had not fulfilled. Pace was afraid the French, to injure him, would publish in England that a treaty had been made between themselves and the Swiss, but ' they may lie at their pleasure after their accustomed manner.' Some people in Zurich thought he might be a spy, for he produced no letters of credence. He would, he said, at least die faithfully discharging his commission against the enemies of his country. Sir Robert Wingfield thought it was wonderful he escaped alive, remarking piously that the religion of a good servant (such as Pace was, and as Sir Robert felt himself to be) makes dangers sweet to him.

We get an idea of the secrecy of the matter from a letter written by Wolsey to Giglis at Rome. If the French King complained to the pope when they met at Bologna, as they were planning to do, that Pace's mission was a breach of treaty, he was to say that Pace had gone on Wolsey's authority alone, to see if the French intended any injury to the pope. At the interview at Bologna Francis did complain to the pope of Pace's being sent to the Swiss. Pace, who was nothing much in Rome three years before, was now being talked about by pope, emperor, and king. Wolsey thought he could not afford to speak the whole truth about his mission. When the Venetian ambassador mentioned to him a report that had reached him, of large sums of money being sent through Flanders to the emperor, on the ground that it was a breach of neutrality (Venice being at war with the emperor), Wolsey, the Duke of Norfolk confirming his statement, denied it was for the emperor. He said it was to buy fine armour, and ornaments for the King. The Archbishop of Canterbury added his confirmation to their statement ' with an oath.' Giustinian was not satisfied, and went to Wolsey again, but he reiterated his statement that the money was not for the emperor. He said he would tell the Venetian the truth, as became a cardinal, on the honour of the cardinalate ; the money was indeed for armour and costly furniture, and a quantity of very fine jewels, which Maximilian was selling cheap. Henry would not help the emperor to keep Brescia or Verona from Venice ; those who said such things lied in the teeth. Giustinian had, on the whole, a high opinion of the English statesmen—compared with others of the day—and thought that some of them, at least, would not affirm an untruth upon oath. And they spoke the truth in saying the money was not for the emperor ; Wolsey did not intend him to get a penny of it. Giustinian asked that the money should be held back, until Venice had recovered the two towns ; he said there would be many more opportunities of buying the jewels from Maximilian ; for he was always in need of money. But however fairly Henry and Wolsey were behaving towards Venice, they were playing a double game with Francis. At this moment they were talking of Wolsey's and Suffolk's going to Paris, to congratulate him on his glorious achievement at Marignano, and to ask him to be godfather to the child to whom Queen Catherine was hoping to give birth.

The 100,000 gold crowns were being sent, partly by bills, and partly by bearers. The bills were to be paid at Augsburg, a place ill-chosen, since Wingfield, to whom they were jointly payable, had to be moving through Swabia, Bavaria, or Tyrol, with the emperor ; and Pace had to be with the Swiss ; but it was a place where money was easily found. Just before Christmas Wolsey began to send great sums through Flanders. Its passage was brought to the notice of merchants by the rate of interest rising in London, and falling in Antwerp and Bruges. Couriers were coming and going, and Henry and Wolsey tried to escape questions. Pace assured the emperor that Henry had 100,000 gold crowns at Antwerp, ready for the Swiss, so Maximilian asked his daughter to send over to Antwerp to inquire of Thomas Spinelli and others if this was true. If so, she was to get it handed over secretly to Fugger's factor, and the bill sent to Jacob Fugger at Augsburg, for payment to the imperial treasurer, either at Augsburg or Constance. He found it difficult to make up his mind, whether it would best serve his turn to side with Francis or Henry, but he would get any money there was about. The point which turned him towards England was that the army of Swiss, that Henry was willing to pay to follow him into Italy, might help him to keep his towns, Verona

and Brescia, which were very rich, and were the key to what he
wanted in Italy.   Venice knew this and was afraid.   By the end
of 1515 he had pretty well decided on accepting Henry's offers ;
but Pace had strict orders not to let him have any of the money
that was coming for the Swiss.   Wolsey had by then arranged
with Frescobaldi to pay further sums to Pace and Wingfield,
when the army had reached Italy.   It would have to come down
from Augsburg through Trent after the army.   The Frescobaldi
firm were finding difficulty in providing it.   Henry and Wolsey
were as innocent about matters of exchange as Elizabeth was,
until Gresham instructed her.   It was only when the English
sovereign took into service such a man as Gresham, whose
antecedents led him towards patriotism and straight dealing, as
well as his own profit, that the English sovereign could walk
safely on Bourse.   Perhaps Gresham gave Elizabeth an advantage over other sovereigns from which the British empire still
benefits.   If so, it was because the English merchant-class, and
the English sovereign-class, in the sixteenth century, were fonder
of their native land than their kind were anywhere else.

If Pace was to convince the emperor and the Swiss that he
was acting for Henry some sort of credentials would have to be
sent to him.   He had a servant named Thomas Cotton, who is
first heard of as travelling between him and England, and probably followed his master out in the late autumn.   At the beginning of 1516 Pace sent him to England for a commission.   Pace
had some trouble with Michael Abbate, who turned out badly ;
at least he was suspected by Wolsey of being a French spy.   Pace
thought he was not, and at the most his fault seems to have been
that he was too fond of using what Sir Robert Wingfield called
his ' lavas ' tongue.   Even at that he seems only to have been
trying to impress the friends of the emperor and Francesco
Sforza with Pace's importance.   At another moment the French
spread it that there was no Pace at all among the Swiss, and that
it was all a plot of Cardinal Schiner's to make it thought that
Henry was backing him.

By the end of the year the eight cantons had ratified the
treaty with Francis, and after the diet Pace went from Switzerland with Schiner and Sir Robert Wingfield to Augsburg, to see

the emperor, and to take over money which had arrived. Pace
and Schiner did not tell Sir Robert more than they could help
about what was going on, which rather hurt his feelings ; but he
told Wolsey that Pace was wise, discreet, and diligent. The
going over of the eight cantons, and the friendly meeting between
Leo and Francis at Bologna in December, had an effect 'favourable to the French in Switzerland ; but there was to be another
diet in January, at which the five cantons might declare for Pace.
In Italy Francis was so satisfied with the pope's friendship that
he withdrew the greater part of his army, leaving a garrison in
Milan, under Bourbon, and sending Lautrec to help the Venetians
to retake Brescia and Verona from Maximilian.

Antwerp was full of rumours at Christmas-time about what
was going to happen. Henry was known to be sending great
sums to Upper Germany, but even Knight, the important English
agent in Flanders, did not know that the money was going to
the Swiss. He did not know what Pace was doing, and thought
the money was for the emperor. Much more was known in
Italy, where the news had come through from Venice ; but
Wolsey did not even tell Giglis the facts. In Antwerp the news
always got about when great sums of money were moving, and
it was rumoured that anything from 20,000 to 100,000 gold
crowns, or more, were going through. Every one on Bourse
was talking about it, but they did not know the exact sum, or
its destination. On 5th January Knight advised Wolsey that
the merchants in Flanders were saying that neither Frescobaldi,
nor any other Italian banker, could furnish half 100,000 crowns
in Upper Germany, nor could even the Fuggers or Welsers, the
two greatest German firms. Knight would have preferred that
the money should go through Welser. The Swiss were by this
time raising their price to 120,000 gold crowns, which would
bring out 15 or 20,000 men, and that was what Wolsey promised
they should have. The exact amount promised to the Swiss
does not matter to Pace's history. When recruiting began the
100,000 crowns, or more, divided itself into monthly ' pays,'
which had to be made in advance. To keep Pace's account at
Augsburg, or wherever payment was to be made, well replenished
had to be Wolsey's care. Two members of the council at home,

Ruthal and Fox, assured the Venetian ambassador that this money was not being sent to be used against Venice, and the ambassador was finally convinced that the object of all these plans was ' to make some stir in Italy against the most christian king,' who was Venice's ally, and not directly against Venice. When at last Knight in Flanders heard what Pace was about, he said that, if he carried it through well, Wolsey would be able to dictate peace to whom he would. Wolsey ardently desired to be recognized as the peacemaker of Europe.

Wingfield stayed with the emperor at Augsburg, to draw more money as it came in. Schiner and Pace—two churchmen —went to Constance to meet Galeazzo and the Swiss captains, to discuss recruiting, and they wanted the emperor to be at Constance while the diet sat ; for his presence on the frontier would influence the deputies. The actual arrival of money at Augsburg, on the heels of Pace's promises that it was on the way, did Henry's reputation so much good that there was said to be no prince like him. All others differed from him as shadow does from substance. Pace was very pleased with the King, and showed him how judicious letters to pope and emperor would further enhance his reputation. He was surprised and pleased that the King and Wolsey had not let him down. The January diet came to no useful decision in favour of Henry and the emperor's cause, but Pace and Schiner concluded that the five cantons would readily enlist, and that there was a chance of filling up from the other thirteen. Only 17,000 men were needed, and their confidence grew with their stay in Constance. Pace wrote to his old antagonist in Rome, Giglis, to tell him how to advise his holiness ' quod si non faciet, reputabo eum non modo oculis sed animo quoque caecum.' Some of Maximilian's councillors were receiving pensions from Francis, so Wingfield asked Wolsey to let him and Pace have £100, to distribute among them as they thought best.

On 31st January Pace wrote to Wolsey from Constance that all went well, and that he had every hope of raising a large body of Swiss, to march at once, even more than he needed. All would march under the popular Galeazzo, whom alone they would have for leader. They would not only fight the French in Lombardy,

6

but pursue them into France. He wanted bills payable at sight, and said that if there was any difficulty in getting merchants to pay money out by exchange it must be sewn in the coats of secret messengers ' after the manner of Italy.' This would save the heavy charges and losses on exchange. He was an astute observer and thinker, and there is much in his apology for the delays of the cantons in coming to a conclusion in comparison with Henry's quicker decisions ; ' for they be a community and their matters hang in many thousand heads and a prince's but in one.' [1] There was little chance of the diet coming to a conclusion, which would send an army to fight for one prince, now that two were trying to buy them. Pace was sure that Zurich would come into the field for Henry, whatever the other cantons might do ; but it is to be suspected that the most pro-English of them thought that English troops were coming to fight beside them in Lombardy ; or at least were going to invade Picardy at the same time. Just when Pace was confident of success, arrived an emissary from Francis to bribe Galeazzo himself, with the offer of 10,000 crowns in cash and as much in yearly rents, if he could win the Swiss over to Francis. Galeazzo said he was pledged to the emperor and the other allies, and he immediately disclosed the offer to Pace. Henry seemed at the moment the richer, and the prompter to produce money. When French money came the Swiss treated it as if it was what was due under the Dijon agreement. It is not interesting to search out which of the payments made to London merchants were to go to Pace, and which to defend Tournai and Calais. Here goes over the best part of 100,000 gold crowns, taking four or five to go to a pound sterling. Things got hot and strong at Constance in February 1516. Maximilian had promised to be there, and had broken his promise. The Swiss captains, who had come to make plans, said he never kept promises. Pace thought if it had not been for himself they would have gone home. Maximilian, according to the original plan, was to have marched in command of the whole army, including the Swiss, for he was no mean commander, but they would not have it so. His command had to be confined to his own army, which was composed of lans-

[1] *L. and P.*, ii. 1466. An important letter by Pace.

quenets, cavalry, and artillery, all Germans. The Swiss were to
be led by Galeazzo, and Pace would go with them (really as
security for their pay), ' for him they do esteem for his wisdom
and faith, and me for my King's money and a little more because
they do evidently see now that I was not sent into this country
to deceive them.' The Swiss would not trust the emperor about
money, and warned Pace that they did not get more than 40,000
florins of the 100,000 crowns which Henry had given him for
them on the last campaign. This was what Wolsey had suspected. About 100,000 crowns for 20,000 men seemed to the
Swiss to represent the value of a good war to them. Galeazzo
regarded himself as going into Henry's service, at Pace's offer ;
he was soon speaking of ' our King.' Pace and Schiner felt they
must abandon hope of preventing the men of the eight cantons
serving the French, for they had ' the teat in their mouths,' and
would not let it go except for a great bribe. The diet did not
come to a unanimous decision as to which King should be served,
and recruiting must go as best it could. Such a state of affairs
might not last until there was a battle ; for the diet was at all
events not anxious for Swiss to fight Swiss. Pace had proved
his King to be the best paymaster, and his army of Swiss was
therefore likely to outlast one enrolled for Francis. His men
were likely to march and to fight.

Everyone who was going wanted to be on the move, especially Pace, who feared some one might buy his Swiss over his
head at the last moment. He wanted to go and fetch the
emperor to Constance, but the Swiss thought—or pretended to
think—he was trying to get away. So Schiner, Galeazzo, and
Pace all wrote to stir the emperor up. On the whole, Pace
thought this holding off was not a sign that he was going over
to Francis ; for he believed he feared England more than Hell.
As the Swiss would not let Pace out of their sight, Galeazzo
had to go into Germany to hurry the emperor up. When he
got back to Constance, Pace was delighted to hear from him
that there were victuals, artillery, and cavalry all ready. So
enrolling of men could begin on 15th February. Seventeen
thousand Swiss were to be raised for Henry, and they were to
assemble at Chur (Coire), some twenty-five miles above Milan,

whence a three days' march would bring them into Lombardy. Pace had feared the expedition might be hurt by the emperor's slowness ('these Almayns be so diligent [dilatory?] in resolving their matters, that they had liever lose a great city, than to arise from their dinner to defend the same'); but he became enthusiastic about the expedition, and asked Pace to come over and see him. He said his daughter, the regent of the Netherlands, had told him he was greatly trusted by Wolsey, which one would have thought he had known for some time. He left Pace in complete charge of the enlistment. Schiner wrote Wolsey a commendation of Pace, who had made war with France possible, and whose wisdom and constancy had won the esteem of the emperor, the Swiss, and every one in those parts. He was aiming a blow at France on England's behalf. Schiner hoped to catch Francis in north Italy, and punish him ' on the scene of his trespass,' at Marignano.

Money went like water, and the Swiss, even more than most soldiers, became unruly and lazy when unpaid. Complete victory was so near that it would be a shame to lose it for a few thousand crowns. One can imagine these three men at Constance, talking over the enterprise, and writing letters to fill up time. They were excited—the *condottiere*, the cardinal, and the secret agent ; the two ecclesiastics filled with hatred of France, and of opinion that they were saving Christendom from the overlordship of the French king. As soon as the seventeen thousand men were enrolled they were to march. Pace arranged this, with a nobleman and two captains Maximilian sent over to draw up plans. Pace not only threw his whole strength into his duties, but wrote to the pope, the King of Spain, and Wolsey, to remind them of theirs. He even wrote to the haughty cardinal of Gurk, at Potnoy, intimating that he did not believe that the emperor would desert the Swiss. This, of course, meant that he was longing for an assurance on that point ; Gurk showed the letter to the emperor, who wrote to him that of course he would not. It must be remembered that at this time there was peace between England and France, and the French ambassador would sometimes surprise Henry with Maximilian's and Ferdinand's ambassadors talking over this expedition. The King would saunter off arm-in-arm with Norfolk and Suffolk, as if it was all about nothing. ' Money, money, money ! ' was the cry of these men at Constance. If the Swiss offered themselves they had to be taken, although the ranks were full ; otherwise the whole nation would pretend to be offended, and one lost those one did want. In the middle of February the emperor wrote to Pace from Potnoy. He was establishing posts to Constance to keep them in touch. Pace and Galeazzo had to go over to Zurich, on the chance of the diet coming to any conclusion which would bind the mercenaries to serve Henry or Francis ; but there was no such answer. Eight cantons should be expected to enlist under Francis, and five under Henry ; but Pace had a month's pay in hand, and good credit for the rest. Francis' Swiss, if they were not paid, were not so likely to fight ; but there was always the anxiety that a diet might recall all the mercenaries from both armies.

News of the death of Ferdinand, King of Spain, arrived on 18th February, but it made no difference to the marching of the expedition ; for the Swiss had not trusted him, and they had not expected to get any more money from him. Had the expedition, however, not been in preparation at this moment, Francis would have descended on Naples, the investiture of which the pope had promised him on Ferdinand's death. Pace could congratulate himself on having achieved this great success, in accordance with Wolsey's policy. According to More in *Utopia* the French King was ever after ' fugitive Naples ' ; such men as he and Pace thought his aim was to keep Milan, conquer the Venetians and all Italy, and then win Flanders, Brabant, Burgundy, and other countries.[1] A letter from More to Erasmus, at Basel, written on 17th February, says : ' Pace is on an embassy in your part of the world ' ; and that Henry had a great affection for him, and hoped for his safe return. He was high in favour of King and cardinal, and all men of worth.

When the enlistment began recruits poured in. Schiner told Wolsey that, within a month of their arrival in Italy, he would hear of a complete rout of the French. The Swiss would

---

[1] *Utopia*, Book I.

winter in Italy, living on spoil, and then invade France. But it had been a costly business for all who had tried to buy the Swiss. They simply swallowed the money. Schiner went to the emperor, and Pace and Galeazzo went to meet the Swiss at Chur ; and on 15th February gave them the first month's pay in advance. By 19th the emperor was going down to Trent, on the Italian frontier, at the head of lansquenets, cavalry, and artillery. Pace was in high spirits—nothing but delay in the arrival of the money could save the French from defeat. If Henry and Wolsey could see what he did, they would not miss the opportunity of crushing France for a million of gold ; things were improving hourly. Francis was likely to have some of the best-known Swiss military leaders in his army, but Pace claimed to have the most valiant men of all the cantons with him, and not only of the five forest cantons. The captains said they would set forward with good will, having the King of England for their master, for he had never deceived them. Pace felt he would nearly die of sorrow if all these preparations were to be undone by lack of money. This would be the greatest enterprise ever undertaken against France. He felt he was going, not merely to war, but to take part in an actual hand-to-hand conflict. He wrote to Burbank that he hoped his friends at home would pray for him ; he joked to Burbank about ' Summer shall be Green,' who was Sir Robert Wingfield. He wrote amidst the noise of arms and drums, and the Swiss officers were dropping in for meals and drinks. He asked Burbank to tell Wolsey not to believe that ' Summer shall be Green's ' inventions could hinder him in setting out on the expedition. So at the moment of starting we come upon something like a quarrel between Sir Robert Wingfield and Pace. The nickname was probably taken from a popular ballad. We get a letter from Wingfield to Wolsey. Ministers (by which he meant diplomatists or ambassadors) should possess four things —wit, learning, good will, and experience ; ' for my part I am not ashamed to give place to your secretary (Pace) in the first twain, . . . in the third it were too great a shame for me to give place to any, and in the fourth, both to eschew arrogance and comparison, I will leave the judgment of that part to such

as have practised with us both.'[1] This jealousy was unfortunate, and almost worse was a quarrel which was arising
between Schiner and Galeazzo, the former being jealous of the
latter, for supplanting him in the favour, and in the leadership
of the Swiss. Schiner and Wingfield moved down towards
Trent with the emperor. Pace and Galeazzo sent off the first
detachment of Swiss on 20th February,[2] and followed on 21st
with the rest. Pace left the Swiss, soon after they had started,
and rode on to Trent, to meet Frescobaldi's factor, who should
have had money for him. On the way he overtook the emperor,
three days' journey from Trent, and dined with him, Schiner,
and Wingfield. He urged Maximilian not to become friendly
with Francis. Next morning he rode on to Trent, leaving
Schiner and Wingfield with the emperor, who said he would
always be one day's march from the Swiss, and that when the
time for battle came he would be among the first into it. The
emperor caught Pace up at Trent, but Frescobaldi's factor had
no money. Talking to the factor would not do much good, so
Pace relieved his feelings by rounding on the emperor about
the failure of the last expedition, and recommended more
caution this time. Three days after the emperor, came Galeazzo
to Trent, with his seventeen thousand Swiss. All the captains
of the Swiss and Germans took oath at Schiner's lodging, to
live and die together ; the best comradeship prevailed all round,
and the emperor was keen and energetic. The Swiss boasted
that they would soon revenge themselves on the French for
Marignano, but no one was so foolish as to expect that they
would stay in the field if they were unpaid, and half a month
had gone before the pay for the second had come, let alone the
third. Pace had had to disburse much more than he had
expected the Swiss would have demanded, and in that respect
made a worse start than Wolsey at home knew about. He
had spent the money on the Swiss and in ' secret ways ' to induce
them to march. He had several interviews with the emperor
at Trent ; at some of which Schiner and Wingfield were present.
His servant, Thomas Cotton, had returned with credentials for
him and Wingfield, and they presented them to Maximilian

at Trent. Wingfield spoke on behalf of Henry, and Pace on behalf of Wolsey and as the special emissary to whose care the expedition had been entrusted. Then the emperor promised to advance the second month's pay for the Swiss, pending payment by Frescobaldi's agent ; and appointed the Marquis of Brandenburg to go with Pace as a hostage. Thus secured, the Swiss marched into Italy under Galeazzo on 4th March, and Pace rode after them, leaving the emperor at Trent, where he received the Sacrament and kept his Easter, although the festival was not till 23rd, so that he might afterwards devote his mind to military affairs. He expected to encounter the enemy in two or three days. The Swiss marched in the van under Galeazzo, then came the artillery and cavalry, and then the emperor and his lansquenets. On 11th March the army reached Verona which was held for the emperor, the enemy retiring before them. When they reached the Mincio the enemy threatened to oppose their crossing, but were dispersed by serpentines ; and they crossed on 12th, and raised the siege of Brescia. The emperor went slightly out of his way towards Cremona, which he could not take, and, after wasting some time trying to take a fort, reached the Adda on 22nd March, Easter Eve, where he showed great valour in face of the enemy, who were driven back on Milan.

On Easter Monday the army was some nine miles from Milan ; and Schiner and Galeazzo urged the emperor to attack the city, alleging that the enemy could not hold out for two days, the citizens being hostile to the French. They remained where they were that night, and next day the emperor sent for Pace and Wingfield. He appeared ' sore moved,' saying he had news that Francis had offered to cease helping Scotland against England if Henry would break from this expedition. This emperor had had to resort to subterfuges all his life to get money, and he had become so experienced in dissimulating and making false suggestions, that any one dealing with him had to be constantly prepared against surprise. Pace did not yet know him thoroughly. He, Wingfield, and Schiner assured him that what he had heard was untrue ; they would vouch that it was. Pace ought to have carried the dispute into the

emperor's breast, and have asserted that he was putting forward
an excuse which would get him out of what he was disinclined
to go through with.   But, for all his blunt comments on princes,
Pace was never disposed to accuse them of being corrupt, and,
if Maximilian suddenly changed his course, those who knew him
could surmise that he had heard the clinking of gold.   It is a
terrible thing to be an emperor who cannot afford to be independent, and one must pity this ' Pochi Denari,' as the Italians
called him.   Now he appeared to be satisfied that Henry was
not betraying him, but he sat all day in pensiveness, angry
with every one who urged him to set forward.   At night he
sent for Schiner, Wingfield, and Pace, and said plainly he could
not perform his promise to advance the Swiss their second
month's pay, pending the arrival of the King's money.   He
said he had none for his own army and household, and was
therefore compelled to abandon the attempt to take Milan.
Schiner was furious to see the hated Frenchmen slipping from
his grasp, but Pace diplomatically reminded the emperor that,
by retreating when Milan was almost his, he would lose his
chance of getting Italy, Naples, and Navarre for the Habsburgs.
He certainly could not pay Pace's Swiss ; for his captain-general
tried to borrow money from Pace for his own troops.   The
second month's pay had fallen due nine days before, and Pace
had only part of it.   Schiner, Wingfield, and Pace turned to
the emperor's councillors, and urged them to give him the
same advice as they had done, and tell him that no man in
Germany would esteem him worth a groat if he turned back.
So writes Pace in a long letter to Wolsey on the crisis, but this
did not urge the emperor forward, perhaps because he knew his
own value.   Presently came to him a Spaniard, ' a vile person,'
from the Duke of Bourbon, who held Milan, to say that if the
emperor would come and drink with him he would be welcome.
If not, the constable would come out to breakfast with the
emperor.   In answer the emperor commanded the Marquis of
Brandenburg to send a trumpet, and offer battle on the following
day.   Next morning, the Wednesday after Easter, the constable
did not come out to give battle, but said he would come out next
day.   The emperor used this as an excuse for not waiting any

longer.　The enemy evidently expected an attack, for they set about burning houses in the suburbs to prevent the Swiss creeping up to the walls under cover.　The Swiss crossed the Adda under Galeazzo, and took a fort on the way to Milan, killing every man in it.　If the rules of war justified a barbarous act the Swiss showed no tendency towards mercy.　There was fighting on the outskirts of Milan, but, without the emperor's artillery there, and without his cavalry in the open, not much could be achieved.　On the advice of Galeazzo and Pace, the Swiss sent a messenger to the emperor, desiring him, if he was afraid, to put himself into Brescia, and they, with his cavalry, would clear the French out of Italy.　In Pace's opinion his retreat would mean the ruin of Christendom.　He, the cardinal, and Wingfield were almost dead for sorrow.　Galeazzo went so far as to say, if he ran away, he would commit greater treason against all Christian princes than ever did Judas against Christ. The emperor changed his tune, he gave out that he could not trust the Swiss to stand firm, and indeed it was a fact that they had betrayed Ludovico Sforza.　They might or might not be reliable, if paid—they probably would be if well led, for they were fine mercenaries—but, being mercenaries, there was no particular reason why they should get themselves killed for nothing.　If they did not get their English crowns they might seize the emperor ; and his own German lansquenets, being likewise unpaid, were unlikely to protect him ; though they might have fought the Swiss for the possession of such a security. At present the Swiss were holding Pace and Galeazzo as security for their second and third month's pay.　Galeazzo managed to supply some money to keep them going, but Pace considered his life would be in danger if money did not come.　The Swiss saw no more of the emperor, and Pace was afterwards emphatic in his assurance to Wolsey that the French did not drive him back from before Milan.　They did not dare to attack the Swiss, but he retreated voluntarily and shamefully.[1]　His was a ' sudden and wilful departure.'　On 2nd April Pace was at Lodi with the Swiss.　He told Wingfield that if any one asked him for money he was to say he could not give it without

---

[1] *L. and P.*, ii. 1877.

Pace's consent ; he seems to have been putting forward an inducement to the Swiss to spare his life. Maximilian's sudden change of mind may in part be accounted for by the news of the arrival in Milan of Swiss from the eight cantons, to help the French ; but if he had waited he would have found they were no danger. If he had not delayed in trying to take towns and forts, on his way to Milan, this force would not have had time to reach the enemy. A friar was sent out by the Swiss in Milan with a letter to Pace's Swiss, saying Bourbon was strong enough to keep Milan, and urging their comrades to go home, and offering to get them safe-conducts. Swiss must not fight against Swiss, so one or other band of mercenaries had to go. The captains met in the presence of Galeazzo and Pace at Lodi, and sent an answer describing this suggestion as impertinent. On this the Swiss captains in Milan agreed that it was their duty to retire—in point of fact it was unlikely that Francis would pay them, and there was little zeal for his service. Pace had made Henry appear the only prince who could and would keep his promises to pay, and the diet, by being divided as to whom the nation should serve, had really withdrawn the sanction to serve any one. Now it recalled all their country-men. By this time the emperor had decided that the enemy had cut him off from his base, so that Henry's money could not reach the Swiss, nor could supplies come down from Trent. This was indeed the case for some days, and the enemy had closed the roads leading to Germany sufficiently to prevent Pace sending letters or receiving the pay for the Swiss.[1] This Pace stated himself, but the finance-men found it more difficult to have the money ready at Augsburg than they did to carry it through Trent to Brescia. There was no difficulty about the retreat. The emperor left his own army under the command of the Marquis of Brandenburg, and made for Trent, by way of Verona, sending messages to the Swiss as he went. He would soon be with them again, and would lead them against the French. By 10th April he was miles away. He left his guns, but carried off the powder. His army fell back on Verona. He suggested he was going to meet the pay coming down from

[1] Allen, *Opus Epist.*, iii. 37, seq.

Trent and bring it to the Swiss. With him he carried off
Schiner and Wingfield. Schiner went because he was angry
with the Swiss for taking Galeazzo as their leader in his place,
and Wingfield because as ambassador it was his duty to attend
the emperor ; both thought the emperor had disgraced himself.
They left Pace with the Swiss at Lodi, near Milan. Unfortunately, while Wingfield and Pace were so far apart, a packet
from Wolsey, addressed to Pace, was handed to Wingfield. It
seemed urgent, so he opened it, after consulting Schiner, and
among the letters he read was one (now much mutilated)
which greatly upset him, considering that he had loved and
honoured Pace, not only for Wolsey's sake, but also for his
learning. The letter had revealed that Pace had complained
of him to Wolsey and had spoken of him as ' Grene Somer.' The
ambassador, smarting under the scorn, felt he ought to reveal
to Wolsey that he had had to rectify errors of Pace's which
would otherwise have produced the greatest mischief. Poor
old ' Summer shall be Green ' rode over to Trent in a very dejected
state to receive some of the pay. It had been provided at
Augsburg by Jerome Pruen, the Welser's agent, working with
Frescobaldi, and by Fugger, and had been brought down by
Schiner's chaplain. The German financiers had come into the
transaction because the Frescobaldi had not the means to convey
such large sums to Augsburg. Fugger had to lend money to
Frescobaldi.[1] This money was for the balance of the second
month's pay, but money even for the third was on the way.
Leonard Frescobaldi went from England to Germany, and down
to Trent. Part of this money was paid out to Wingfield. A
considerable sum for the Swiss got down to Brescia, which was
the emperor's town ; but it was seized by his soldiers for pay
he owed them, while Pace and Galeazzo were being held as
hostages by the Swiss at Lodi for this very pay. Pace and
Galeazzo were convinced that the emperor would ruin the
enterprise ; they do not.seem to have realized that he was not
coming back, and had ruined it already. They were so miserable
about it that they took to their beds. The money stolen at
Brescia would have kept the Swiss in the field for some time,

[1] R. Ehrenberg, *Zeitalter der Fugger*, i. 96.

and they were loud in their cries against the emperor. Hearing there was money coming down from Trent, the Swiss fell farther back on Bergamo, taking Pace with them. By this time the third month's pay was due. The whole sum Henry had promised was in Flanders on 20th March, but the Swiss began to say the Frescobaldi had been corrupted by the French. By 21st April Wingfield saw the enterprise was languishing, because the ' order and diligent conveying ' of the sinews of war had not been properly looked to. Pace wrote to Wolsey from Bergamo. Wolsey had wished the army to invade France, but that could not be done now, as the emperor had made it impossible to go against Milan ; and the pope, Florence, and Genoa would not come in until Milan was taken. Pace described himself as so oppressed with sorrow and disappointment that he doubted if he would ever see Wolsey again. Only their loyalty to Galeazzo held the Swiss from going over to the French, and Galeazzo himself was so annoyed by the injury done to his reputation by the emperor that even he might go over. Bourbon had destroyed Galeazzo's house in Milan, seized his goods, and set up a painting of him hanging upside down, like a traitor, at the city gate. Schiner was angry with Pace for having refused to give him some of Henry's money for the emperor. Pace had learnt that, wherever his King's money passed, the emperor would try to get some of it, by force or false pretences, saying, if he did not get what he desired, he would go home, ' like as children say they will not go to school without bread and butter.' In Pace's view Schiner dared not refuse the emperor anything, and Wingfield took him for a god, and supposed all his deeds and thoughts proceeded ' *ex spiritu.*' While the Swiss and Pace were at Bergamo, the emperor sent Schiner down to them, and it was said he brought money. So the soldiers crowded round Pace's house, saying they would now fight the French, even if the emperor would not go with them. The cardinal had only brought a small sum, at which they murmured, and some seven or eight thousand started home. The enemy approached Bergamo and compelled the remainder to retreat. Schiner, at this crisis among the Swiss, invited Galeazzo to stifle the quarrel between them, and to forget the past and love him as formerly. The old soldier agreed to do so ; but in a few days Schiner was abusing him in Pace's presence. Pace described the cardinal as a man of great genius, though too passionate. The enemy came up to Bergamo, as the Swiss retired, and were fired on by artillery ; but there was no serious fighting. Schiner and Pace were actually imprisoned by the Swiss, charged with deceiving them, but that night 32,000 florins arrived, and Leonard Frescobaldi came with more in the morning. All the three months' pay was given them.[1] This made things look better ; they had been paid in the largest manner, and they might go against the enemy again, if they were supported by the emperor's cavalry and artillery. At the least they ought to stand firm for another month, which began a few days later. Pace had carried out all his promises.

Galeazzo had been left behind, ill, at Brescia, and when he heard that Pace was made prisoner by the Swiss he prepared to have himself carried to the camp, but, as the French cavalry scoured the country, he had to make part of the journey by the lake of Garda by night. Just at that time news came from Trent that the emperor would not return. So the Swiss abandoned the expedition, and Pace could do nothing but ask them to assure their leaders at home that Henry's promises had been carried out, and urge them never to serve the King of France.

[1] *L. and P.*, ii. lxxvii.

CHAPTER V

MAXIMILIAN

THE scene of this comedy of the invasion of the Milanese was now changed to Trent; and the emperor proceeded to play with Pace, to call his mind from thinking badly of his desertion. He offered to give, or suggested that he should give, to Henry the investiture of Milan; but Pace was sure the people would have none for duke but a Sforza, and that this plan was only an attempt to deceive his King. The offer would be a better one when the emperor had taken Milan; and Francesco Sforza had done nothing to justify the emperor in breaking his promise to give him the duchy. Maximilian afterwards pretended he would not be unwilling to resign the imperial crown in Henry's favour.

The Swiss marched contentedly home under Galeazzo, for they had received all their pay for the three months for which they had served, and had suffered little. Pace had kept all the King's promises, and they had treated him, as events proved, with undue suspicion and unnecessary severity; but every allowance can be made for mercenaries who had already been cheated by impecunious princes. They seemed ready to go against the French again, if satisfactory terms could be agreed. All too late Pace found there were another 150,000 florins for him at Augsburg, but the cavalry and artillery had to be supplied by the emperor, who could not pay them, and the policy of lending (giving) him money had never been found a good one. Pace stayed at Trent with the emperor, who sat devising plans to get English crowns to pay troops to keep his cities in Italy from the Venetians. The impetuous Cardinal Schiner took upon himself to tell the German lansquenets that Henry would pay them

—a thing he was very unlikely to do. He might pay gunners and troopers to support the Swiss, but not German infantry. Some lansquenets had come up to Trent with the emperor, but most of his army lay at Verona and Brescia. The artillery, without gun-powder, had been dragged to Bellinzona. Down to Verona to serve the emperor went some five thousand Swiss, who held Schiner as a hostage. They seemed ready to rely on the emperor for pay, and to fight against the French and Venetians ; even in the face of any contrary decision reached by their diet at home.

The Swiss who had marched with Pace, under Galeazzo, had been three months in the field ; long enough to allow of a smashing victory over the French ; but they had had no oppor-tunity of wiping out the disgrace thrown on them at Marignano, or of getting square on the breach of the agreement made at Dijon. As they marched home they could argue as to the causes of the failure of the expedition. The rank and file cried that they could not be expected to risk their lives unless they were paid, and that their pay had been delayed through the fault of the Frescobaldi. They suggested these merchants had been bribed by the French, and that the emperor had betrayed them, being in French pay, and had gone away leaving them without cavalry or gunpowder. Wingfield likewise attributed the ruin of the expedition to the want of money and gunpowder. Cardinal Schiner hated Galeazzo for having supplanted him in the affec-tions and in the leadership of the Swiss, and, as Pace had come from England with orders to trust this old soldier, and as he had trusted him implicitly, Schiner had come to include him in his condemnation.[1] The failure of the expedition was, in his view, due to Pace, who had entirely submitted himself to the counsel of Galeazzo, 'whose conduct is openly known and noted, that he hath ever been, and ever taken for, a friend of the Frenchmen.' When the King of France was last in Milan he had supped several times with Galeazzo's wife—so said Schiner. He added that most of the Swiss captains chosen by Pace and Galeazzo had been French-favouring, and that a quarter of the money had been wasted in paying foot soldiers too highly. Pace, he said,

[1] *L. and P.*, ii. 2040.

would listen to no one but Galeazzo. Schiner induced the emperor to blame and hate Pace for following Galeazzo's advice, and made the accusation that, to cover his errors, he had written lies to England about the emperor. The truth was that Schiner had become unpopular with the Swiss, because his promises made on behalf of the pope had not been kept, and Pace and Galeazzo had taken his place among them. These charges against Pace were in a letter to the emperor's ambassador in London. Schiner asked him to tell Henry that he (Schiner) had confided certain things of great importance concerning Henry to Pace, under a great oath of secrecy, and that Pace had revealed them. He accused Pace of having told Francesco Sforza of the emperor's offer to give the empire and Milan to Henry—an important indiscretion, as Sforza had been promised the investiture. Schiner's suspicions about Galeazzo were not unwarranted, but it was all a question of money with men like him. They were usually loyal to those who paid them according to agreement.

There was mutual recrimination between these ambassadors, councillors, and soldiers, and Pace described Jacob Villinger, the imperial treasurer, as a very deceitful man, and one of those chiefly responsible for the emperor's bad conduct. The blame for what had happened at Milan was thrown from one to another. Maximilian was laughed at in Milan and Venice. Pace said that such a chance of taking Milan would have moved an ass, but not the emperor. Pace himself ever maintained that the emperor simply fell away undefeated ; and that the Swiss would have stood firm and captured the town. It is very likely that the emperor had thought he would be the gainer financially if he went off and came to terms with Francis. It is possible he wanted to go home to gather in some cash which was likely to be lying about after the death of the King of Hungary, which occurred in March. It is as likely that he thought he might be unable to take Milan castle or do anything that counted against the enemy. He was certainly justified in fearing that the unpaid Swiss might seize him for their pay, and hold him prisoner as his own Flemish subjects had done when he was much younger— or betray him, as these same Swiss had betrayed Ludovico

7

Sforza. He did not want to be led captive to France by Francis, as Francis was afterwards led to Spain by his grandson, Charles. Pace maintained that the failure of the expedition was primarily due to the delay in the arrival of the money. The Frescobaldi did not behave dishonestly or negligently in the matter, but they had not the business connexions in Upper Germany which would have facilitated the exchange of such very large sums of money to those parts. Wolsey should have employed Fugger or Welser from the first, but it was a most praiseworthy thing, and a remarkable one, that all the English gold promised was paid in Flanders when promised. Wolsey explained [1] that the retreat was due to want of money, but that Henry had provided what he had promised through Frescobaldi. He blamed these merchants, and said the King would punish their knavery whenever he got hold of them, but, afterwards, he seemed to realize their position ; they had done their best, and their task was too great for them.[2] It is true that if Wolsey had sent the money in gold by bearers, it might have got there sooner ; but he found it difficult to get so much together quickly, and the roads were dangerous. In point of fact Henry had sent four months' pay, and the Swiss had only earned three and Pace held the balance. Henry was very pleased with Pace for his share in the expedition, and made him his principal secretary, and, to fill his pockets, he was made treasurer of Lichfield. His predecessor as the King's secretary had been Ruthal, who became privy seal. After this Pace seems to have received no more ecclesiastical preferment until 1519, when such rewards were showered on him.

After the Swiss had gone, Pace at Trent found himself in fresh difficulties—this time at the rapacious emperor's suit. He had had a very bad time with the Swiss, mentally and physically, and the season had been a severe one. He had not recovered his health, and was confined to his bed for some days ' as well by meane of a dysease in his legge as oother maladie.' To him in this state sent the emperor for some of his King's money ; his orders were to disburse none of it. Schiner and Wingfield, who had been with the emperor during the campaign, and regarded

[1] *L. and P.*, ii. 1928.
[2] R. Ehrenberg, *Zeitalter der Fugger*, i. 279.

his army as the mainstay of the enterprise, and Pace and Galeazzo only as bad leaders of a subsidiary band of Swiss mercenaries, joined the emperor in his attacks on Henry's purse, which Pace held. Henry ought, they said, to pay the troops the emperor had in Italy, who were to be the nucleus of the next army to attack France. The only argument for lending the money which had weight with Pace was that his refusal might send the emperor into an alliance with Francis. ' No ! ' he said ; his commission from home had been to raise and pay an army of Swiss, and the money had been sent him for their pay. That army of Swiss had marched home, and he had no authority to pay any one else any money. Apart from such a great expense, Henry did not wish to provide money to be used against the Venetians. Pace was to keep what had been sent for other Swiss, who were to be raised for another attempt on Milan ; for Henry and Wolsey supposed at first that there was only a lull or interval in hostilities, and that the emperor, Schiner, Wingfield, Pace, Sforza, Galeazzo and the rest of them were active in preparations. As a matter of fact no one but Pace seriously thought the experiment worth repetition, and few but Galeazzo talked about it as if it was. The emperor, his councillors, and his captains on the one hand, and the Swiss captains and the rank and file on the other, all talked about the fresh expedition ; but not one of them expected to march, and they hoped to talk Henry's gold into their pockets. The emperor was thinking only of Verona and Brescia. Few princes have had to beg for money as persistently as Maximilian had to do, and there were so many beggars with him that at last Pace had to pay more attention to his importunities. At this moment, according to Pace, he had not enough to pay for his dinner, and he might sell himself to Francis. Money was so scarce everywhere, particularly in Upper Germany, that one could not hide a great pile of it at Fugger's bank, and Wingfield said Pace had money. Pace had himself carried from his sick bed to the emperor. He was ill in mind and body. He was not a strong man and ill-fitted for exposure and fatigue, and, least of all, worry. He soon got knocked up, and, worst of all, he worried over everything ; all excitement at success and very depressed when things went wrong, and often too sorry for himself. It gave him some satisfaction to be able to write home to Wolsey that he had had himself carried into the emperor's presence. His determination breathed zeal: he would be faithful unto death to his King. Excitement often carried him through trials Erasmus would have felt himself unequal to; but Erasmus laughed at himself when Pace would have pitied himself. Wolsey in distress acted and spoke as Pace would have done. There were certainly Swiss in Maximilian's army round Verona and Brescia, and they—or some of them—may have been those whom Pace had recruited, which might be a good reason for calling on Henry for their pay, but the expedition was really at an end—had failed. Before the emperor, in the presence of Sir Robert Wingfield, who should have supported him, the sick man at last gave way, and pledged Henry's credit, a thing he had no commission to do. The emperor was to have 60,000 florins belonging to Henry in Frescobaldi's hands, to pay his troops at Verona; but he was to write to Henry to take the blame for the transaction. Pace and Wingfield gave a bond on Henry's behalf. Pace's version was that the emperor had blackmailed him into the loan, by threatening to tell Henry that the recent enterprise had failed through his default, and he was afraid, if they were left without money, Maximilian and Charles would make peace with Francis. He proved to be correct in the latter opinion. He took the emperor's promise to repay Frescobaldi, 'but Caesar pays at the Greek Kalends.'[1] Leonard Frescobaldi's account of the transaction was that at first he was desired ' with good words and afterwards with great threatenings ' to provide 60,000 florins, which he did, sending it down from Innsbruck to Trent. But he and his father would never do business with the emperor, and they looked to Henry for payment. When Henry heard of this transaction he stopped payment, but neither he nor Wolsey ever blamed Pace. They threw the whole odium on the foolish Wingfield, who, by his letters to Wolsey and the King, laid himself open to censure. Frescobaldi had of course paid over the money before the authority was revoked, and stood to lose, and did lose, so that the firm failed in 1518. The exchange in

[1] *L. and P.*, ii. 1896.

this case had been arranged for Wolsey by Thomas Spinelli, at Antwerp, with the Fuggers, to be paid out in Germany by Frescobaldi. Fugger's factor, Bernard Stecher, was crying out in July that Frescobaldi and Pace owed his firm full 60,000 florins. When the matter was referred to afterwards Pace never liked it. He would remind people that he had been ill at the time ; he said he had consented only as a thief does to be hanged, and put out the cold excuse that the emperor would have lost Verona but for this money. He must have realized that Henry did not care two straws whether the emperor or the Venetians held the town, so long as the French did not. Henry would rather that the Venetians should have it, although they were for the moment the allies of France ; for there was an old friendship between England and Venice, and it was good to see Venetian galleys anchored at Southampton and Sandwich. Pace's loan did not save Brescia, which was taken by the French and Venetians under Lautrec, and they soon held all Lombardy and Venetia except Verona. It was part of Pace's commission to further the alliance against France, and it was a pity he was not sent to Venice during this summer, for he was very popular there as Bainbridge's secretary. He might have detached the republic from France, but he was doomed to waste many months among the Swiss. The fact was that the Swiss had learnt they could rely on the promises he made on Henry's behalf; and they would not believe Schiner, after the breaking of the promises he had made for the pope. They knew they could not trust the emperor : Wolsey thought Wingfield a fool, and so Pace was the best man to be employed to keep the Swiss from going over to Francis. The Swiss distrusted Francis, but they knew him to be powerful, and at all events usually able to pay, if he wanted to, which Maximilian was not. Pace's influence with the Venetians and the Swiss was henceforth a force to reckon with, and he was the best ambassador to be sent to either nation.

His illness seems to have given Pace time to think of further developments of his King's adventures. He expatiated on the suggestion made by the emperor that he should resign the imperial crown in Henry's favour. One does not know how far Maximilian thought he could persuade the electors to his choice, or how far he spoke seriously, but it was a matter talked over by him and Pace, who had no authority to speak for the King in any such matter. Within a few months of this—after the death of Maximilian—Pace was sent to support the candidature of Henry among the electors. So it is interesting to see what he thought, when there was talk of putting Henry into the imperial throne, while it was still warm. The business went rather through Wingfield, but Pace saw the letters written to the King, and warned Wolsey, ' whilst we looked for the crown imperial we might lose the crown of England, which is this day more esteemed than the emperor's crown and all his empire.' [1] That ' we ' shows the zeal with which such a faithful secretary would serve his King, and his valuation of the English crown was not much too high, for he regarded France as part of its realm. The part of the emperor's plan which most offended him was the suggestion that, to get the empire, Henry should come with an army, and go to be crowned at Rome. This he thought a castle in the air to get money out of Henry, or to make him fight the emperor's battles. He wanted Francesco Sforza to be set up in Milan as the only man popular enough in the town and among the Swiss. He said if Maximilian would not give him the investiture it was because he wanted to pill and poll the duchy himself, while it was vacant. If Francesco was set up as duke, there was a good chance that he would repay Henry all the money he had spent on the expedition, which would otherwise be lost.

At the end of May Pace went to Augsburg to pick up money waiting for him, a secret sum, to be used only if it was wanted for the Swiss, at the moment a victory was in sight. After a victory Wolsey thought they could live in Italy on the spoils. Galeazzo and the Swiss got back to Zurich in June. He had been continually urging them to march again against the French.

This was Pace's third experience of raising Swiss against the French, and it had no new features and no result ; for from the start he was unlikely to be able to do more than keep them from

[1] *L. and P.*, ii. 1923.

a league with Francis. But he was enthusiastic enough to say that if there was no failure about money, as before, they would march again, and fight not only against the French, but against all the devils in Hell. He did not believe the emperor would start again, and the English government soon determined it would be best to leave him out of it altogether. There was the sending of money, the promising of pay, the disputes as to who should be made Duke of Milan, when they were victorious, and who should command ; and these points were argued till the autumn. Again Henry and Wolsey had kept all promises made to Pace about sending money—except that they had cancelled the order to pay what had been taken by the emperor. There was money for Pace at Augsburg and Innsbruck. All this time Pace and the English government—except for the early outburst against the firm by Wolsey, on account of the delay in paying out—had confidence in the integrity of the Frescobaldi. They valued the advice of the partner Leonard, who travelled extensively in connexion with the arrangements. Leonard had complete confidence in Pace, and wanted any fresh money to be under his complete control, at Basel, out of the emperor's reach. The emperor soon showed himself capable of ill-treating Pace, although a privileged representative of the King of England, in the hope of getting more money out of him ; and it became certain that, if he was to join in the expedition, Henry would have to pay his troops. In the middle of June the Marquis of Brandenburg and Villinger came to Pace at Augsburg from the emperor, to ask for pay for lansquenets and cavalry. He would not help them.

Galeazzo and Pace wanted to march next time without the emperor, who 'doth as often times change his mind as the weather-cock doth change his turn.' They hoped he would be asked to send only as many soldiers as he could himself maintain. The force of the army would be in the Swiss. A great deal of harm was done to Pace by the statements made to the emperor about him by Schiner, who was annoyed that Henry's money should be kept to pay the Swiss, who were no longer under his leadership, and had become a separate English-paid army. He stirred the emperor against Pace over the withdrawal of the order to pay the 60,000 florins, and over Pace's constant refusal to supply more. The quarrels over these points went on for weeks without the emperor getting his way. When Schiner came out of Italy he could cause Pace greater distress. In the middle of June Pace was at Meiningen, and Schiner was at Trent. Frescobaldi showed Schiner the original letter from Henry, engaging to pay 60,000 florins, and, as this had been counter-ordered by Henry, Schiner told Maximilian this must be because Wingfield and Pace had warned the King not to trust the emperor. The emperor sent three councillors to remonstrate with Pace, and they eventually ordered him to leave the court next day and not to tarry in one place for more than two days. Pace said he would obey, but complained that such treatment was harsh to the King of England's representative. It is Pace who tells the story, but it seems as if, when the councillors were going out, one of them turned round and said the whole matter could be pacified, if Pace would lend the emperor 25,000 florins in Henry's name. Pace put it that if he was only allowed to remain on payment of money it would be a great ' rebuke ' to the emperor. Next day Jean Hesdin, Margaret of Austria's chamberlain (who may have been one of the three), was sent to him, but Pace was obdurate. Sir Robert Wingfield was good enough just then to put in a word for Pace with the emperor, saying he did not think he had any more money to lend, though of course he had—a secret store with Fugger at Augsburg—and that he was sure he desired nothing but the emperor's honour. But Wingfield was in his heart very displeased with Pace, and, although he disclaimed any animosity towards him, he wrote to Henry pointing out his defects. He repeated that Pace did not like to hear the emperor praised, and that he seemed ill-qualified for his new office of principal secretary to the King ; for the ' name of secretary hath the foundation upon the knowledge of such things as ought to be kept secret.' He believed Pace to be indiscreet in what he revealed. Wingfield was too eager to find fault with Pace ; it was a case of an old kind of public servant being outstripped by a new kind. This appointment of Pace's, and some hint that he was to be well rewarded, had inflamed Wingfield's jealousy. He maliciously told their King that these honours conferred on him, for his handling of affairs lately, would very likely lead the emperor to think Henry was falling away from his friendship. Wingfield said he had always defended Pace in public. At the end of June the emperor, Pace, and Wingfield were at Constance, and the emperor sent for the two English ambassadors, and told Pace he had heard that he, Francesco Sforza, and Galeazzo had slandered him to Henry, and cooled their friendship. He would allow Pace to leave his court on the King's business when he liked ; but before he left he must pay some 2000 or 3000 florins, which he was supposed to have received from Frescobaldi, out of the 60,000. Pace denied that he had slandered the emperor, and refused to hand over the money. Frescobaldi said Pace had taken 10,000 florins for the Swiss. After this the emperor would not speak to Pace, saying that the counsel of ' his school-master '—[Galeazzo]—had endangered the enterprise in Italy. Wingfield thought fit to write to Henry that the emperor was surprised that such important business should have been en-trusted to such ' a proterve and dyssymulyng person ; for what-soever he saith now, within an hour, he turneth it of another or rather into twenty divers fashions.[1] But he hath gone to school with that ballyd Gallias, which betrayed and sold his master that brought him up.' Leaders of expeditions were fond of accusing each other of vacillating conduct—when they failed. Pace had brought such a charge against the emperor, and com-pared him with a weathercock. It is fair to say of Pace that he was very apt all his life to blow hot and cold suddenly. He was not as well balanced as a statesman or diplomatist should be. Wingfield was right in this, and the tendency was noticed in Rome eight years afterwards.[2]

Fortunately for Pace, Henry continued to regard Wingfield as chiefly to blame over the money being lent to Maximilian, and spent by him on the defence of Verona. He pointed out to Wingfield that a demand for repayment might make the emperor an enemy, ' and if it does it will be through your having lent him the money.' As it had been used for the defence of the emperor's towns Henry was not inclined to reimburse the Frescobaldi ; he hoped Wingfield and Pace would lay aside

[1] *L. and P.*, ii. 2104.　　　　　　[2] P. 241.

their animosity. ' For, to be plain with you [Wingfield] we now evidently perceive, more by your own writings than by the relation of any other, that ye, having better opinion in yourself than your wisdom or qualities can attain to, not only by elation of a glorious mind, moved by the instigation of envy and malice against our secretary Mr. Pace, have more considered your appetites than regarded our commandments, weal, profit, and surety, as it appeareth evidently, as well by the advancement and laying out of our money without commandment, as in continual practises by you daily made and driven, to put us to further expense, and the emperor in comfort, to require more money to our intolerable costs and charges.' [1] He had put into the emperor's head that Pace had spoken ill of him ; hence Pace had been, or was likely to be, turned out of Germany. He was envious of Pace's advancement. As to advancement, the King wrote that Pace deserved it, having obeyed his commands better than Wingfield had done. Even if he had not done all this good new service among the Swiss, and even before his departure from England, Henry had intended to make him principal secretary, in consideration of his learning, wisdom, and activeness.[2] Wolsey must have formed a very high opinion of this young man's abilities and character, on a very short personal acquaintance ; but there was much talk about Pace even among people who had never seen him. If any danger or inconvenience came to Pace out there Henry would attribute it to Wingfield's fault, and he would be punished for it. The King had written to tell the emperor that Pace had never written anything against him. Wolsey followed this with a flattering letter to Pace, and entrusted him with further business—to make friends between the emperor and the Venetians, and to treat with the pope by letter, or through Giglis, to get him to join the league against France. He took it for granted these two old enemies had made peace, and would work well together.

The emperor's appetite for Henry's money was insatiable. Pace thought that he was in danger of his life for refusing it. Probably he had not recovered from his illness and exaggerated

---

[1] *L. and P.*, ii. 2177.   [2] *Ibid.* ii. p. xcvii. and No. 2177.

his difficulties. The regent of the Netherlands, the emperor's daughter, Margaret, heard some money was going through her government from England to Pace and seized it. Apparently Henry came round to being ready to pay one half of the 60,000 florins borrowed from Frescobaldi, if the emperor would pay the other, but the latter said he could not do so. He was sorry to be the cause of Frescobaldi's ruin.

But a gradual change was coming over the emperor's plans. Young Charles and Margaret of Austria were negotiating with Francis, and Maximilian began to nibble at the bait thrown to draw him after them. Pace was ill again in August, at Constance, and longing to get home. He wrote to Ammonius that if he was not recalled soon they would not see him alive again in England. He was to endure another year's exile. It rained so hard in Constance that he was expecting another Flood. He was tired of his mission, and tired of doling out money to the many who came to ask for it. There were scores of beggars, the emperor being the worst. All the gold of Midas would not have satisfied them. He sent letters for Ammonius to deliver to Erasmus, if he was in England.

Henry seemed on better terms with the Habsburg family after Ferdinand's death, and he lent money to the Brussels court. He wanted to get young Charles, now King of Spain (as well as lord of the Netherlands), and the pope to join him and the emperor against France. This league was to provide something like 40,000 angels a year, to keep a large Swiss army on foot. But Francis and Charles signed a treaty at Noyon, on 13th August 1516, and after that it seemed unlikely that the Swiss expedition would ever start. England was cut off from Italy and Upper Germany, and from the pope and Venice, except by sea. The treaty left Milan in French hands, and Henry with no chance of recovering the money he had spent on backing Francesco Sforza. Francis was strengthening his political position every day in the autumn of 1516. It seemed wise to get Maximilian down to the Netherlands to break up the treaty of Noyon. So Wolsey decided to let him have some journey-money through Pace. The negotiations at Noyon gave French agents the chance of spreading, among the Swiss, that the emperor Charles and Henry were on the point of making peace with Francis. The Duke of Savoy, the chief agent, went to Berne, and kept open house and spent money to win the Swiss over to France, but Pace was able to persuade them that Henry and Wolsey would not approach Francis, with a view to making peace, while he remained among them with a commission to levy them against France. Henry was the paymaster, so it mattered less to the mercenaries what the other princes planned, who were all Henry's debtors. Zurich and four other cantons still stood for Henry. Pace got a diet held in October and asked Wolsey for money to entertain the delegates. He hoped for a little more peace when Schiner went to England as ambassador from the emperor. The King and Wolsey had asked Galeazzo to make friends with the cardinal, and the old soldier wrote professing his willingness to do so, but pointed out that it must all be the cardinal's fault, for he had never displeased him. He promised it should be between them as it had been before the cardinal began to pursue him with hatred and injustice. The object of Schiner's visit to England was to get a treaty between the emperor and Henry, which would bring money to the emperor. On 29th October, he (on behalf of the emperor), the Spanish ambassador (for Charles), and Henry signed a treaty, by which the allies were to keep up a Swiss army against France for the defence of the church ; Charles not to be expected to do anything contrary to the treaty of Noyon. Schiner's restoration to power, as a recognized Swiss leader, had the effect of inducing Galeazzo to enter secret negotiations with the French, and he went over to them at the end of the year, as Schiner had long said he would do. He had been without means for a long time, and had lost his property in Milan. Wolsey should have sent him money, but Henry was cooling from any marching of the Swiss. He and Wolsey scarcely hoped to do more than keep them from Francis, but it was necessary to play with them, and perhaps keep them in pay. Francesco Sforza was afraid his duchy would be given to Henry, and Pace was to tell him Henry had no real intention of taking it : but the duke began to listen to Francis' offers to buy him out. With so much talk of alliances the Swiss feared they might be in the unthinkable position of getting money from neither side, instead of from both.

Pace was ill and tired, and found himself left to plan an expedition which was not likely to start. He thought, rightly or wrongly, that attempts had been made to poison him at Zurich. An inquiry was held into the charge. A citizen of Milan, named Antonio, had made a statement and was examined. He deposed that a Milanese of infamous life, named Bosso, had been sent from Milan, by the French general's secretary, to Zurich, with a poisonous powder to be given to the English ambassadors. Bosso reached Zurich in October, and told Antonio about it. He offered him a large reward to administer it, saying it would not kill, but only deprive men of their senses. The ambassadors under its influence would behave in such an extraordinary manner that the Swiss would think them mad, and would turn over to the saner French. He especially urged that a dose should be given to Pace, because he did his King's business admirably and cheaply, and disturbed all the attempts of the French, who had to spend large amounts in trying to get what they wanted.[1] Pace sent home this report and advertisement of himself. When Antonio refused Bosso threatened to get him murdered. Bosso said a noble exile of Milan had written home from Zurich telling how everything was managed in Pace's house, and what servants he had. He explained that the powder could be easily given to Pace, without his suspecting anything. Bosso bound Antonio to secrecy by the most unheard-of oaths, but when he definitely refused to do the deed, Bosso said he would not do it either. He could not be found when wanted, and, if he existed at all, was probably mad.

After the treaty of Noyon there was no longer any chance of keeping any cantons pro-English, unless the emperor would coerce them by preventing the importation of corn, wine, and salt. Perhaps the emperor, when he got down to Flanders, would prevail on Charles to break up the treaty. It was in that hope that Henry had paid for his journey. Then came the news that the emperor, instead of averting the effects of the

[1] *L. and P.*, ii. 2517.

treaty, had joined in it, and on 29th November all thirteen cantons entered into a treaty with Francis at Freiburg. The position was that Henry, Wolsey, Wingfield, Schiner, and Pace wanted war with France, while the emperor, Charles, and the pope wanted peace with her, and the Swiss wanted to sell their services well. Later on there would be war between Charles and Francis. When Schiner and Wingfield heard the rumour that the emperor had joined the treaty of Noyon, they obtained an audience and told him what they had heard. He said he had done all he could to break up the treaty, but he was a poor emperor, and he had had to wait too long for money from England, and that he had joined the treaty when he was ' despaired by the demeaning of Master Pace,' and the answers he got from Henry. No doubt Wingfield was glad to be able to tell Henry that Pace was to blame. Giglis in Rome, Henry's ambassador as he was, took this opportunity of saying it was Henry's fault for not giving money to Schiner, to take to the emperor. His experience was that the English government never opened their purses in time. The treaty between Francis, the emperor, and Charles was proclaimed at Brussels, just before Christmas. Again England's allies against France had gone over to the enemy ; the history of 1513 had repeated itself. England was isolated, but Flanders was secure for a time. Wolsey's fear was that Francis might retake Tournai, and there was talk in Paris that that was what he intended to do in the spring.

Pace was expecting to be recalled, but he went on entertaining the emperor's ambassadors at Constance, and wrote ' as they have dealt subtly with me I have somewhat dealt craftily with them,' and by spending money he had got possession of all their secrets. They tried to bluff him that the emperor had not made any peace with Francis without Henry's consent. He was still keeping in touch with the Swiss, and was negotiating with the pope to bring him into an alliance against France. This latter matter was much impeded by his letters being intercepted by the French spies in Italy. These spies were all over Italy and Flanders, and they had tried to catch Schiner going to England, and he had to travel disguised. In May

Anchises Visconti, Galeazzo's nephew, went to France, and when he got back to Switzerland, he described to Pace questions Francis had asked about him. Pace was so flattered by the notice taken of him that he passed the report on to Wolsey. It is certainly remarkable that the name of this secretary of the king who at the most had only proved himself, so far, a very good ambassador, or agent, and a scholar, should be in the mouths of his King, the French King, the emperor, the pope, the doge, Margaret of Austria, Wolsey, Thomas More, Jacob Fugger, and Erasmus. Francis made ' wonderful inquisition ' of his person, his stature, and so on, complaining that he had caused him to expend 2,000,000 of gold. He might have added he had prevented his seizing Naples, at Ferdinand's death, and getting the pope under his thumb, and had done something towards preventing his taking Tournai, and perhaps Flanders. Apparently Francis would have given Pace piles of gold to bring him to peace with Henry, and as for Wolsey, he should be secured in his Tournai revenues. He offered Pace a safe conduct to Milan, and honourable attendance through France to Calais gates. It seems as if Anchises had followed Galeazzo into French pay, and that Pace was being sounded to see what Francis could do with him.[1] As for the going over of the emperor, and Charles, to friendship with Francis, Pace thought it was needless purchasing the fidelity of those who had none. Charles was ' an idiot,' and his council corrupt; he had anticipated that the emperor would behave in this way. Time began to hang a little heavily on his hands at Constance in spite of his attention to the book he was writing—*De Fructu*. He made a point of collecting, and sending home, news from all quarters—from Rome, the East, France, Urbino, and Ferrara. He was alarmed at the diplomatic triumphs of Francis. The pope was reluctant to oppose him; Maximilian was too old and Charles too young, even if they had the desire. Spain was on the verge of revolution; the Swiss were becoming Francophile; the Italian states were disunited. Pace thought that Henry and Wolsey alone joined him in seeing what the world was coming to. Henry told his ambassadors in Flanders to put

[1] *L. and P.*, ii. 3247.

before Charles' councillors, that driving the French out of Italy concerned Charles even more than him ; but the victor of Pavia was still only seventeen years old. In the meantime here were the Holy Roman emperor, the king of Spain, the ruler of the rich Netherlands and the Swiss mercenaries, all holding out their hands to Henry for money, and getting it ; just as the pope and the doge begged him for moral support and sympathy. And this was at a time when the English archer was not quite so useful as he had been, and the English fleet had not been built. England had been breeding splendid men to go into public life—middle-class people—More, Wolsey, Tunstal, Ruthal, men of the highest honour and sagacity, and of great industry, bent on making England great. Perhaps Richard Pace's name should be put amongst the best of them.

Every prince and republic might get money from Henry, but private individuals, who served the crown, sometimes found difficulty in getting what they seemed to have earned. Pace referred in his letters to promotions which he had received from the King on Wolsey's recommendation, and complained he had not received their emoluments. His pension was badly paid : by pension he of course meant salary. Wingfield was making the same cry, when he and Schiner were with the emperor in Flanders. Now he had gone home, and Schiner, as soon as he got back to Constance, got Pace to write to Wolsey about his pension. Galeazzo had gone over to the French, because he was starved in Henry's service. Yet Henry was the best paymaster of all princes. In July Pace's anxieties were a little lightened by the pope's sending to raise six thousand Swiss to fight against the Duke of Urbino. This would keep them out of Francis' service, but Pace thought his holiness had behaved with dishonour over the matter, in trying to raise men behind the backs of the leaders. He never failed to write what he thought of the great, whether pope, emperor, or king of Spain. The Swiss thought the pope had not paid them their usual pensions, due under treaty, and called off their comrades. Maximilian interfered with the levies hoping ' to pluck some money from the pope.' The pope could of course excommunicate the Swiss if they refused to help him against the Duke of Urbino, so they

had to harden their hearts to endure such a punishment.   Thus
was a road made for Luther and Calvin.

The year 1517 was the most useless to Pace of all his active
life, but for the writing of his book *De Fructu.* He was most of
it at Constance, and he found he had to spend more than he
cared to on drinks, for the German and Swiss captains.   In his
book he referred to their custom of drinking—called by some
' superfluous drinking '—a pastime that gave him no pleasure,
but duty demanded hospitality.   When the captains came to
him at Zurich to offer their services, ' I made them, . . . after
the manner of their country, the best cheer I could devise for
the King's honour.'   *De Fructu* was not published till he had
left the country, but he offended the Swiss and Germans by what
he wrote.   He had all the poor man's contempt for anything
that rendered a public servant less efficient.   In July Paulus
Bombasius, his old master at Bologna, came to Zurich, and he
hated the country and found his only comfort in Pace's ' frequent
and most loving letters ' from Constance, which made him think
he was in Athens.   He seems to have been with Pace at Constance in September 1517, and he liked *De Fructu.*   Pace dated
a very long letter to Erasmus on 5th August.   From it several
quotations have already been made.   He longed to get home.
' I have been leading a very dreadful life, and one out of sympathy with my nature ; for I have been engaged in war—which
has nothing in common with the Muses—and in it there has been
more zeal shown in spoiling than in fighting ; and I have been
engaged in the negotiations of princes, in which every care was
taken that no good should result.' [1]   In October he wrote to
Colet, and his letter shows he was expecting to be on the move
at any moment.   Another ambassador had arrived to relieve
him early in September.[2]   He wrote to Wolsey from Constance
on 6th, and he started soon afterwards.   His return had been
eagerly looked for by Erasmus and More, who could not find
out what he had been doing so long at Constance, and it closed
another chapter of his life.   We shall hear little more of Galeazzo
Visconti ; Francesco Sforza got into the ducal throne of Milan ;
the Duke of Bourbon will play a leading part again, but one

---

[1] Allen, *Opus Epist.,* iii. 39.   [2] *Cal. Ven. St. Paps.,* ii. 420.

8

unexpected from him.   The Swiss remained on good terms with the King of France, who seemed destined to possess the world, or at least to share it with the Habsburg, unless the Tudor could save some of it for the English people.   It took a long time for the English to appreciate the growth of the Habsburg power, probably because it was not centralized.   In Pace's dreams he seemed to drive the French before him.   He had first heard of such a thing from Cardinal Bainbridge, his old master : it was in accordance with an old tradition, which Wolsey was to follow, perhaps too long.

CHAPTER VI

A LEAGUE OF NATIONS

PACE came home by way of Antwerp,[1] and saw—perhaps stayed with—Peter Gilles, the famous clerk to the magistrates; though Peter was ill at the time, and had recently been married. Erasmus had come down to Flanders to be near Quentin Matsys of Antwerp, who had painted his portrait, with that of Gilles, as a present to More. He was at Louvain and had not heard Pace was going to Antwerp. 'If only I had known that Pace was there,' he wrote, ' —for so much I learn from his letter—I should have flown over at once.' [2] It was More's whim to picture himself in Gilles' Antwerp garden listening to Raphaell Hithlodaye's description of the island of Utopia, and we may guess that Pace knew that garden well. Under Gilles' hand in Quentin's portrait, now at Longford Castle, is *Antibarbari*, Erasmus' book, part of the manuscript of which Pace had lost. From Antwerp Pace went to Bruges, and made friends with Marcus Laurinus, dean of St. Donatian's there. 'I am glad More and Pace please you,' wrote Erasmus to him, ' such persons would please me, even if they were Scythians!' [3] Pace stayed some time in Bruges, and seems to have travelled slowly for one returning to his King from an embassy. He was enjoying a delightful change of scene. More was at Calais, on public business, much against his will. 'This is the way,' wrote Erasmus to Gilles, ' that kings make their friends happy, this is what it means to be favoured by cardinals! Thus they kept Pace over two years on a mission to the Swiss.' [4] More went over to Bruges to see Pace in December. It seems clear that Pace

---

[1] *L. and P.*, ii. 3857.   [2] Allen, *Opus Epist.*, iii. 166.
[3] *Ibid.* iii. 170.   [4] *Ibid.* iii. 142.

115

travelled home through Antwerp and Bruges in October, November, and December, arriving in England a little before Christmas. A letter written at Windsor which was placed in the Calendar of Letters and Papers, as if dated October 1517, seems to make him home by then, but it was afterwards transferred to 1521. Further confusion might be caused by Erasmus' statement in November that Pace had written to him from Marseilles,[1] which might receive some colour from Francis' offer of a safe-conduct for him through France ; but Erasmus was inaccurate about the dates of letters. Pace may have gone to Marseilles on his way home in 1515 and have written then. Budaeus, the scholar in Paris, heard from Pace from Bruges, in a letter dated 9th December, when he was expecting the publication of *De Fructu* ; and he was told afterwards, evidently wrongly, that he was going on an embassy to Rome.[2]

Pace could be sure the humanists would welcome him on his release from the Swiss. He came home, the King's first or principal secretary, to sit in the council, and the author of *De Fructu qui ex Doctrina Percipitur*, which he had written at Constance, far from books, and the last place in the world favourable to composition. He had dedicated the book to John Colet, dean of St. Paul's, and it was printed by Froben, Erasmus' publisher at Basel, in 1517. With it was printed and bound the oration he had made at Venice, in 1504, in favour of the study of Greek. Perhaps he went to Basel on his way home to put the matter through with Froben. By Langton's help he had learnt to love Letters ; he already knew many prominent Englishmen—Wolsey, More, Tunstal, Latimer, Linacre, and the men in the council and about the court. He knew a score of foreign humanists, who had been referring to him in their letters for the last three years, and had corresponded with him, and sent him messages ; had let him see their manuscripts, and taken his opinion on the work on which they were busy. As long ago as his Ferrara days he had entertained Erasmus. His conversation amused the humanists, and they

---

[1] F. M. Nichols, *Epistles of Erasmus* (trans.), iii. 183, and Allen, *Opus Epist.*, iii. 161.

[2] L. De Laruelle, *Corr. de G. Budé*, p. 35.

admired his character and sought his company. Erasmus only saw him once again—when he was going through Flanders— but when Pace was broken down in health and at the end of his public career Erasmus wrote of their Orestes-and-Pylades friendship.[1] In those days similitude of studies was reckoned ' the most perfect foundation ' of friendship. Pace had had the good fortune to get in the way of studying Greek, the heart's desire of scholars, and now he was more than the friend of humanists—he was an author. He could meet Erasmus on a different footing, but unfortunately, when the Dutchman read *De Fructu* in January or February 1518, his feelings were sorely hurt by it. In the anecdote already referred to,[2] in which an English sportsman decried Learning for the little money she brought her votaries, Pace had put Erasmus among the needy : ' The learned are all poor ; even Erasmus the most learned of them all, as I hear, is needy, and in one of his letters calls " this Damned Poverty " his wife.' Mr. P. S. Allen suggests that this scene was imaginary, because the letter in which Erasmus mated himself with Poverty (Epistle 421) was not written until after Pace had gone to Switzerland ; whereas it is quoted in a scene in England, in which Pace pretends to have been present.[3] Another passage which annoyed Erasmus was the account of Pace's defence of his arguments in a dispute alleged to have taken place in a hypocaust at Constance, in the hearing of the drunken Germans ; a patronizing and impertinent attitude in a younger man, he thought. He told Warham that Pace had traduced him for his poverty, though in his own estimation he was (at the moment) as rich as Midas. All the same he pointed out Warham's duty was to remove his poverty. He would beg and complain of being called a beggar in a breath. Henry should send him some money to buy a nice quiet horse to take him to Venice.[4]

He wrote to Pace himself : ' You have made me thoroughly well-known by the badge of poverty—when to myself I seemed a sort of Midas. . . . But having exposed me in your book, you ought to help me to drive back this disgrace. Urge up

---

[1] Allen, *Opus Epist.*, vi. 191.   [2] P. 46.
[3] Allen, *Opus Epist.*, iii. 218, footnote.   [4] *L. and P.*, ii. No. 3988.

Moecenates among all those with whom your deserts bring you in touch.'[1] Possible Moecenates were Warham, Mountjoy, and Colet, and he could not let Pace know how displeased he was, while he needed his influence with them.

He wrote to Beatus Rhenanus : ' As for Pace's very feeble little book, I can hardly say . . . how ashamed and angry it makes me. . . . I know all his learned friends will deplore it with me sincerely ; but meanwhile he enjoys good fortune, is rich, and is the favourite of King and cardinal.'[2]

This is what Erasmus wrote to Sir Thomas More : ' I can hardly say whether I deplore or wonder at what has happened to our Pace ; that he should think of publishing that little book in which I miss that judgment in which I did not think him lacking. I am sorry for his reputation . . . for your England, I know, has for a long ·time looked for a different kind of genius from her children, and for myself, whom he names so often, no doubt in a friendly way, but so that if he had been an enemy he could not have hurt more. . . . Has he not weighed in his mind that one has a sacred duty when giving a friend's name to the world and to posterity ? . . . Does he think everything wranglers utter over their cups is proper to be published for the world to read it ? ' He suggests that, knowing him so well, More should give Pace a hint not to make such an abuse of literature again.[3]

Erasmus wrote to Pace's old master, Bombasius, at Zurich regretting the publication of this book. His friends expected very different fruit from Pace's learning and ability. If his aim was serious, there was nothing serious in it ; if jocose, there was nothing witty. It was loosely put together, and Erasmus objected to the jests about his unpopularity with the theologians, as he did to those about his poverty.[4] He had thought better of Pace than this book warranted : ' I have known Richard Pace as a man of character, pure as snow—honourable, free, bound extraordinarily to a friend, a man of many tongues, and of much learning.'[5]

[1] Allen, *Opus Epist.*, iii. 242.   [2] *Ibid.* iii. 251.   [3] *Ibid.* iii. 218.
[4] *L. and P.*, ii. 4007 ; Allen, *Opus Epist.*, iii. 254.
[5] Allen, *Opus Epist.*, iii. 254.

While Pace was young, and before he had attained his
present position, Erasmus had praised his character and ac-
complishments in the dedication to Lord Mountjoy of the first
enlarged edition of *Adages*.[1] This had been as long ago as the
Ferrara days of 1508. Erasmus found another fault in *De
Fructu* : Pace gave away the little trait of snobbishness in his
character, which made him carry in his pocket, to show people,
the letter which Henry had written him—the scene described
as taking place at Ferrara. But Erasmus had not read *De
Fructu* when he first began to show some annoyance with Pace.
On 2nd December, in returning to his pet complaint against
him the loss of the *Antiburburi* manuscript—he wrote : ' I
scent that Pace's nature is changed, although he feigns his old
friendship. . . . Pace in his letter to me, boasts of his book,
entitled *De Fructu Studiorum*.' [2] It was the loss of *Antibarbari*,
as much as the indiscretions in *De Fructu*, which angered him,
and he was a little jealous of his becoming the King's secretary.
He was a man of moods—hot and cold by turns for a friend—
but usually warming to him after a little trouble. He was
at Louvain when he wrote these letters, and he was never
happy there in the winter. Three years afterwards a pamphlet
against Pace was in circulation in Germany and Switzerland.
entitled *Apologia in Pacoeum*, and when he heard of it Erasmus
wrote to John Botzeim, that whatever his old friend had said
about the Germans was in joke without any ill intention, and
that he had jested on him (Erasmus) as well, and that the whole
thing was written ' *ex tempore*.' [3] Pace had brought Erasmus'
name before patrons in England, and had to be forgiven.
Erasmus was getting old and had published many books ;
Linacre was completing the manuscript of his translation of
Galen ; More had published *Utopia* in the preceding year, and
Froben was printing another edition. Erasmus said that
scholars were ready to accept any book which came from
Froben's press, and *De Fructu* came from it. But this book of
Pace's would not have been read by many ; few copies would
have been sold, and one of them might pass from hand to hand

[1] Allen, *Opus Epist.*, i. 445.   [2] *Ibid.* iii. 162.
[3] *L. and P.*, iii. 816, and Allen, *Opus Epist.*, iv. 262.

among a score of the little band of readers. And it was not another *Utopia*. One is tempted to think Pace wrote it to be able to say he had written an original book, and was an author, like his friends, and that he might therein show his scholarship and his standing among the great and learned. He was at pains to show that he was scholar enough to write in Latin, that he had read much in the classics, that (above all) he possessed Greek, that he was well versed in ancient history, the Bible, and the Fathers of the Church ; that he had studied at Padua and Bologna, and met well-known men there ; that he could count Bombasius, Erasmus, More, Linacre, Tunstal, William Latimer, William Stokesley, Andreas Ammonius, John Clerk, and a great number of other scholars among his friends ; that he was familiar with foreign lands, had served the King of England, could speak of Julius and Leo from first-hand knowledge, could laugh in his sleeve at princes and rich men, was Langton's pupil, and was fond of music. His avowed object was to prove the fallacy of the proverb ' *Doctiores* are not *sapientiores* '—which was a sort of text or an excuse for giving the book to the world. What little interest it has for us now is in the few details he gives of his own life, and in a story or two—about Erasmus or the fox-hunting Englishman.

About the same time as *De Fructu*, Pace wrote *Conclusiones de Veniis Pontificum et consilio de bello in Turcas suscipiendo*, which Erasmus sent to More, in March 1518. It was printed, but there is no copy in the British Museum.

Pace found plague in London and the sweating sickness. ' Some,' says Hall, ' were merry at dinner, and dead at supper.' According to Sir Thomas More there was less danger on the field of battle than in London, and Michaelmas term had to be adjourned. Wolsey was ill, on and off, for quite a long time with the sweating sickness and its after-effects, and overwork. Fox had to advise him to give up working after six o'clock in the evening, which corresponded to nine in our day. His absence from court threw Pace into closer touch with the King. The court moved from place to place, and the King's secretary followed the King and the court—to Windsor, Abingdon,

Esher, Richmond, Reading, Woodstock, Farnham, Easthampstead—to avoid air that might be tainted.

When Pace went out to the Swiss in 1515 the political state
of Europe had seemed easy to estimate. Francis ruled over
a country with a population five times as large as that of England
and with ten times the wealth. He had just won a splendid
victory over the finest infantry in the world, and there was no
reason why, if left to himself, he should not overrun Italy,
take possession of Naples, and establish his influence over the
pope. He might not carry his arms over the Pyrenees, or
the Rhine, but he was sure to covet the Low Countries—including Tournai, Wolsey's bishopric—and Calais, which was the
English bridgehead to the continent, and the Flemish seaboard. It has always been an accepted theory in English
politics that it is unwise to allow the ports on the Belgian
littoral to fall into the hands of a great military power. This
argument for curbing France had not so much weight at that
moment as usual, for those ports were already in the hands of
such a power, if Charles proved a great ruler ; but there was
a traditional friendship based on trade between England and
Flanders, and one based on family ties between Henry and
Charles. Against the victor of Marignano, Pace, this envoy
of the English King, spending two miserable years among the
uncouth Swiss, had tried to band together these Swiss, the
emperor, the pope, Venice, and Charles, the young ruler of the
Netherlands and Spain. He had not had much to do with
Charles, but he had tried all the others and they had fallen
away from him. Now the position was that the Swiss had
entered a perpetual pacification with Francis, which might
prove real ; the emperor was old and approaching death and
had gone over to a friendship with Francis ; the pope was
busy with a private war at home ; Venice had got too luckily
out of her Cambrai troubles to want anything but peace ; and
Charles had entered the treaty of Noyon with Francis. Maximilian was to die fourteen months after Pace's home-coming,
and for the last few months of his life his existence did not make
much difference to England's policy. Francis and Charles
were the two great powers to be watched. Francis possessed

one compact country, though parts of it had been lately added
and might not be very loyal.   Charles ruled the Low Countries,
Spain, Naples, Sardinia, the Austrian heritage, and a part of
the new world ; but parts of Spain and the whole of the Netherlands were inclined, just then, to be too independent for a
ruler forced towards war.   Henry and Wolsey and the council had
to make up their minds what to do.   Should English policy
be a continued opposition to France, open or secret ?   Would
it be well to ally England with Charles against France ?   Would
it be better to stand aside and risk these two giants joining to
prey on England ?   Either or both of them might work up
Scotland to attack England.   It was impossible in 1517 to
tell which of the two was the stranger ; it was not even settled
eight years afterwards, at the battle of Pavia, which marked
the end of Pace's career as a diplomatist, and of his active life.
Wolsey could not look into the future, and it proved him a
great statesman, if he realized that a great struggle was bound
to come between Habsburg and Valois, and if he could weather
every storm.   There were two storms which had a great effect
on England's future, which every schoolboy knows all about
now, but Pace, with all his knowledge of Europe, would hardly
have thought their beginnings worth more than a discussion
over a sea-coal fire in winter.   An Augustinian monk had
begun an agitation in Germany, and Queen Catherine had
failed to give the country a male heir to the throne.   Charles
was the monk's prince and the Queen's nephew.   In 1517,
Luther's agitation had not gone far and there was time for
Catherine to have a number of sons ; she was only six years
older than Henry.   Wolsey decided to make a peace treaty
with France, to gain time to see what was going to happen in
Europe ; but the peace or alliance was to be of such a nature
that a friendship with Charles at the same time would not be
incompatible with it.   Universal peace would be best of all,
if it could be established.   Warham, Fox, and the older councillors would have kept England out of continental affairs
altogether.   Wolsey intended to interfere a great deal.   So
Warham, Fox, and other experienced statesmen had gone out
of the council, and it soon consisted of Wolsey, as chancellor ;

Ruthal, Bishop of Durham, as privy seal ; the old Duke of Norfolk, as treasurer ; Pace, as ' Mr. Secretary ' ; the Duke of Suffolk, Lovell, Marney, and a few more, to fill up the chamber in which they met. The sweat had carried off Ammonius, the secretary for the Latin correspondence, in August, and perhaps this had something to do with Pace's recall, for he now looked after that correspondence, but everything of importance was decided by Wolsey. Wolsey could not read letters in Italian, and no one at court could read those in Spanish ; they had to call in one of the queen's confessors.

Negotiations for peace with France stretched from Pace's home-coming to the Field of the Cloth of Gold, in the summer of 1520, but we have not yet come to that vale ' twixt Guynes and Arde.' The money which had hitherto been spent on Swiss was now spent on England's navy. Let us hope that Pace had something to do with the building of the great ships. Wolsey said that Henry had spent £80,000 before September 1516 on setting up Maximilian and the Swiss against Francis.[1] Financing foreign mercenaries may have become more difficult than it had been, for the result of Henry's refusal to repay the money-men what they had advanced to the emperor at Trent was the failure of the Frescobaldi, soon after Pace got home. In October 1517 arrived ambassadors from Francis to conduct preliminary peace negotiations, but no business could be conducted in London on account of the plague ; and Henry did not like to meet even ambassadors for fear of infection. In November he dismissed all his court, and all the queen's, keeping only three favourite gentlemen and a Crutched Friar from Cà Memo at Venice, who played the organ. London began to groan at the loss entailed by the prolonged absence of the court, and by Christmas there was fear of a recurrence of the riot of the spring—Evil May Day. Taxation had been very heavy, and economies were being introduced to avoid it. The King had thought it best to keep no ' solemn Christmas,' as the fewer people round him the better.

Pace, the King's new secretary, received a grant of arms on

[1] L. and P., ii. 2404.

12th February 1518,[1] which enhanced his reputation—made a
gentleman of him—and after that he began to be very busy
with affairs of state. The King's secretary was often called
by his Christian name, as Master Richard, for Pace, or Master
Peter, for Vannes, who did some of the Latin correspondence.
Pace was soon in touch with Sebastian Giustinian, the Venetian
ambassador, who had come to England when he came home
in 1515. They talked about the conquests by the Turks and
the Signory's desire for the repeal of duties on Candia wines
brought to England. Giustinian reported to the senate that
he had lately received a visit from *one* Master Richard Pace,
who had been for a long time the King's ambassador with the
Swiss, and had been brought home, and was in great favour
with the King, and was honoured by all the great men, and had
the third seat in the King's privy council ; Wolsey and Ruthal
alone were above him. Giustinian went on to remind the
senate that Pace had been secretary to Bainbridge, who was a
very great friend of Venice, and, he said, the archbishop's soul
really seemed to have transmigrated into Pace, who evinced
so much affection towards the Signory, that more could not be
desired.[2] He had told Giustinian that he considered he had
received at Venice greater honours than really became his
private capacity, for he had been allowed in the *Bucentaur* on
Ascension day, and invited to the doge's banquet, and entertained constantly by the Signory, solely because he was known
to be an Englishman.[3] He was therefore loud in his praises of
Venice among Englishmen, even telling the King and the cardinal
that seven years would not pass before Venice was mistress of
Italy. But Pace warned the Venetian to be on the look out
lest Francis should betray Venice. Giustinian thanked Pace
for his visit, and for his goodwill towards the republic, but
piously reminded him that God alone could decide which states
were to rise and fall ; and said to be mistress of Italy was the
last thing Venice thought of ! He assured the Signory that

---

[1] *L. and P.*, ii. 3941. The editor considers this 1518 new style.
[2] Sebastian Giustinian, *Four Years at the Court of Henry VIII.*, ii.,
trans. by Rawdon Brown.
[3] *Cal. Ven. St. Paps.*, ii. 1000.

Pace really was devoted to Venice, for he had known him in
England, before he went to the Swiss, and was his friend.
Giustinian suspected that Pace had been sent to him by Wolsey
to warn him that Francis—Venice's ally—might negotiate
with Maximilian—Venice's enemy—to her prejudice. Pace
had told Giustinian that he had actually been present when such
a thing had been discussed between Maximilian and Francis'
representatives. But the Venetian would not believe it, for
Maximilian was then Henry's ally, and it was very unlikely
that such a discussion would have been opened when Henry's
ambassador was present. However, Giustinian reported that,
knowing Pace's character as he did, he did not think he lied,
but that he was in error, and that Maximilian had given him
this information, and that he had handed it on to Henry and
Wolsey, for they had already mentioned it. Probably Pace had
heard some one, who might have had a roundabout right to
call himself Francis' representative, making some such suggestion to Maximilian. Pace told the same story at Venice
afterwards. As a matter of fact, the negotiations, which had
been going on since Pace had left Maximilian, had resulted in
the restoration to Venice of what she had lost to the League
of Cambrai. It seems as if this Ascension day visit to Venice
was paid when Pace was a student at Padua or Bologna. He
does not seem to have been at Venice on Ascension day in any
later years.

England had nothing to fear from the Turk, and had no
intention of going on a crusade ; but, since the First Crusade, it
had been the habit of Christian princes to talk as if they wanted
to start on one, if only they could overcome some other Christian
prince first. Europe was little disturbed at this moment.
Francis had his eye on Tournai, but there had not been such a
good prospect of peace among Christians for a long time. The
Turk, however, was getting dangerous, had overrun Syria and
Egypt, was threatening Hungary, and was building a fleet to
take Rhodes and sweep the Mediterranean. The reports about
the Turk came through the Signory and Giustinian to Henry
and Wolsey, but when Venice renewed peace with Sultan Selim
the ambassador thought it wise to say nothing about it, and let

them find it out for themselves ; for they and the council were
hugely suspicious, and detested all who made friends with the
infidel. Venice's desire for the repeal of duties on Candian
wines led to audiences for the ambassador with the King and
Wolsey, after previous discussions with Pace. Wolsey promised
Giustinian that the matter should be referred to Pace and Sir
Thomas More to negotiate, and Giustinian described them as
' the most sage, most virtuous, and most linked with him
[Giustinian] of any in England,' but he suspected this promise
would not be performed, because Pace was known to be devoted
to the Signory, and More to justice, and therefore likely to
decide against England.[1] In May 1518 the three Venetian
galleys reached England, for the first time since the League of
Cambrai, and in June Henry went down to Southampton to
receive them. The *patrone* and the masters of the galleys and
the Venetian ambassador went to meet the King, and the
patrone made a speech in Latin, and he was answered at the
King's order by a counsellor, who was one of the finest scholars
of the court. This has been supposed to be Tunstal, but it
might have been Pace, who had carried on the negotiations
about the repeal of the duties and was thought a very good
speaker on such occasions. After the speech-making they all
went with the King to the house in which he lodged. Before
he went on board Henry prudently sent the Earl of Surrey to
tell the *patrone* to send all the sailors from the ship, as plague
was reported to be among them, and to have all the gunpowder
carried on shore, and that no guns were to be fired while he was
on board. Then, after dinner, he went with all his court into
the flagship, which had been hung with tapestries and silks.
There were some three hundred persons present, and they ate
sweetmeats spread for them on tables. The King walked
round the tables and to the poop, where he tasted cakes and
confectionery, which were afterwards offered to the rest of the
lords and great personages. The guests sat at tables, ' which
they cleared of confections,' and the Venetian glass vessels,
which had held the wine, were distributed among them. Then
the sailors performed feats on slack ropes, to the great wonder

[1] *Cal. Ven. St. Paps.*, ii. 1010.

of the English spectators, unaccustomed to such performances. Next day Henry got them to fire their guns, and marked their ranges, being very curious about such matters, and there were fireworks in the evening.[1] Only one galley landed her cargo at Southampton, instead of two as had been expected, and the others went on to Flanders, and what merchandise there was proved to be of very poor quality. Wolsey complained about it to Giustinian, so that this wise ambassador advised the doge to send him a present of some dozen small handsome carpets which he needed. This coming again of the Venetian galleys pleased every one.

For months Pace was in attendance on the King, often receiving dispatches from abroad at first hand and acquainting Wolsey with their contents, and he had to make reports to Wolsey which are varied and interesting. The sweating sickness and plague continued through the summer, and the court continued to move from place to place. Henry preferred Windsor, for he could easily ride up to London for business and back again ; and he liked Abingdon, because it was so far from London that no one came to talk about death. When the court got to Woodstock, at the end of June, Pace wrote Wolsey, on 28th, that all there were free from plague. But by 11th July two persons had died of it, and more were infected, one being servant to a yeoman of the King's guard ; the house appointed for the King and Queen's next night's lodging was infected. People were dying everywhere in the neighbourhood, not only ' of the small pokkes and mezils, but also of the great sickness ' [plague]. Pace was anxious about the servants attending Princess Mary at Enfield. The only thing for these royal persons to do was to rush from place to place—Woodstock, Wallingford, the Moor, Enfield, Wanstead. The council, through Pace, called on Wolsey to devise ' such gistes as shall be most for the King's surety and my Lady's.' ' We have daily advertisements here, other (either) of some sweating, or the great sickness, from places very near unto us, and as for surfeits and drunkenness we have enough at home.' Giustinian had the sweat twice in one week, but he was

[1] *Cal. Ven. St. Paps.*, ii. 1041.

not at court, and two of his servants died in his house at
Lambeth.

Officers of the household were responsible for the housing
of the court, and the moving of it, but sometimes the arrangements brought duties to Pace ; the court could not go to
Woodstock for lack of ' horse-meat ' there, or he had to find
out from Wolsey which of the royal palaces had been infected
with plague. An Abingdon resident might be put out of his
chamber by the King's harbingers, and would seek redress
from Wolsey, through Pace. He wrote letters for the King,
and read letters and dispatches to him, and had to get his
signature to documents sent down by Wolsey. He found that
after dinner was the best time to get the King to attend to
business, and dinner was about noon. On one occasion Wolsey,
through Pace, offered the King one of the children of his chapel,
named Robin, and Henry was so pleased with Pace's report
on him that he had him sent to court ' notwithstanding his
disease.' Then Pace wrote to the cardinal : ' My lord, if it
were not for the personal love that the King's highness doth
bear unto your grace, surely he would have out of your chapel,
not children only, but also men, for his grace has plainly shown
unto Cornish that your grace's chapel is better than his,
and proved the same by this reason, that if any manner of new
song should be brought unto both the said chapels to be sung
ex improviso, then the said song should be better and more
surely handled by your chapel than by his grace's.' [1] William
Cornish was master of the King's boys. Henry had himself
composed a Mass or two, and could play several instruments.
He liked Pace for his knowledge of music, and Polydore Vergil
said Pace's being ' musicus et facetus ' pleased the King in-
credibly, and led to Wolsey's being jealous of him.' [2] A
knowledge and love of music was valuable to an
ambassador reaching a foreign court, and stood Pace in good
stead many a time. The roll of those who were musicians was
a brilliant one : Giorgione, Leonardo da Vinci, Julius, Leo,
Clement, More, the Duke of Urbino, Isabella d'Este, the Duke
of Ferrara, and Reginald Pole. Henry kept the organist from

[1] *L. and P.*, ii. 4024.   [2] *Angl. Hist.* (1651), p. 65.

the Venetian Crutched Friars with him, even when any attendant might carry the plague. Later, another organist from Venice (S. Marco), a natural son of the Governor of Cyprus, who played most excellently, came to England in the hope of being treated as the Crutched Friar had been, but his performance pleased Henry so little that he gave him only twenty nobles, and he hanged himself. He played wonderfully on the harpsichord, and had brought his instrument by land from Venice at great expense. In 1515 there was at court a Brescian, to whom Henry paid three hundred ducats a year to play the lute. Henry was ever looking for lute-players. The music-room at Greenwich Palace was provided with organs, harpsichords, and other instruments. Records exist of payments made by Henry for musical instruments, and he was specially pleased to come across any new kind of them. He would sometimes, when on progress, borrow the organ from the parish church. After his visit to England Cardinal Campeggio extolled at Rome the music at the English court. Pace would tell Wolsey any news about Henry's enjoyment of music : ' The King hath now good pass-time by the new player upon the clavicords that Monsieur Rochpotte hath brought him (who playeth excellently) and likewise by the gentleman of Almayne, who was with his grace at Woodstock and hath now brought hither (Windsor) a new good and goodly instrument, and playeth right well upon the same.' [1] When Wolsey's singing-boy arrived at court at Abingdon, just before Easter, Pace spoke to Cornish to treat him honestly (kindly). ' Otherwise than he doth his own.' [2] Cornish, when he heard the boy sing, did ' greatly laud and praise ' him, not only for his ' sure and cleanly singing, but also for his good and crafty descant,' and also praised his teacher, Pigott, the master of Wolsey's chapel. When the court was going to Abingdon, it was difficult to get fodder enough for any but the King's horses, and Cornish ' hath made a merry supplication unto the King's grace for a bottle of hay and an horseloaf.' [3]

Pace had interviews with Queen Catherine, and was able

---

[1] Ellis, *Letters*, Series III. i. p. 200.
[2] *L. and P.*, ii. 4044.   [3] *Ibid.* ii. 4025.

9

to convey Wolsey's compliments to her. Sir Thomas More
and Dr. John Clerk, Dean of the Chapel Royal, joined the court,
and Pace had to write to Wolsey from Abingdon to desire him
to write to the lord steward that these two might have their
daily allowance of meat, which had been granted by the King.
' Here is such bribery that they be compelled to buy meat in
the town for their servants, which is to them intolerable, and
to the King's grace dishonorable.' Pace himself was little
better off. Clerk was not the same man as Pace's colleague in
Bainbridge's service, but they were together later, in Rome.
Pace had to attend the royal chapel, where he enjoyed the
singing, even if it was not as fine as in the cardinal's chapel,
and he liked a sermon when it showed ' both substantial and
profound learning,' and if the gesture was ' apt and convenient.'
He was pleased and amused once at Newhall when the King's
almoner, preaching before the royal household, brought in the
ballads, *Pass time with good company* and *I love unlov'd.* The
members of the council supped together, and the King and
Queen, supping later, would sometimes send for a favourite to
amuse them while they sat at table or after the meal—perhaps
More or Pace. Being by the King's side, Pace could and did
send the royal commendations and thanks to the chancellor ;
but such a go-between stands the risk of rising to fame and
sinking suddenly, if he is so unfortunate as to incur the chief
minister's displeasure or jealousy. For months there was no
proper service of posts between the court and Wolsey ; and
Pace had to report all manner of things. He asked that the
Queen's chaplain might be left with her as at that moment she
had no other to say matins with ; he asked Wolsey to speak
to the Duke of Norfolk in favour of an Irish gentleman that he
might have a place in the customs at Bristol ; he told Wolsey
of the first whispers that the Queen was pregnant. The Duke
of Suffolk and the Dowager Queen of France, Henry's sister,
were rather under a cloud since their secret marriage, and
Suffolk was afraid that Wolsey would treat him as disloyal to
the King. They came to court at Abingdon in April at the
same time as Buckingham and Shrewsbury. It was Holy
Week, and ' carding and dicing . . . is turned into picking off

arrows over the screen in the hall.' In these times of dearth and sickness entertaining important people was difficult; Wolsey and Pace had had correspondence on the matter, and the King had told these great personages how little lodging and ' horse-meat ' there was, and therefore they brought few attendants. Lovell and Marney were at court, and the King held councils, although Wolsey was absent. When he left the council, Fox had advised Wolsey to keep it with the King; but the sweat upset arrangements, for the King avoided London, and the chancellor could not leave it for long. After Suffolk had received the Sacrament at Easter, he spoke to Pace about accusations, which had been made against him by enemies, such as that he had assured the French ambassadors that Tournai should be restored to them. He told Pace with an oath that he was guiltless of this, as he was of any disloyalty to Henry, and of accepting the protection of Francis. He was most anxious to keep in favour with the all-powerful minister, and tried to make Pace a go-between, he ' did speak with me very effectually of one the same matter which I have declared unto your grace in time past, viz. of faithful amity to be established between your grace and him, confirming with solemn oath, in most humble manner, the most faithful love and servitude that he intendeth to use towards your grace during his life in all manner of cases touching your honor.'

While Pace was in Rome there had been decisions of Consistory and of the Lateran Council to send a legate to England to persuade Henry to take part in a crusade, and Bainbridge had almost been appointed. The matter had dragged on for five years, and on 5th March Giglis informed Pace from Rome that on the previous day the pope had ordered Cardinal Campeggio to proceed to England as legate. On hearing this from Pace Henry at once said it was not the rule of this realm to admit legates *a latere*, but if Campeggio came only to preach a crusade he would admit him. This was a wise decision, but Henry and Wolsey had no intention of being moved from their daily routine by such a negotiation, and the pope was horrified to find not only that the English archers were not preparing their bows, and that no English crowns were being collected, but that his letters were not being answered expeditiously. Zeal for crusades had died out in England during the Wars of the Roses, or perhaps even during the Hundred Years' War. The pope complained every day to Giglis, said he did not get an answer to his letters in less than two months. Giglis wrote to Pace and said that in Ammonius' time he got better letters written at Wolsey's dictation. Since then things had been neglected, but he seems to blame Wolsey more than Pace. He had been told to write everything of importance to Ammonius, and to give credence to his letters, and he wished Pace had been quite in Ammonius' position. If Pace was too busy to write at length, could he not give directions to the papal sub-collector in England, or Peter Vannes ? As a matter of fact Vannes had been writing some of the letters. On 11th April Wolsey wrote to Giglis that it was not usual to admit any foreign cardinal to exercise legatine authority in England, but Henry would waive the objection, seeing the necessity for the crusade, provided that he (Wolsey) was joined with him in equal authority by papal mandate, and that all the faculties conceded to legates *de jure* were suspended. On 15th April, before Wolsey's letters had had time to reach him, Giglis wrote again reproving Pace, who of course was acting under orders. Still no answers ! This backwardness displeased his holiness, and was ill-timed and dishonourable to the King and the cardinal. Wolsey had moved astutely ; he had made it clear that no foreigner would be admitted to England as legate, except under special circumstances, and had thereby preserved his own pre-eminence in England. He had courteously advised that this was one of the exceptional cases, but he had entirely taken away Campeggio's majesty by compelling him to share it with himself ; and Wolsey being the greater, in or out of England, would naturally take the lead, probably to the relegation of the other to the background. Wolsey, even if no longer legate, would stay in England to enjoy the prestige that office had conferred on him, when the other went back to Rome. This appointment was the foundation of Wolsey's greater glory, and as it put him above all other subjects, so when he began to fall, it was at it and its illegality that their jealousy urged his enemies to point.

Campeggio reached Calais when the court was at Woodstock, and when Henry heard of it, he made Pace write to Wolsey telling him to ride a few nights afterwards secretly to meet him at Greenwich, to talk over several matters. He wished Wolsey to make provision there for their suppers, ' for he will depart hence secretly, with a small number of his chamber, without any such persons as should make any provision for him.' The King's servants in London were to be sent down to prepare Greenwich Palace. Wolsey had not seen the King for some months, and Pace slipped in, at the end of the letter, a hope that he would take the opportunity of reminding him of his necessities. Campeggio crossed to Deal, and went through Canterbury. At Greenwich he was welcomed by Norfolk and Ruthal, and entering London on 29th July he was received by More, with a Latin speech in Chepe, and by the Bishop of London, the Bishop of Lincoln, and the cathedral clergy, at Paul's. But the King and Wolsey were not present for fear of the plague, and Pace was with the King. Campeggio was lodged at Bath Place.

Henry received the two legates on 3rd August at Greenwich in great state, with the lords spiritual and temporal and ambassadors. The necessity for a crusade was exposed, and Henry expressed his approval ; but a crusade could not be made until there was universal peace, and the legates waited to see that brought about. Two matters choked the way to peace. Francis had been stirring up Albany in Scotland against Henry, and Henry had been considering stirring up the Swiss again against Francis, and he had tried to keep them from enrolling themselves under Francis' banner. The former question would be settled by the treaty with France. Henry's efforts to set the Swiss against Francis were more secret, and therefore more difficult to prevent. Cardinal Schiner had stayed with the Swiss after Pace's departure, and continued to work them up against France, and he sent a messenger to Pace in the hopes of bringing Henry in again. A report from Rome of January 1518 to the Signory, founded on a statement made by Michael Abbate,[1] said that Pace was again among the

[1] *Cal. Ven. St. Paps.*, ii. 999.

Swiss, about Christmas-time, with money to buy their services
for Henry. Abbate was misinformed, although in March,
while negotiations were going on with France, there was a
plan to send him, and he was on the point of going in April.
The Swiss were not all keen on their alliance with Francis, but
the treacherous Galeazzo was trying to win Francesco Sforza
after him. Certainly no more than eight cantons really favoured
the French alliance, but Henry had benefited by experience,
and was no longer anxious to pay a Swiss army unless the
emperor, the King of Spain, and the pope contributed, and at
the moment he thought the wiser course was to be at peace with
France.

Apart from the scheme to raise mercenaries, Henry had
promised Charles to send an ambassador to Germany to watch
the electors, lest Francis should get himself elected emperor
at Maximilian's death. If Francis heard he had sent an agent,
it would prejudice the chances of peace with him, and Pace
was too well known to travel unobserved, so Henry and Wolsey
hesitated about sending him, when the emperor asked for him.
He might be captured by the French ; he did not want to go,
and thought he could do better service to the King in England. They kept changing their minds. Pace himself wrote to
Wolsey from the court at Abingdon, in the middle of April,
that Henry wanted him to go to Wolsey, and then to the Swiss.
Money was to be provided for him by the Welsers, and no one
was to be made privy to his instructions but Ruthal. He would
go through Liège, disguised, with only two companions, and
no luggage ; but when among the Swiss he would play the
ambassador properly, and outshine his rival from Francis.
This was the plan Pace sketched out with the King at Abingdon.
Giglis had quite forgiven Pace for accusing him of murdering
his master, and while wishing Henry would send some good
man to reside among the Swiss, he said : ' I do not suggest
Doctor Pace, who is so cultured that it would be a crime to
keep him among such boors.' Margaret of Austria was indignant that Henry had not sent an agent, and Maximilian
himself wrote to Henry asking him to send some one to the
Swiss, that by community of action the two of them, with

Charles, might bring them over to their side. In July most of the princes of the empire were at Augsburg, and it would have been a good time for Henry to send an agent to work for Charles' election. Pace was not sent at that time to influence either the Swiss or the electors.

All else gave place in interest before the negotiations for peace with France. Pace played but a second part in them under Wolsey, but not an insignificant one. It seemed a momentous change of policy ; England and France—so long at war—were to enter into a friendship, which was to lead to a universal peace among Christians, and a combined resistance to the infidel, who came on apace. Peacemakers are always blessed, but doubly so when Europe is on the point of dividing itself into two great camps, as it was then. The French commissioners, who had come to London in the autumn of 1517, just after Pace's home-coming, had opened negotiations, which were conducted with more or less secrecy for twelve months, and meanwhile the greatest suspicion lived among the negotiators and among the onlookers. Was Francis stirring up trouble in Scotland ? Was Henry enlisting Swiss ? Were either of them trying to prepare the way for his own election to the Imperial throne, or had Henry promised to support Charles ? Was either of them arming against the other or some other power ? The pope and Venice were easily alarmed. The difficulty most openly and fairly dealt with by the negotiators was the fate of Tournai. Commissioners came and went. The birth of a French prince gave an opportunity for politeness and signs of friendship, and Henry made promises not to stir the Swiss against Francis, who promised not to support Albany in Scotland. In July articles of agreement were drawn up, based on a marriage between the Dauphin and Princess Mary and the surrender of Tournai. Point after point was put before Henry by Pace in Wolsey's absence. On 1st September came Stephen Pencher, Archbishop of Paris, a very learned man, who knew Erasmus and liked him, and the Seigneur de Villeroy. Next morning Giustinian hurried to Wolsey and found him already with the archbishop and three or four English councillors, and they were shut up for a long time in a stormy discussion. When

the meeting broke up Giustinian tackled Pace, who had probably been at it, to find out the real state of matters.[1] He asked
why the archbishop had come, seeing that peace and the
nuptials were settled ; not that he believed they were, but he
wanted to ' draw ' Pace, who replied that the archbishop and de
Villeroy had come to negotiate, and not simply to ratify what
had been agreed. Giustinian regarded himself as in Pace's
confidence, and pumped him to find how far off complete agreement might be. Pace told him that other ambassadors would
ask for Mary's hand, and that the difficulties were still about
Tournai ; he had no doubt that peace and the nuptials would be
concluded, and that Tournai would be surrendered to France.
The Venetian asked whether the surrender of Tournai constituted one of the conditions of the peace, or if it would form
part of the dower of the princess. Pace said it was not the
custom of the English to purchase peace from Frenchmen, and
that no one ever dreamt of giving Tournai *in conditionibus
pacis*, but that it would be ceded on certain terms as dower.
Giustinian did not inquire what these terms were for fear of
appearing too inquisitive. Pace told him the treaty would
include the pope, the emperor, the King of France, the King of
Spain, and the King of England, places being reserved for many
other parties including Venice. Sir Thomas More had recently
been admitted to the privy council, and found that Wolsey
conducted entirely the final negotiations with the French
ambassadors, and only told the others what had been arranged,
so that even the King hardly knew what was going on. The
Seigneur de Bonnivet, admiral of France, arrived in September,
with another ambassador, to lead the Archbishop of Paris and
the Seigneur de Villeroy, and in their train, according to the
chronicler, Hall, came many ' young fresh galantes of the court
of France,' and a great number of rascals and pedlars and
jewellers, who brought over hats, caps, and diverse merchandise,
not usually on sale in England, all under colour of their being
the ambassadors' ' trussery,' but really to sell them. They
opened their wares at the Merchant Taylors' Hall, where the
ambassadors were lodged, and made it like the pound of a mart,

---

[1] *Cal. Ven. St. Paps.*, ii., under dates mentioned.

which angered the shopkeepers. All told, this embassy seems to have numbered some twelve hundred persons. ' These gentlemen of Fraunce were very freshe,' says Hall. The King gave public audience to the French ambassadors at Greenwich ; and Campeggio and all the other ambassadors were present, and afterwards there were daily conferences. On 2nd October the terms of a treaty of universal peace were agreed. When this document had restored peace to Europe, all princes and states would arm against the Turk. It was signed for England by Henry, Wolsey, Warham, Buckingham, Norfolk, Suffolk, and several others, including Sir Thomas Boleyn, Tunstal, Richard Pace, and Sir Thomas More.[1] Two days later Pace was among those who signed the treaty of marriage between Mary and the Dauphin.

On the 3rd October, which was a Sunday, the King with a great train of gentlemen richly dressed, and attended by Campeggio, and the French, Spanish, and Venetian ambassadors, went in procession to St. Paul's.[2] Mass was celebrated by Wolsey, as legate, before all the bishops and abbots of the kingdom—so thought the Frenchmen. The ceremony was too magnificent for description. After the Mass Pace made a ' grave ' oration in Latin which was printed in 1518 by Joannes Gormontius as *Oratio Richardi Pacei in pace nuperrime composita et foedere percusso inter invictissimum Angliae regem et Francorum regem Christianissimum in aede divi Pauli Londini habita.*[3] ' Elegant ' was another epithet applied to it, and it was ' a good and sufficiently long oration ' delivered excellently. It was less a sermon than a scholar's tribute in the Latin tongue to Henry and the legates. Pace, after ten months' close attendance on Henry, thought him—or felt bound to call him—a great King, and a worthy successor of other great Kings. The dean, John Colet, a better preacher, was sick to death, and Pace was probably filling his place. Colet had said in a sermon, ' pacem iniquam praeferendam bello aequissimo.' Pace put forth that Nature had intended Henry to be a great leader in wars, and a great completer of wars. He complimented him on his fine

---

[1] *L. and P.*, ii. 4469.   [2] *Ibid.* ii. 4479.
[3] J. H. Lupton, *Life of John Colet*, p. 228.

frame, and was kind to the legates. The King sat beneath him, near the altar, in a pew of cloth of gold, and on the other side of the high altar was a throne for Wolsey, and a lesser one for Campeggio. After the sermon the King and the French ambassadors swore to the treaty of peace. The great ones dined with the King at the Bishop of London's house, adjoining St. Paul's, and after that he returned to Durham House in the Strand, below Charing Cross, where he lodged. Wolsey went on to his own house, York Place, now Whitehall, followed by the whole company, who sat to a sumptuous supper, the like of which Giustinian supposed was never given by Cleopatra or Caligula. The banqueting hall was decorated with huge cups of gold and silver, and Giustinian fancied himself in the tower of Chosroes. After supper there was mummery. Twelve men and twelve women came dancing in, all masked, and turned out to be the King, his sister, the dowager Queen of France, and great lords and ladies. It was such a scene as Shakespeare has brought before our eyes. They danced till midnight. Pace should have been at the dinner given by the King at the Bishop of London's, but perhaps not at the supper and revels at Wolsey's.

On 5th October, in the queen's great chamber at Greenwich, Bonnivet, representing the Dauphin just born, espoused Mary, two years old, after Tunstal had given an address on marriage and its obligations.

Within a week of the peace Pace had told Giustinian that the Spanish ambassador had tried to upset it : but, as he pointed out, Charles had four months allowed him to come into it if he wished to do so. Queen Catherine was absent from the festivities, because she was pregnant. The English government were relying on her to give birth to a prince, otherwise this new marriage plan might give England to France, but little importance was attached to the plan and the Queen brought forth a still-born daughter.

Pace had been corresponding with Budaeus in Paris during the summer, and a letter written just at the time the French ambassadors were starting for London shows that he had been suffering from fever, and he continued in bad health for some time.[1] The ambassadors returned to Paris delighted with his

---

[1] L. De Laruelle, *Corr. de G. Budé* (1907), p. 38.

eloquent discourses.[1] He attended to the arrangements for the departure of the ambassadors to Paris, and then disappeared from court till Christmas eve 1518, and then he wrote again to Wolsey. He dined several times with the Venetian ambassador at Lambeth to discuss the duties on Candian wines. Arrangements had to be made for the handing over to the French of Tournai, and for the great meeting between Henry and Francis, which was to be held somewhere across the channel. Giustinian felt that the King and his ministers cared nothing for news about the Turk, and he reported to his senate that they were so reticent that he was unable to elicit the slightest matter of importance from them, unless by accident they allowed it to escape. Some dispute arose concerning the Abbot of Westminster which brought Pace up to London, and he took Campeggio's son to call on Wolsey. Wolsey was ill again in February 1519—so ill with the ' murre ' that he could not hold up his head. Pace had to deal with appointments in the church, with the examination of prisoners he suspected of being spies of Richard de la Pole, and with the disposal of the Queen of Scots.

In March Count Horn came to London as ambassador from Charles to ratify the universal league for peace, and public audience was given him, in the presence of all the other ambassadors, and a great number of lords and prelates. The two cardinals, being newly recommissioned as legates by the pope, were received *de novo* by the King. Campeggio's son, the protonotary, delivered an elegant oration in the pope's name, alluding to the peril from Sultan Selim. One of Charles' ambassadors addressed the assembly, and Henry's reply was made by Pace, who alluded to the pope, ' tamquam *comitem* confoederationis,' and in pretence of mitigating what might seem arrogance, he added, ' *Comitem*, et quod maxime optavit hic sacratissimus Rex, *Principem* confoederationis.' In point of fact the pope was being brought willy-nilly into this English-made peace. Pace might thank him for having chosen to conclude and ratify the confederation in London, instead of Rome,[2] but his holiness had not so intended. In answer to Charles'

[1] L. De Laruelle, *Corr. de G. Budé* (1907), p. 46.
[2] *Cal. Ven. St. Paps.*, ii. 1178.

ambassador, Pace said Henry was content to include his master
among the chief confederates.   It is Giustinian who makes this
report to show the Signory in what standing Henry was then
among princes.   He saw that Wolsey was responsible for it all,
and he suspected his sole aim was to be called the arbiter of
Europe.   Wolsey had attained his object by getting the treaty
ratified in London.   He had delayed Campeggio's work for the
pope's suggested five years' truce for a crusade, which after
this manœuvre was no longer talked of.   On 20th March the
articles were signed by Henry and by the legates and Charles'
ambassadors, and the Venetians came into the league in April.

CHAPTER VII

THE FRANKFORT DIET

THE court lay at Greenwich all May 1519, and the council were very busy; Wolsey, though suffering from dysentery, going down twice in three days. Then Pace suddenly disappeared, and it was thought that it was the business engaging the council so earnestly that had sent him abroad; but other troublesome matters were in the wind. During the last three days before he started—while he was packing up—Henry had made a great change in his court. He dismissed four of his chief lords-in-waiting, who had been his very soul, ' youths of evil counsel.' This measure was deemed of as vital importance as any which had been carried out for many years, and Giustinian wrongly regarded this dismissal as being connected with Pace's departure.[1] The council had indeed decided during these sittings that these young men must be removed as being too ' familiar ' with the King. A lot of young gallants had gone to Paris with the French ambassadors, and had learnt bad manners there. They rode with Francis through the streets, throwing eggs, stones, ' and other foolish trifles,' at the people, and when they returned to England they were, says Hall, ' all French, in eating, drinking, and apparel, yea, and in French vices and braggs.' No particular accusation was brought against these ' minions,' they were simply told by the lord chamberlain to go, and England was saved from what greatly afflicted the French court. Wolsey and Pace had been planning this change for months. Four ' sad and ancient knights ' took their places in the privy chamber, and several lesser officers of the household were changed. Perhaps their influence with the King was bad,

[1] *Cal. Ven. St. Paps.*, ii. 1220.

but, bad or good, Wolsey would allow no rival near the King's ear. And they had not confined themselves to introducing French manners, dress, speech, and jests, but advocated a pro-French policy ; thereby doing what of all things was most likely to offend Pace.

Maximilian had died in January 1519, and all the year excitement prevailed as to who would succeed him as emperor. There were several candidates who appeared within measurable distance of election—Charles, Francis, Henry, the Duke of Saxony, the Marquis of Brandenburg, the Archduke Ferdinand of Austria, and the King of Poland. As soon as his grandson, Charles, was declared of age, Maximilian had begun to plan for him the succession to the imperial throne, which old age told him would soon be empty ; but while Pace was with him he had held out the suggestion that Henry should become emperor at once, on his own resignation, or later, as his successor. Pace had seen that he had as his object the getting of money from Henry ; and the electors were by no means certain to follow his advice. He was not rich enough to buy them ; he could only promise them money. Even when Pace went back to Rome to wind up Bainbridge's affairs there were rumours about the election ; and Francis put it about that his candidature was being backed by Henry, then his new ally, and that Pace was working for him. At the time of his death Maximilian held promises from four of the seven electors to vote for Charles. Then the bribery had to begin over again, and Charles sent huge sums from Spain, by bills through Spanish merchants and the Fuggers, Welsers, and Hochstetters. Charles and Francis were now the two great men of Europe, Henry having a place only as great as Wolsey's policy might make it. Francis was sure to come in to try to wrest the imperial crown from his great rival, and the English could not allow—or thought they could not allow—the King of France to reach such great authority ; which he was quite likely to do if the pope held Charles to an oath, taken as King of Naples, not to become emperor. So long as Charles was hindered in this way Henry must find a candidate to oppose Francis, or run in the race himself. The election had to take place at Frankfort, and the

electors, who decided who should be King of the Romans, or
emperor-elect, were the Cardinal-Archbishop of Mayence, the
Archbishop of Cologne, the Archbishop of Treves, the King of
Bohemia, the Duke of Saxony, the Count Palatine of Bavaria,
and the Marquis of Brandenburg. The popular idea outside
Germany was that these men would sell their votes to the
highest bidder. No doubt they pretended to be going to vote
for the best paymaster, but other considerations came in, for
princes, ecclesiastical and lay, were not entirely devoid of a
decent desire to discharge a public duty satisfactorily ; but
no one was wise to approach them without a pocket full of
money. Pace knew that. The electors were all Germans,
and therefore likely to elect a German to what was a German
dignity, and had been in one German family—the Habsburgs—
for eighty years. The duty of the next emperor would be to
repel the Turk, coming from east and south, and therefore he
should be powerful, a great military leader ; and he would
have to deal with the heretic Luther, and it seemed wise to
pit German against German. If Charles was not entirely
German, Francis was not German at all. One would hardly
have suspected Henry of being German. Charles had the
Habsburg mouth without a doubt. His grandfather was the
Habsburg Maximilian ; his father, the son of the daughter of
a Burgundian-Valois father ; his own mother was Spanish.
He was born at Ghent and brought up in the Low Countries
by a very Habsburg aunt, herself educated in France. So he
seemed a sufficiently cosmopolitan prince to lead Christendom
against the infidel. That is probably what the electors, and
every one else in Europe, thought about it all the time, but the
Duke of Saxony was more German than he. Francis claimed
that his victory at Marignano had proved him to be the greatest
military leader in Europe, and that he should therefore command the Christian army against the Turk. He promised the
English ambassador that, if elected, he would personally lead
the crusaders into Constantinople within three years. Charles
was still under twenty, and had no military achievement to his
credit, but he thought he had Henry's support, and was talking
about supporting Wolsey for the pope's throne in return when

it was next vacant. Maximilian and Charles had been urging Henry to send a secret agent, according to promise, to watch the electors in Germany, and Pace had been on the point of going. Henry had told Pace to write to Wolsey that he did not want Francis to be elected, but he would leave it to him to devise how to prevent it. After Maximilian's death an invitation reached Henry to take part in the contest, whereupon a French courtier remarked that the electors knew the King of England had 'a good mine of gold, on which account they wrote this to him.' As the time for the election drew near, Charles' ambassador in England complained that Francis was trying to get the imperial crown by violence and tyranny, and was making warlike preparations ; whereupon Pace was ordered to be ready to go to Frankfort.

At such news those Englishmen who thought it their duty to check Francis' ever-increasing power sprang to activity with amazing zeal ; it always had a most stimulating effect on Pace. He became another man, and any sickness or disability was at once forgotten, or at least thrust aside. Henry hurried off a letter to the Elector of Saxony, who was far from the Rhine, stating his view about the election to be that in their choice the electors ought to be guided by what would be for the good of Christendom. He introduced Richard Pace, his secretary, who would be at Frankfort and would explain his views touching the election. On 12th May Pace wrote from London to Wolsey, who was sick with dysentery, asking for instructions as to his behaviour towards the Count of Nassau, whom Charles had sent to Germany to look after his interests in the election. Should he tell him as much as he was going to tell Charles' aunt at Brussels ? If Nassau got to know something was being hidden from him he would become suspicious. Pace was to make overtures to Margaret which Nassau had better not hear of. At the last moment Pace went off in a scramble. He had a final interview with Wolsey, but no final instructions. Wolsey promised to post off letters to him that night, and he was to leave a servant in Flanders to take them on. Wolsey had promised him a proper commission this time, but Pace forgot to remind him and started without it. He was sorry he had forgotten, but, for the last two days before he started, all his wits were in Germany. He set out either on 12th after writing to Wolsey or next day. Giustinian did not hear of his departure for five days, and came to the conclusion he had gone to the Swiss again ; and even Campeggio, who was usually full of news, did not know for certain the object of his mission, for Wolsey had kept out of his way all the time. Perhaps the dysentery was only an excuse for doing so. Wolsey could not refuse an interview to the French ambassador, who had a very bad opinion of the intentions of the English government and came out of it feeling sure that Pace had gone to counter Francis at Frankfort. The Duke of Norfolk said Henry was taking steps to secure the freedom of the election. That was the part Henry wanted to play—his only interest was to help the electors to discharge their duty freely. There was such confusion at the court through the recent changes of officials that information was less easy to get than usual. The man in the street, who looked upon Charles as Henry's nephew, supposed Henry had sent Pace to support him.

At Dover Pace found a French post, who tried to persuade him that the French hostages were sending him to France to get some money for them. Pace believed they were sending him to inform Francis of his [Pace's] departure, and to ' put suspicious bruits in his ears ' ; so he made secret arrangements for him to be detained at Dover, until he had got a good start. He wrote to Sir Thomas Boleyn, the ambassador in Paris, telling him, if any ' sinister report ' of his journey came that way, to give out that he was only being sent to be present at the coming election. If no report came, Boleyn was to keep quiet. Pace felt this was a wise precaution for his own safety, for Francis might capture him, and, perhaps, destroy him. He wrote to ask Wolsey to write to him regularly. He had been on three missions for his King, and experience had taught him that lack of instructions was as usual, and as embarrassing, as lack of money. His commission was dated 20th May, and only reached him in Germany, after the diet had opened. Put shortly, it set out Christendom's need of a leader against the

10

Turk, and the King sent Pace, his chief secretary, to remove
any cause of discord among the electors, moved to do so by
papal briefs.[1] Pace's private instructions were longer, and
are in two existing documents, one much mutilated.[2] He was
to do his best to bring about Henry's election ; he was to
promise the electors money in that event only. He was to praise
the king as suitable for the dignity and office. He was to take
letters of credence to the Swiss and to find out from Schiner
and his friends if they would favour Henry's election, though
it is difficult to see what the Swiss could do in the matter otherwise than by force. He was to find out which electors favoured
Charles and which Francis. When he spoke with those who
favoured Francis, he was to speak as if Henry favoured Francis ;
and when he spoke with those who favoured Charles, he was to
speak as if Henry favoured Charles. Neither candidate must
think Henry was against him, and he was to be careful not to
say the wrong thing in either case. He was to approach the
pope's ambassadors on the basis of letters recently received
from Giglis, and to join with them in preventing the election
of either Francis or Charles. He was ' by provident and cir-
cumspect drifts' to procure the electors to choose Henry,
' which is of the Germany tongue,' or one of their own country,
and not to translate the empire, which had been in Germany
seven hundred years, to a strange nation.[3] So Francis was not
to have it, even if Henry had to call himself a German to prevent
it. An eavesdropper heard what Pace actually said to one of
the electors when he was convinced that Henry had little
chance. He urged the election of a German, or at least of one
of German descent, and if it came to a question between Charles
and Francis, then it must be Charles. Wolsey probably had
little expectation of Henry's being elected, and that part of
Pace's instructions was really a ' brag,' which it was usual to
make when sending an agent on such a mission. One could
never tell, however, what might happen at an election, whether
at Frankfort or Rome.

Pace took ten hours crossing the channel, and was very
sick, but on reaching Calais he was soon ' very whole by the

------

[1] *L. and P.*, iii. 239.   [2] *Ibid.* iii. 240, 241.   [3] *Ibid.* iii. 241.

reason of the same sickness.' He told Wolsey he would endeavour to remain so, as it was not the time to be sick. He
wrote to Wolsey from Calais on 14th, and, leaving next morning, was at Bruges on the 17th, and wrote at once to Schiner.
He went on to Brussels, where he interviewed Margaret of
Austria, and assured her of Henry's friendship towards herself
and her nephew, and she was enthusiastic in her gratitude.
She promised to arrange for him to be conducted to Germany.
She, Montigny, and the vice-chancellor, told him all their
plans for the election. They said the Count Palatine, the Archbishop of Mayence, and the Archbishop of Cologne had promised
their voices to Charles ; but Pace perceived by their faces, and
their vacillations, that they were not so very confident. At
the Brussels court people would have him believe that Charles
had the pope's favour, in spite of the oath, that of the Archbishop of Treves, who feared his lands near Luxemburg might
be ravaged, that of the Elector of Saxony, and that of the Elector
of Brandenburg. After pondering and considering, he could
see no certainty. He went to Antwerp on 20th May, saw
Erasmus, and got from him letters of recommendation to the
Archbishop of Mayence, to Anthony de Bergis, and to the scholar
Bannisius, telling the latter that he was an excellent scholar in
both tongues, a favourite, for his unspotted character, with
his King, the cardinals, and the pope. Erasmus gave him
another such letter to the Elector of Brandenburg. He arranged
with Gualterotti for payment of money, where he might want
it, and received 1000 florins across the counter. He went on
to Malines, and perhaps Erasmus travelled a short distance
with him ; [1] anyway, their talk gave Erasmus a very favourable
opinion of England as the home of scholars and patrons, and
he could think of nothing else for a long time. From Malines,
Floris of Egmont, Lord of Isselstein, accompaned him, at Margaret's order, to Cleves, where he hired four guides to take him
to Düsseldorf. These fellows proved ' strong thieves,' and when
he parted from them he was afraid they would follow him. So
he gave them some of his money to prevent their taking it all.
This experience, and the knowledge that there had been many

[1] Allen, *Opus Epist.*, iii. 597.

robberies recently on the road between Düsseldorf and Cologne, induced him to hire some armed men. He had asked the magistrates of Düsseldorf for guides, but they replied he was ' a Frenchman,' and should have no guides of them. They meant that he was supporting the French King, but he persuaded them that he was the English ambassador by showing them an English noble. After this convincing proof, they said he might have the whole of Düsseldorf town to take him to Cologne, for England must surely be supporting Aragon and Burgundy against France. He reached Cologne on 29th. The air was full of rumours—that Francis had sent an ambassador to Frankfort with three hundred armed horsemen ; that the pockets of the Archbishop of Treves and the Count Palatine were mysteriously full of French crowns ; that the Swiss were arming for Charles, and the Swabian league too, headed by John of Sickingen.

On the day of his arrival at Cologne he had an interview with the archbishop of Cologne, who would not let him go to any hostelry, but had a chamber prepared for him at his castle outside the town. On his arrival there he was met by the archbishop's chancellor, and some of his council, who explained that the archbishop was at Mass, or he would have been at the gate to welcome him. When Mass was finished the archbishop hurried to Pace's chamber, before he could leave it to pay his respects ; that seeming to be great courtesy. The host dispensed with ceremony, but was careful to make Pace sit at his right hand. Pace delivered the King's and Wolsey's letters, which were in Latin. The archbishop confessed plainly that ' he had not greatly exercised the Latin tongue,' and desired that his brother and his chancellor who managed everything for him might be present at the reading of the letters. The chancellor read the letters, and Pace, on Henry's behalf, urged the propriety of the electors' discharging their duty fairly and honourably to choose a good leader of Christendom. The archbishop consulted his counsellors for half an hour in private, and returned an answer praising Henry and Wolsey for what they said in the letters. Touching what Pace had said on Henry's behalf he said every prince in Christendom ought to be grateful for such advice to the electors, especially the electors themselves; for his part he would follow it. He said he thought that Henry would gain great honour by having sent Pace on such a splendid mission. Pace dined with the archbishop, and thought he could not have been better, or more honourably entertained, if he had been elected emperor himself. They were rather merry at dinner, and, in the middle of it, the archbishop asked what Henry had agreed with Francis in the new treaty made in London. Pace explained that it was intended to be a universal pacification, and was not limited to Henry and Francis. French agents had been representing that these two would make war on Charles, hoping to bring the electors over to what would seem the stronger side. Such talk annoyed Pace and he was glad to be able to queer the pitch for all Frenchmen. He could soon write—' it is now great jeopardy here to speak one good word of a Frenchman.' The archbishop would not let Pace hurry away after dinner, ' because it was a fervent hot day,' but kept him to supper, and they talked on, and although the elector never actually said who he was going to vote for, Pace had no doubt it would be Charles. Pace thought he had not made a bad beginning with the electors, and went to bed with the thought that the archbishop was a very good and sub-stantial man. He went up the Rhine to Frankfort—no one could ride for fear of robbers—and there was pestilence every-where and great heat. Francis was sending money daily to buy the electors, but Charles sent even more. Pace saw Francis had little chance, and he kept up the pose of neutrality. He wrote to Wolsey on the boat, as they were approaching Mayence, and on landing called on the cardinal archbishop of Mayence, and his brother, the Marquis of Brandenburg, just as they were preparing to set out to Frankfort. The archbishop promised to see him at once, and received him nobly before he left; but the marquis asked for further information as to who he was, and wanted to see his letters of credence, which made Pace ' somewhat muse and study.' Considering that if he got no interview he would get no information, he sent his credentials along, and the marquis, having read them, sent for him at once, asking him to come secretly to his lodging close to the church of

Our Lady. This he did at 9 o'clock at night ; but the secrecy demanded of him was not respected. De Bonnivet, admiral of France, Francis' chief election agent (who had been in England, as ambassador), was allowed to hide himself behind the tapestry. He heard Pace speak in favour of the election of Charles, which he regarded as an unfriendly act to Francis, and he had no doubt he had spoken in similar terms to the other electors.[1] Anne Boleyn's father afterwards reported this to Wolsey from Paris.

Brandenburg received Pace graciously, in a ' little secret closet,' and after making apologies for demanding his letters, listened to his ' Proposition,' which was the same as that which he had made to the Archbishop of Cologne. Brandenburg gave his answer in Latin, ' right well for so great a personage,' says Pace. Perhaps Brandenburg had forgotten it at first, but he and Pace had met in Maximilian's army in Lombardy, three years before, and in Germany. After his formal answer he saw Pace privately, and told him Francis would not be elected, although his brother, the archbishop of Mayence, was working for him.

Pace started up the river again next day, and, on reaching Frankfort, hunted up the archbishop of Treves. Treves saw him at once, and received him graciously, before his council, but had private talk with him as well, saying Henry was not excluded from being elected. Pace felt free to open out with him on the matter, and, according to his instructions, showed reasons why Henry should be elected. Treves said that if such statements were made to all the electors Henry's candidature would be well considered. This was really the first encouragement Pace had received, even to dream of Henry's election. He had begun to suppose that to keep Francis out was the most he could achieve. He saw the count palatine, and found him wholly French. All ambassadors and strangers were ordered, according to custom, to leave Frankfort as soon as the majority of electors had arrived. Henry had addressed a joint letter to the electors, but it could not be read, for they were never together

[1] *L. and P.*, iii. 530.

until they assembled for the election, by which time outside influence had to be cut off. When Pace went down to Mayence he had had no communication from Wolsey since he left England. The Duke of Saxony reached Frankfort on 11th June, and then the procurator of the King of Bohemia. Pace missed them both. Saxony was neutral, and had not sold his vote, Bohemia was sure to support the Habsburg.

Pace was in much doubt as to how the electors would vote. He thought if Henry had come in as early as Charles or Francis he would have had a good chance. He felt that these two had fought each other so hard that both might lose. He went about Mayence talking to every one, the count of Nassau, the bishop of Liège, and Charles' other agents, to whom Margaret of Austria had recommended him, the count palatine's brother, and the papal ambassadors. He said he liked the legate about as well as Schiner liked friars. He met Ulric von Hutten; he could not see the cardinal of Gurk as he had taken ' a medicine.' He got to see a copy of an oration the French ambassador, who had his headquarters at Coblenz, had not had an opportunity of reading to the electors. In the neighbourhood of Frankfort was a considerable army to support Charles, and the barons on the Rhine were ready to rise for him. Mayence was over-full, and Pace had to pay heavily for his little room and for his servant's meat and drink. The archbishop of Mayence sent him a welcome present of wine and meat. Like the cardinal of Gurk, Pace was not feeling very well, and he promised Wolsey to expel his disorder, as the times and the business required nothing so little as that he should fall sick. It was very hot on the Rhine in June. Feeling ran very high against Francis and the French, among all Germans, and infamous songs about them were written in Latin and German. French messengers were caught at night on the Rhine with money on them. Merchants who had promised to pay money on Francis' account were caught and imprisoned. No letters came from Wolsey, but all sorts of rumours disquieted Pace, in the absence of news, however foolish they might seem. It was said that Francis had an army ready to invade Germany; that English troops were being sent to help him; and that Pace was there to help him be made emperor, which was the same rumour as had followed him to Rome five years before—an odd circumstance. The heat and worry were too much for the delicate Pace ; and being unable to expel his disorder, as he had hoped to do, he wrote to John Clerk, dean of the chapel royal, who was in attendance on the king, saying he was ill. The King was concerned at this news. ' Master Pace's sickness and his feebleness runneth marvellously in his mind,' wrote Clerk, from Windsor, to Wolsey. And fearing he was not doing well Henry decided to send Clerk to relieve him, and they talked his journey over late at night and both slept on the plan. Wolsey was delaying about doing anything until he heard again from Pace.

On 13th June the archbishop of Mayence wrote assuring Wolsey that he would follow his advice and vote for the fittest man for the dignity. Some people told Pace Henry would be elected, but nothing would move him to consent to promise money to the electors ; until the archbishop of Mayence sent a message that Henry had come in late, but there was still a chance for him, if he would pay a sum equal to that which Charles had at Frankfort—420,000 gold florins. Pace promised the money should be forthcoming if Henry was elected, and arranged with Herman Rynk, the Hansa merchant, to pay the money for Henry, and gave his own promise and bond, and wrote to Wolsey for confirmation.[1] He thought that if the money had been with him when he got to Germany he could have procured Henry's election. But the people were in favour of Charles, and if Henry was elected Pace thought he and his retinue would be killed. He saw that Henry would have to live in Germany, which would be the ruin of England. It was only on 20th June that he received Wolsey's letter, dated 9th, with the King's commission and other documents, but by that time Henry was keen on being elected, and was anxious lest Pace's illness should impede his cause. Wolsey had arranged for payment out to Herman Rynk, by way of exchange. He sent Clerk to Pace with letters confirming the bond and promise he had given. The electors would not expect Rynk

[1] *L. and P.*, iii. 318.

to pay the money promised them unless he had this proper confirmation.

By 20th June nothing had been done in the diet but to sing the Mass of the Holy Ghost ; there were delays caused by the discussion as to who should represent the King of Bohemia. Meanwhile Francis offered double what Charles had promised, and then Charles' agents increased their offer. Some hot-headed people—the mutilation of the letter has prevented our knowing precisely who they were, but they seem to have been councillors of the archbishop of Mayence—suggested that Pace should raise an army against Charles. It would not have been his first experience of that kind, but he declined, because he had not got the money, and because it would cause animosity between Henry and Charles, and Henry would stand to lose by it more than he could gain if he was elected.

On 28th June, at 7 o'clock in the morning, Charles was elected King of the Romans, and his agents let Pace know at once at Mayence. Pace hurried off a short letter to Wolsey by the post who was just starting. A sudden assurance by the papal legate and ambassadors that the pope had put aside the Naples question, and that Charles had his holiness' support, had turned the scale. Pace went over to Frankfort next day to congratulate Charles' ambassadors. ' I have so handled them that they have written unto their king that my coming hither hath done unto them good service.' He persuaded the Duke of Saxony, the archbishop of Mayence, and the archbishop of Cologne, to tell these ambassadors that Henry's letters, his own ' proposition and other secret practices ' had greatly helped their master's cause, and they promised to tell this to Charles, now King of the Romans—emperor he was usually, though prematurely, called. An English agent had written to Wolsey from Barcelona to give an account of the interview he had had with Charles, whom he had told the reasons Henry had for sending Pace to the electors. Charles had expressed satisfaction, recognizing that he would not work for Henry, unless it appeared that Francis was outstripping Charles.[1] Pace was told by merchants in Frankfort that the emperor

[1] *L. and P.*, iii. 312.

had spent 1,500,000 florins, and had given promises of more.
Soon afterwards Henry granted Herman Rynk and his son, the
Hansa merchants, a substantial annuity in survivorship, out
of the petty customs of the Port of London.   It was a member
of this family who commissioned the portrait of Henry VII
in the National Portrait Gallery.

Pace was anxious to leave the town, for there was much
sickness in it ; it was very hot, and there was lawless violence
in the country.   He tried unsuccessfully to get a complete
copy of the conditional articles or terms agreed on between
the electors and Charles' representatives.   He started home by
Cologne on 4th July, on which day he reached Mayence.   There
he received letters from Wolsey, telling him that the pope had
promised Henry to procure a postponement of the election,
to give John Clerk time to get out and Herman Rynk time to
advance money to bribe the electors.   As it was, Henry's
letters to Rynk only reached him that day.   On 8th July Pace
wrote to Wolsey from Cologne.   There were all sorts of rumours
about great men seizing lands they wanted, before the new
emperor had got the power to prevent them, and about those
who had been at the election lying in ambush to punish and
rob each other.   The roads were alive with robbers between
Cologne and Maastricht ; and Pace was lucky to travel with
the Bishop of Liège and the count of Nassau from Cologne to
Brabant, for they had a hundred horsemen.   A body of men
that Pace put at eight thousand hung round them.   The Duke
of Juliers came out against these brigands, but the travellers
had to ride from morning till night for two days.   The count
of Nassau entertained Pace at his town of Diest, and said he
would be Henry's faithful servant in all things which had to
be treated between him and the emperor.   Pace reached
Antwerp on 22nd July, and waited there for further orders
from Wolsey.

Erasmus had been upset by the criticism of the young
theologian, Edward Lee, and Pace had tried to end the quarrel
by a series of letters, and with that object he interviewed him
now at Antwerp.[1]   These humanist scholars were very touchy

[1] Allen, *Opus Epist.*, iv. 201, 256.

under criticism. In August 1520 was published by Froben, *Epistolae Aliquot Eruditorum Virorum*, etc., containing letters from More and Pace to Lee, written in the controversy.[1] The dispute was one between literary men, and only concerns Pace the diplomatist in showing that when returning from a mission he could interest himself suddenly in such a matter ; but Erasmus felt he had stood by him like a brother in it.

The people of Antwerp were very pleased that their margrave was now the emperor—they called him Keizer Karel. Erasmus was still at Antwerp, and Pace brought him a letter from Ulric von Hutten, written at Mayence, but, as on several other occasions in his relations with Erasmus, something went wrong. He did not deliver the letter ; Erasmus saw it first in print.[2] Pace went to Malines to wait on Margaret and received her thanks for what he had done for Charles in Germany, and her whole court received him well. His letter to Wolsey about his reception throws light on his methods of diplomacy—' and in very deed they have no cause to complain upon me, for I did never speak against the king catholic in the said election, considering that it was sufficient to me to have the electors speak against him, and allege reasons why he should not be elected ; and surely they would not have elected him if fear of their persons had not driven them thereunto, and evident ruin of all their nation if they had elected any other king.' [3] He called Wolsey's attention to his adroit management, that, when Charles was elected, it seemed to his ambassadors that it was partly through his exertions made at Henry's orders. Charles had instructed his ambassadors in England to thank Henry for sending him for that purpose.[4] In the same spirit the English ambassador in Paris told Francis that Henry had worked for his election, until it appeared hopeless.[5]

Margaret and her courtiers evidently liked Pace, and pressed him to stay at Malines for a couple of days ' in continual feasts and drinking, but it is not for my purpose to be sick

[1] Allen, *Opus Epist.*, iv. 210 and 233.   [2] *Ibid.* iii. 613.
[3] *L. and P.*, iii. 398.   [4] *Ibid.* iii. 419.   [5] *Ibid.* iii. 416.

ex crapula.'   On 28th he started for Calais, and at Dover, after a rough crossing, he met Sebastian Giustinian, who had handed over his commission as Venetian ambassador to Antonio Surian, and was on his way home to the Adriatic.

CHAPTER VIII

CLOTH OF GOLD

WHILE Pace was away the court was in the country. The King had been amusing himself in such simple ways as running races with the French hostages, and people were pleased, for before the changes in his household had been made he had been losing too much money to them at play. Charles' subjects in London wanted to celebrate their sovereign's election to the empire, and some of them were trying to light a bonfire, when the crowd took offence and insulted them. Very likely there were Frenchmen in the crowd, but the Londoners had been in bad temper since the Evil May Day riots, and Wolsey was rather afraid of them. He consulted the Lord Mayor about keeping order in the city, and the rejoicings were confined to some jollification among the Italians, Germans, and Spaniards, who gave wine to the people. The occasion called for a solemn Mass and Te Deum in St. Paul's, at which Wolsey, Campeggio, the dukes of Buckingham, Norfolk, and Suffolk, and the ambassadors were present.

Pace waited on the cardinal before going to the King, and they agreed on an account of his mission, for his highness' consumption. Pace found Henry staying with the Duke of Buckingham, at Penshurst, on 10th August. When he went for audience the King was back at his old gaming with the hostages ; but he soon sent for Pace, and received him ' lovingly,' and asked for all the news of the election. Pace gave him. it should be noted, the account he and Wolsey had agreed on beforehand.[1] That he saw home-coming ambassadors before they had been to the King, was a complaint made against

[1] Ellis, *Letters*, Series III, i. 195.

Wolsey at his fall. Henry was amazed at the huge sums Charles had spent on his election—which Wolsey and Pace may have agreed to exaggerate, and said he was glad he had not been elected at that price. He called Suffolk and his host, and told them about it. Pace told Henry that of the three papal ambassadors, two had certainly taken money from Francis ; and showed on what his accusation rested. Henry seemed convinced. For some reason Pace particularly disliked one of these ambassadors. ' After this communication, his Grace sported with me merrily of my journey in most loving and familiar manner, and that done, went to supper, and spake of me many better words than I have or can deserve.' A less skilful agent than Pace might have wasted a lot of money at Frankfort to no purpose. He had spent something in costs to Rynk, and something on his diets and journey. He constantly, throughout his working life, reminded Wolsey how much money he saved the King, and how much distress he caused Francis by doing so.

He took back the duty of writing the King's letters from More, who had been doing his work in his absence, and Wolsey's continued bad health threw extra work on him. He had conferences with the emperor's ambassadors, headed by Hesdin, Margaret of Austria's chamberlain, and the Bishop of Helna. He pleased them so well that they commended him to Charles, who, just before sailing from Spain to visit England, a little later, wrote his thanks to Pace for his good offices,[1] and promised rewards to Wolsey, a pension of 1000 florins to Ruthal, one of 800 to Pace, and one of 300 to Brian Tuke.

Pace soon made the acquaintance of Surian, the new ambassador from Venice, who had had it from Giustinian that he was a staunch friend of the Republic.

During the next few months Pace was sometimes with Henry in the country, sometimes in London, sometimes at Greenwich. In September 1519 the court was at Newhall in Essex, and there was masking, in which part was taken by Suffolk and a number of courtiers, including Pace's old friend Sir Robert Wingfield. Hall says of them ' all these were some-

---

[1] K. Lanz, *Actenstücken etc. des Houses Habsburg*, p. 176, seq.

what aged, the youngest man was fifty at the least. The ladies had good sport to see these ancient persons maskers.' This was another result of the recent changes at court. Wolsey was usually at York Place, and Pace would come up for the day to transact business with him. On 9th November Pace was very unwell and could not go up to see Wolsey—it was fever 'joined with another troublesome passion.' Perhaps it was partly on this account that Henry ordered that, if there was pressing business, Wolsey should send for Pace, but that at other times he was to remain at court.[1] London was an unhealthy city, and the palaces, and manor-houses were insanitary—even worse were the inns in Germany, at which Pace had to lodge. Courtiers and ambassadors expected to be ill.

Sir Thomas More had himself been on an embassy when, writing to Erasmus, he had referred to Pace among the Swiss, hoping some great good fortune was in store for him. More compared the case of churchmen sent as ambassadors with that of laymen like himself. The former had no family to provide for, while they were away, and had a large field of ecclesiastical promotion open to them on their return, which cost the King nothing. Erasmus at this time spoke of Pace as 'provehendus haud dubie ad summas dignitates.'[2] Several lucrative benefices were given him in 1519. On 4th February he was made rector of Barwick-in-Elmet, near Leeds, but he resigned in the same year. When, in February, the marquis of Dorset asked Henry to write to the Bishop of London, to get his brother the archdeaconry of Colchester, the King said he thought it would be better bestowed on Pace, and told More to write for it ; and this without Pace's having asked for it, or having known about it. But he thought it as well to write to Wolsey at once, to get his favour in the matter, and he was successful. This he likewise resigned on his return from Frankfort. On 21st March he had been made a prebendary of Exeter. On 12th May he was presented to the living of St. Dunstan's, Stepney, which stretched from Mile End to Thames, and from Whitechapel to Bow, and was one of the richest livings in England. He held it till 1527, when he resigned it.

[1] *L. and P.*, iii. 504.   [2] Allen, *Opus Epist.*, iv. 262.

On 22nd October he was made prebendary of Finsbury, or Halywell, in St. Paul's. On 25th October, on the death of Colet, he was made dean of St. Paul's.

In a famous sermon Colet had laid it down that such an ecclesiastical office as this last ought not to be held by a man who was busy with affairs of state, and who had obtained distinction in them. This was precisely the position of Pace, whose social position and comfort soon rested on plurality. The dean and chapter of St. Paul's owned much land, and the dean had important business to transact, but Pace—busy with affairs of state—left everything to the sub-dean—the worst possible thing for the chapter. While he was dean, Wolsey, as legate, deprived St. Paul's of the honour of entertaining convocation of the province of Canterbury, by summoning it to meet at Westminster. Peter was said to have robbed Paul. Rewarding good public service at the expense of the church had been a practice since the conquest. The church still produced the servants of the crown. The great seal had almost always been held by an ecclesiastic ; the chief ambassadors had been made from the same class, and their salaries, apart from benefices conferred on them, were neither attractive nor regularly paid.

Pace had greatly admired Colet, for his love of letters, for his school, and for his selection of its high master, William Lily, and he dedicated *De Fructu* to him. Foxe, in his *Acts and Monuments*, speaks of Colet and Lily as very learned men, and then of William Grocyn and William Latimer as their successors, and then of another couple whose names were not unworthy to be remembered with them—namely, Thomas Linacre and Richard Pace. Erasmus told Ulric von Hutten that More, Mountjoy, Linacre, Pace, Colet, Stokesley, Latimer, Tunstal, and Clerk were a credit to Henry's court, and that England was to be envied for her scholars. He had no love for courts, but he would have been glad, had he been young again, to return to England. ' Aula Regis plus habet hominum eruditione praestantium quam ulla academia.' [1] He wrote to Tunstal, ' I should deplore More's fortune in being dragged to the court, but that, under such a King and with so many learned men for

---

[1] Allen, *Opus Epist.*, iii. p. 596.

companions and colleagues, it may seem not a court, but a temple of the Muses.'[1] He described Pace's character as akin to More's.'[2] The French ambassadors surprised Francis' court, when they returned to Paris, with their description of the important place given to ' *les savants* ' by Henry ; and they praised the elegance of the discourses they had heard Pace pronounce.[3] His education and long residence in Italy had given Pace an advantage, which Erasmus thought would have embellished Sir Thomas More but England benefited less by his learning than it did by that of More, Linacre, Colet, or Lily. He gave pleasure to none but scholars, musicians, and the King. It was at the end of his life that he studied Hebrew, Chaldean, and Arabic, but even at this time he knew the five chief languages, Latin, Greek, Italian, French, and German. In April 1520 he was made lecturer in Greek in the university of Cambridge, with a yearly stipend of £10 ; but he does not seem to have lectured there. Such a position was suitable to one whom Erasmus spoke of as ' utriusque literaturae callentissimus,' and ' amicorum doctissime et doctorum amicissime,' and ' vir . . . insigni utriusque literaturae peritia praeditus.'

According to Erasmus, Greek was taught without molestation at Cambridge, thanks to the chancellor, John Fisher, who did for that university what Wolsey did for Oxford. In 1518, at the end of Lent, Wolsey and Pace were with the King and Queen at Abingdon, when a deputation from Oxford University waited on them ; and the queen accompanied by Wolsey visited the university.[4] In 1521 Wolsey attended the queen on her progress to Cambridge.[5] In March of the same year More joined the court at Abingdon, just when news came from Oxford of the founding of a society of Trojans, to oppose the introduction of the study of Greek. Lent sermons had been preached in St. Mary's, attacking Greek ;[6] for the old-fashioned scholars— scotists and thomists—regarded it as likely to let in heresy, and

[1] Allen, *Opus Epist.*, iii. p. 303.
[2] *Ibid.* iii. p. 357, and F. M. Nichols, *Epistles of Erasmus*, iii. p. 422.
[3] L. De Laruelle, *Corr. de G. Budé*, 1907, p. 46.
[4] R. Fiddes, *Life of Cardinal Wolsey*, p. 179.
[5] *Ibid.* p. 186.   [6] *L. and P.*, ii. 4042.

as promoting a wrong interpretation of Scripture. But the preaching against it was stopped by the King. A preacher before Henry was so foolish—probably from ignorance of the court—as to denounce the study of Greek. Erasmus tells the story.[1] Pace cast his eyes upon the King, to observe how his majesty was affected.[2] Henry smiled upon Pace, to show his contempt for the preacher. After sermon Henry appointed a solemn ' disputation ' between the preacher and Sir Thomas More, on the use of the Greek tongue. When More had opened the disputation the preacher, instead of setting forth his case, fell on his knees before the King, and begged pardon for having given offence in the pulpit, excusing himself by saying that what he had said had been prompted by the Spirit. ' Not the Spirit of Christ,' said Henry, ' but the Spirit of Folly.' Henry asked the delinquent if he had read any of the writings of Erasmus, and when he confessed his shortcomings said, ' Why, then, you are a very foolish fellow, to censure what you never read.' ' I have read,' explained the preacher, ' something they call *Moria*,' and Pace broke in, ' Yes, may it please your highness, such a subject is fit for such a reader.' The King dismissed him ordering that he should never again preach at court. He had not expected to find Saul among the revolutionaries : he did not know the way the wind blew at court. Music and Greek were the fashionable hobbies.

William Latimer had written Erasmus from Oxford, that Fisher thought of learning Greek from him, but could only give a month to it, which was not enough, in spite of all his genius. Grocyn had spent nearly two years without intermission in the study under the best masters ; Linacre more ; Latimer himself six or seven, and he did not scruple to confess his ignorance. Latimer forbore to speak of Tunstal and Pace, who were kept longer at it than might have been expected, considering their abilities, by the ignorance and negligence of their teachers.[3] Anthony à Wood speaks of the attributes of several of the English scholars—of the devout and worthy gravity of Grocyn, of the ' much-learning ' and acute judgment of Linacre, of the

---

[1] *L. and P.*, iii. 566 ; Allen, *Opus Epist.*, iii. 546.
[2] Allen, *Opus Epist.*, iii. 547.   [3] *Ibid.* ii. 442.

familiar eloquence of Tunstal, of the candid civilities of More, of the good manner of Pace.[1]

There was already enough new matter in the air to frighten ecclesiastics and laymen—even those who were wide-minded enough to favour the teaching of Greek. The doings and sayings of the Wittenberg monk had not been forgotten, as similar doings and sayings had so often been, and quite a party in Germany approved of them. The King and John Fisher were for a bout with Luther. The pope excommunicated him in June 1520, and in April 1521 the emperor met him at Worms. Wolsey caused Pace to make a copy of Luther's *De Captivitate Babylonica* for Henry, and take it down to Greenwich with the pope's bull and brief against him. Pace saw Henry was dis_pleased with the book, and therefore at once showed him the bull and brief. Henry told, or reminded, him that he had undertaken the defence of the church, and was engaged in writing a book against Luther's doctrines, and said that this new work of Luther's made it the more necessary. At Greenwich Palace Pace would find the King reading Luther's books and preparing his answer to them. It was in Latin and was entitled *Assertio Septem Sacramentorum,* and can now be seen in a glass case in the Vatican library. Some said Fisher, More, and Pace wrote it, or at least had a hand in it, and it could hardly be that one so constantly with the King as Pace was did not furnish him with some ideas, but Henry's early studies in theology had made him quite as capable of writing such a book. It is just as likely that he got points from Wolsey, Tunstal, Stephen Gardiner, and Edward Lee. This was Erasmus' view; when he told Cochlaeus that many had doubted whether a King was likely to be learned enough to write such a book.[2] This Luther business was worrying even the humanists, and Pace and Erasmus corresponded on the subject. Erasmus wished that some 'Deus ex machina' would end the tragedy, which the monk had so inauspiciously begun; for he had been too bitter, and had given the old-fashioned theologians a whip to beat him and moderate reformers with. It was in this letter to

---

[1] *History and Antiquities of the University of Oxford,* Bk. 2, p. 17.
[2] *L. and P.,* iv. 5412.

Pace that Erasmus made his famous admission that he himself had not the strength for martyrdom, and likened himself to St. Peter.[1]

According to Beccadelli, when Reginald Pole, the King's cousin, went to study at Padua university in 1519, Pace proved generous enough to resign in his favour the deanery of Exeter and other benefices.[2] But he had not yet been made dean. It has been thought, probably incorrectly, that Pace managed the young man's estates while he was away. Anyway, when Pace went back to Italy he knew Pole well.

Pace was now very well off, and always had plate, furniture, and a good household ; and he took all he wanted on his embassies. The year 1519 saw him at the peak of his prosperity— in favour with King and cardinal, rich, successful, and as well in health as ever he was to be.

Great preparations were being made for the meeting between Henry and Francis on French soil, which had been planned when the ambassadors were in England. The excitement and rivalry over the election at Frankfort had still further postponed what had already proved difficult to fix. The place and time were matters of conjecture ; none could state them until both monarchs had made up their minds. Although there was no breach of the amity made between Henry and Francis, the greatness of Charles—which might prove equal to that of Francis— made it certain that Henry would not turn his back on him, even if no other ties had made him his friend. Henry and Wolsey wanted to be friends with both, and they thought it well to meet both, but in such a way that the meeting with Francis should seem the more important. From this grew the planning of the Field of the Cloth of Gold. It might—and did— prove wise to meet Charles twice ; to make up for this one glorious meeting with his rival. After the struggle at Frankfort both Francis and the emperor was anxious to make an ally of Henry. Henry had abandoned all thoughts of the empire— for the new emperor was barely twenty—but not of recovering Guienne and Normandy, and even the crown of France. Charles

---

[1] *L. and P.*, iii. 1392.
[2] L. Beccadelli, *Vita Reginaldi Poli* (1563), p. 8.

could help him to these and Wolsey to the papal throne. But such ambitions stirred these great men against France less than a wholesome dread of seeing her grow to such strength that her king could dictate to Europe.

The date of the great meeting was at last settled, for the summer 1520, and Henry wrote to all such lords, ladies, and gentlemen as should be present, and all began to prepare. The arrangements were made by Wolsey ; it was to be between Guines and Ardres. The grounds for the pavilions and tilt-yard were chosen in January and three thousand English work-men were sent over to Calais. Great quantities of food and wine were ordered, and soon little else was talked of but cloth of gold, finery, arms, and fashions, so that many ' broke their backs with laying manors on 'em for this great journey.' Long before the meeting, it was settled that among the councillors of the long robe was to go the King's secretary—(who should be Richard Pace)—and he was to take twelve servants and eight horses. If Pace was not the secretary mentioned, he would go as Dean of St. Paul's. ' Mr. Secretary ' is mentioned several times, as for instance among the king's chaplains, and again among the councillors' chaplains. He would have been included among the King's council—anyway Pace was to go, and to be well attended.

On 8th April the King appointed a commission consisting of Ruthal, Tunstal, Pace, and More to conclude a treaty of intercourse with the emperor's ambassadors in England, and it was signed in the chapel at Greenwich on 12th April. At the same time Henry appointed the same four commissioners to arrange a meeting between himself and the emperor ; and this treaty was sworn at the same time as the other.

Henry, the queen, and the court started from Greenwich towards the sea on Monday, 21st May. They reached Canterbury on Friday, and on Saturday news came that the emperor's sails had been sighted off Dover, and Wolsey went to receive him. Henry rode to Dover early on 27th, Whitsunday, and both sovereigns rode to Canterbury, and joined Catherine. They kept Whitsuntide there, until the Thursday, and then Charles re-embarked at Sandwich. At the interview an alliance was planned, which was far more likely to bear fruit than anything said or done at Guines.

On the day Charles departed Henry sailed from Dover with Wolsey, the great nobles, the chief men in church and state, and reached Calais at 11 o'clock in the morning. On Monday, 4th of June, he went out to Guines, to the lodging which had been prepared for him. Francis was at Ardres, and between Guines and Ardres the two kings first met on the Thursday. Pace slept in one of the 2800 tents which had been pitched. He must have known the whole thing was humbug, so far as it was supposed to bring peace, and must have been glad that it was. To wind up the proceedings on 23rd (Saturday) Wolsey sang Mass, before the kings and queens, in a chapel erected during the night, in front of the stage from which the spectators had watched the jousts. He was assisted by the Archbishop of Armagh, and the Bishop of Durham (Ruthal), and several other bishops. Four French cardinals, and many ecclesiastics. ambassadors, lords, and ladies were present. After the Elevation, the Host was seen floating high in the air over the tiltyard, to the surprise of those who did not know how it was done. Before the surprise had died down Pace, turning towards the two kings, from the stage where Mass had been sung, proclaimed the plenary indulgence conceded to all who had attended the Mass. He said this divine service had been performed to the glory of God and of the noble meeting, and he prayed God to render this peace between the two kings perpetual. He preached in Latin, Wolsey pronounced the benediction, and the kings went to dine with the queens and their courts.

Next day, Midsummer day, the meeting broke up. Henry and the court returned to Calais on Monday 25th, and stayed there until 10th July, when he with Wolsey, the papal nuncio, the French ambassador, Buckingham, Suffolk, Dorset, Ruthal, and the members of his council, and many lords and gentlemen, and a great following, rode to Gravelines in Flanders. There they met the emperor and Margaret of Austria, who were accompanied by the Cardinal of Toledo, de Chièvres, the Count Palatine, the Duke of Alva, the Marquis of Brandenburg, and many knights and gentlemen. There is reason to suppose that Pace was sent to the emperor, on some mission, directly after the Field of the Cloth of Gold, and that he returned with the emperor's party to Gravelines. On Wednesday, Charles and Margaret came with the English to Calais, and there were revels, to which, the chronicler Hall says, several French gentlemen came masked, quite unknown to any one in authority. They were evidently helped in by some English courtiers, who preferred an alliance with Francis to one with Charles, and they were thus enabled to get to know more things than they should have done. The chief secretary, Pace, is mentioned as being present on this occasion. A treaty had been made at Calais, by which Charles was to marry Princess Mary, already espoused to the Dauphin ; but this new arrangement was even less likely to lead to a marriage than the other, because by this time Henry knew Catherine would not bear a son, and there was not the slightest chance of England giving herself to Charles. Charles departed on 13th, and next day Margaret wrote to Pace from Gravelines about requests made by some of Henry's subjects in Calais. Soon Henry and the English returned home. Erasmus had hoped to get to Gravelines to say good-bye to More and Pace, before he went back to Basel ; but he was not well enough to leave Antwerp.

After all this business and excitement Wolsey went on pilgrimage to Our Lady of Walsingham, and Henry did a lot of hunting. Pace stayed at court to attend to business, and there were so few councillors that Ruthal had to be sent for, when Francis began to fortify Ardres, in spite of the recent meeting. There were revels and feasts for weeks. Pace was amused because the Marquis of Dorset came to court at Windsor, to hunt with the King, ' with legs not so meet for the hunting as is his kendal coat,' for he had the gout in them. Henry rose to hunt at 4 or 5 o'clock, except on holy days, and hunted till 9 or 10 at night, ' He spares no pains to convert the sport of hunting into a martyrdom.' Pace had to attend to general business—Irish affairs, the Venetian galleys, the questions raised by Luther, regulations and statutes against aliens, the housing and attendance of the Princess, plague at Woodstock, Scotch affairs, the election of abbots, quieting the fears of the

Venetian ambassador when cannon were put on ships, the plans
of the French hostages to escape, news from Spain, Italy,
Switzerland, Hungary, and the Levant, the safety of English
ships near French ports, piracy by the French and Spaniards.
His letters disappear from the calendar in October 1520, and
on 7th January Antonio Surian reported from London that
he was expected back from the emperor, to whom he had been
sent on a mission by the King.[1]   Henry was anxious at that
time that Charles should not go with an army to be crowned
in Italy, and perhaps Pace was sent on this matter, or to attend
his German coronation at Aix.   He might have gone to find
out what Charles proposed to do about Luther at Worms, or
to arrange loans of money which Charles wanted from Henry.
But in May following Surian informed the Signory that Henry
had sent Pace as his ambassador to Francis.   He was mistaken
in that, and so he may have been in the other case.[2]   In fact
Tunstal was sent to Germany and Jerningham to France.   The
King spent Christmas, 1520, at Greenwich with great royalty,
keeping open court, and himself jousted against all comers,
and with the Earl of Devonshire and four others withstood
sixteen oncomers.

   The Duke of Buckingham was to be charged with treason ;
preparations for clearing him from the steps of the throne,
for that is what it amounted to, had been in the making for
two years.   The matter went before the council, and Wolsey
and Pace had corresponded about it.   Henry summoned him
from Gloucestershire, and he came to Windsor ; where he slept
the night, so much afraid that he could eat little breakfast in
the morning.   He rode to Westminster, and took his barge to
York Place, but Wolsey would not see him ; so he went on to
London, where he was arrested, on 15th April.   Pace had written
to Wolsey about him on the previous day.   He was put in the
Tower, and on 13th May he was taken by barge to Westminster
for trial.   He was sentenced to death, and taken back to the
Tower in the evening, through the streets on foot, with the axe
turned towards him.   He was executed on Tower Hill on the
morning of 17th May.

[1] *Cal. Ven. St. Paps.*, iii. 151.   [2] *Ibid.* iii. 204.

When, in April, at Greenwich, Pace took news-letters from Germany into the King's study, he found him busy ' *in scribendo contra Lutherum*, as I do conjecture.' More importance was just then being attached in England to Luther's agitation, and certain learned men were ordered to examine his works, with the result that Henry ordered the pope's bull against him to be read, and his books to be burnt at Paul's cross, on 12th May. Wolsey and the bishops rode to the great church, and were received there by the dean (Mr. Richard Pace) and the canons, in their vestments, and the cardinal was censed, standing beneath a canopy borne by four doctors. Wolsey went to the high altar and made oblation. Then he mounted a scaffold, erected at the cross, round which were 30,000 people, according to Pace, and sat beneath a cloth of state, with the papal nuncio and the Archbishop of Canterbury at his feet on his right side, and the emperor's ambassador and Ruthal on his left. John Fisher, Bishop of Rochester, preached the sermon in condemnation of the errors of Luther ; and many books were burned in the churchyard during the sermon. It was this sermon which Pace translated into Latin ; he regarded the teaching of Luther as a pestilent heresy and schismatic. He sent a copy of his translation to the pope, with a covering letter.[1] This translation was printed with Fisher's works in 1597. Nearly twenty years after the sermon, when Fisher had gone to the block for opposing the King in his attitude towards the church, it was called in by proclamation ; and Sir Thomas Elyot, the author of *The Gouernour*, wrote to Thomas Cromwell, who then ruled everything, that he had a copy of Pace's translation, which he had bought more because of his regard for the translator than for its subject-matter.

In the spring of 1521 the wars between Charles and Francis began, and both sent ambassadors to Henry, calling on him to intervene ; for the signatories to the treaty of London were bound by it to make war on the aggressor. Henry decided to send Wolsey to Calais to decide who was the beginner of the hostilities. Wolsey saw Francis' ambassadors before he started, and they seemed to think he would act justly ; but it was a

[1] P. Balan, *Monumenta Reformationis*, etc., No. 98, or p. 255.

foregone conclusion that an alliance with the emperor against
Francis would be the result of his journey.   Charles' ambassadors
were brought to Windsor by Sir Richard Wingfield, and lodged
in the house of the dean of the chapel.   Pace joined them at
supper.   Henry had been hunting all day and had sent Pace
to them at this late hour, promising an audience first thing next
morning.   Pace and Sir Richard Wingfield called for them
between 10 and 11 o'clock next morning and took them to
the palace.   They had to wait in the anteroom, for the King
was engaged with the Duke of Suffolk and the Earl of Worcester.
Pace came out to inform them that after Mass the King had
found himself in such good appetite, in consequence of the
exercise he had taken on the previous day, that he would dine
before he gave them audience.   Dinner was set before them in
the anteroom, and Suffolk, Worcester, and another noble sat
down with them.   After dinner Pace ushered them into the
King's presence, and Henry made various excuses for not
helping the emperor ;   at all events before Wolsey had come
to a decision at Calais.   Just before Wolsey started, Henry was
informed that the pope and the emperor had made a treaty.

Wolsey crossed to Calais on 20th July, taking the great seal
with him ;   and Pace was left in charge at home, for Ruthal,
Tunstal, and More went with Wolsey.   So many of the wisest
counsellors going to an arbitration, in which England was the
arbitrator and not a party, was a sign that something else was
being planned.   Soon Henry complained of the return of pains
in his head ' and reaumes falling out of the same,' and told
Pace he would not be able to write to Margaret of Austria with
his own hand, and that he could tell Wolsey to order the
matter as he pleased.   Sickness prevented his binding himself
to anything.   Francis sent messages to Henry, hoping to get
his alliance, and Pace wrote all things out to Wolsey.   Henry
had tried to keep the peace in Europe, and so was liable to be
blamed by any one taken by surprise when hostilities began,
and hostilities usually began with raids intended to be surprises.
While Wolsey was away the King saw all the letters that came.
It is true that Pace could not get him to business one day, because
certain harts were so lodged for him that he must needs hunt

them, and, on another occasion, Pace advised Wolsey that the
King had deferred writing letters with his own hand on the
previous day, ' for the saying of his matins *in honorem Divae
Virginis*, and this day harts and hounds let his grace to do
the same ' ; but he paid special attention to business. Yet he
was not able—and Pace's position was not strong enough to
make him able—to answer all letters of importance in the
absence of his great chancellor ; and some—from Francis—
were sent over by Pace to Wolsey, for him to draft the answers
in French, and send the drafts back to Windsor for Henry to
write out in his own hand.[1] Wolsey sent over drafts of letters
to Charles and Margaret, with the request that Henry would
write the fair copies, and send them back by the bearer. Henry
did not address them, or put wax on them, for fear the French
might see them and recognize what they were, and Pace made
an E on the one packet and an M on the other.[2] It was Pace's
wish that all correspondence on very important matters, in
Wolsey's absence, should pass under Henry's sign and seal for
his own protection. He was really acting as chancellor, and
being Wolsey's nominee on the council and in the King's
service, he wanted to safeguard himself from having blame
thrown on him when Wolsey returned. He always supported
Wolsey : ' It was lately the King's pleasure to dispute with
your grace ; now it is his pleasure to hold his peace, whereof I
am for my part right glad.'[3] The dispute had been caused by
Wolsey's too great trust in France's treatment of English ships
going to Bordeaux. Even the domestic comfort of the King
was in Wolsey's hands. Henry was very short of money.
Taxes were not coming in, and it was very difficult to borrow,
so Henry thought of going up to London to keep the term in
the autumn ; for there was much complaining about the prolonged absence of the court, and he thought a return might
bring in revenue. There was, however, fresh plague in London
' which some calleth the new murre, and some the wild fever',
which indeed is as wild a sickness as ever I suffered,' wrote
Pace ; and it was dangerous to go there. Pace suggested that
Wolsey should send the great seal home by Tunstal, the Master

---

[1] *L. and P.*, iii. 1425.   [2] *Ibid.* iii. 1459.   [3] *Ibid.* iii. 1629.

of the Rolls, to facilitate business and the borrowing of money. Pace was scared of the plague. Young Lord Grey died of it, at court at Windsor, and one of the King's German servants. A Spanish friar of the Order of St. Jerome, who was reputed by his order to be a saint, and able to still tempests, and work other miracles, came to court, presumably to expel the plague. He had an hour's talk with the King ; but Pace did not know the result, except that Henry esteemed him more a friar than a saint, whatever that might indicate. Pace thought he had more Spanish impudence than learning. The administration of justice was delayed by the plague, and by Wolsey's absence with the great seal.

Francis hoped to influence Wolsey, in the arbitration, through Henry at home—a thing he was scarcely likely to do, with the anti-French Pace at his elbow. Charles' case with regard to the hostilities in Navarre and the Ardennes was listened to and put before the arbitrator, Wolsey, by Pace, as that which commended itself to the King. English agents in Flanders had urged Henry to send 4000 archers to help the emperor against Francis. Henry liked the idea well ; and so no doubt did Pace, but he cautiously wrote to Wolsey, ' No such aid can be sent till the convention at Calais is concluded, as it would be a manifest derision to treat of peace and send men to make War.' [1] There needed no ghost come from the grave to tell Wolsey that. But all who were consulted—including Wolsey— agreed to prepare the archers, to be ready when he had found in the emperor's favour, and had concluded a treaty with him. The names of nobles possible as commander-in-chief were passed about. More and Sir William Sandys were let into the secret of what was coming, but Pace was the link between the King and his absent chancellor. Pace wrote enthusiastically to Wolsey about the plans he had talked over with the King. When other things had been concluded for the invasion of France, Henry and Charles ought to destroy the French navy.[2] Henry and Pace wanted this suggestion to be made secretly to the emperor. They regarded it as a ' high and great enter- prise, if it may thus by wisdom and good policy be brought to

[1] *L. and P.*, iii. 1429.   [2] *Ibid.* iii. 1440.

pass.' It was thought best to give out that the archers were being prepared to conduct the emperor to Spain ; and, that being so, the number might as well be raised to 10,000, but Henry wanted the emperor to pay for the additional four or five thousand. Wolsey went to Bruges, to meet the emperor ; and Erasmus went over, hoping Pace and Warham had come with him, and he met More, Tunstal, Ruthal, and Mountjoy.

Wolsey decided that Francis had been the aggressor in the hostilities. On 25th August articles of agreement, subject to the approval of the pope, were signed at Bruges by Wolsey, and by Margaret for Charles, and on 24th November a secret treaty was made at Calais, between the pope, the emperor, and Henry, by which Henry undertook to invade France in the spring. Wolsey returned to England on 28th November, and found Pace very contented. For a time Wolsey had feigned friendship with France, but that was all over, and a great alliance was being formed against his old enemy. It seemed as if France was doomed. The old medieval alliance of pope and emperor was strengthened against her by the addition of young Tudor England. Wolsey joined the king at Bletchingley, and was made Abbot of St. Albans as a reward for his work at Calais. Pace recounts how he had gone, at Windsor, to find the King and give him letters from Wolsey, and caught him just as he was going to shoot. Henry read the letters, and led Pace by ' his secret way unto the park.' The letters were to the effect that Wolsey would like to have the vacant abbey. The King admitted that he had been put to great expense on his recent mission, and said he would rather give it to him—secular priest though he was—than to any monk. Pace—striking as usual while the iron was hot—begged him to sign the letter to the pope at once, and the King promised to sign, if Pace brought it to him at evensong-time. Needless to say Pace brought it, and it was only then that Henry remembered that within the last few days he had granted the monks his licence and *congée d'élire*. Pace had not reminded him of this, but met the difficulty by pointing out that the grant was as yet of none effect, because the letters patent had not issued. Perhaps he had taken care they should not issue. This satisfied the King, who signed the letter to the pope, and told Pace to tell Wolsey he was to have the abbey. Pace was zealous for his patron, and had subdued himself entirely into a secretary, acting between the King and his minister. Wolsey seems to have been pleased with the way he had conducted affairs during the five months of his absence. There had been difficulty at one moment. Sir Thomas More came home in October, and told Pace that the cardinal was displeased with him for reading his letters to the King ' diminutely,' for obtaining the King's favour for a canon to be prior of Marton Abbey, and for obtaining an office in chancery for a servant of Tunstal's. Pace wrote to Wolsey and hoped he would accept this explanation. He had only read Wolsey's letters ' dimin. utely,' or fully, to the King when ordered to do so. The King had read all Wolsey's letters with great diligence, and Pace's answers. Wolsey complained of Pace's answer to one of his letters. This was the King's own answer. Pace had written something very different, but when Henry saw it, he had disapproved, and made Pace bring the correspondence into his privy chamber with pen and ink. There he had dictated what he wanted written, after reading Wolsey's letters, some of them three times, and marking certain parts that called for an answer. Henry had told Pace he was to dispatch what he had dictated and not meddle with it. So Pace considered himself blameless, ' especially at such time as he (Henry) would upon good grounds be obeyed, whosoever spake to the contrary.' Pace said he had never given the King false information about Wolsey's letters, ' for though I lack wit, yet for faith and truth I dare compare with any servant the king hath.' He did not, he wrote, interfere with the election of the canon, but wrote by the King's direction, to the dean of York, that he should be elected prior, in preference to an outsider. As for the office in chancery, he did not know it was in Wolsey's gift, until More told him so. He had acted in this at the instance of his faithful friend, the absent Tunstal, Master of the Rolls, who he thought deserved well of the King. Pace ended the letter by begging Wolsey to lay aside all suspicion ; he had no servant or friend living who could have served him better than he had done.[1] Wolsey forgave him, and

[1] *L. and P.*, iii. 1713.

everything was soon all right again. Pace had described himself as glad that his services had been acceptable to Wolsey, and
stated, in a letter to him, that, though he could not write so
wisely as might be required, he was at all times ready to move
the King to answer Wolsey's letters with convenient diligence.
No tongue, he wrote, could express the King's satisfaction with
the service Wolsey had rendered at Calais. Wolsey had asked
him to write to him privately and secretly, and if he had not
often done so it was because he had nothing to report secretly.[1]
Everything had gone well while he was in charge, ' without any
ill-bruit or murmuring,' and the commonalty had no knowledge
that a war against France was being prepared, and were glad to
be at peace with Flanders. It did not seem necessary to take
much notice of the commonalty.

The allies—they may now be called the imperialists—took
Milan, and all the Milanese and the Florentines and other Italian
states joined them. France would probably have been over-
whelmed when Henry's army moved in the spring. But Leo
died on 2nd December 1521, the league was broken up, and Pace
was dispatched to get Wolsey elected pope. Just before he
started, he was made prebendary of Combe, in Salisbury, and
in the previous year he had been given the living of Llangwrig,
Montgomery.

This was Pace's last embassy. In October he had written
to Wolsey,[2] ' I have not written to you lately, having been very
ill, and almost out of my mind for want of sleep and appetite ;
but I will not fail to advertise you of all occurrences,' and he
was half dead when he came home again. So before going with
him to Italy it is well to gather up fragments of the more
pleasant parts of his life, shining through sickness and worry,
while he was at the court. He had kept up his correspondence
with Erasmus, whom he told about the King's book against
Luther, which Erasmus was anxious to read. Again and again
Erasmus asked plaintively for the return of the ' trifles ' he had
left with him at Ferrara, and he begged him to spare no expense
in recovering them. Erasmus did get some of them, and Roger
Ascham found the lost part of Book II of *Antibarbari*, about

[1] *L. and P.*, iii. 1543.   [2] *Ibid.* iii. 2, 1629.

1550, at Cambridge.   He offered it to Froben, who had already
brought out a complete edition of Erasmus' works, and had no
use for it.[1]   Pace was really very unfortunate in his relations
with Erasmus.   When he was with Maximilian, before Milan, he
had in his possession certain letters from Cardinal Grimani and
Cardinal St. George, which Ammonius had sent him to be
delivered to Erasmus.   He sent them, but they disappeared—he
thought the messenger had been killed.   Erasmus recommended
Peter Luscus to Pace for some reward from the King, but he
had no opportunity of putting in a word for him.   Erasmus
sent Pace his *Paraphrase of the Epistle to the Corinthians*, and
Pace found he had never understood St. Paul before.   He
wished Erasmus would explain the other epistles in the same
manner.   They exchanged views about editing *The New
Testament*, and Erasmus wrote letters he hoped Pace would
show to the King.   They corresponded about Polydore Vergil's
works, published by Froben in 1521, and Vergil's preface to his
Adagiorum Liber was addressed to Pace.   When More received
comedies and tragedies from Erasmus he passed them on to
Pace.   We come across some small personal details of interest.
Pace had in 1521 his own agent in Rome, named Aloysius
Gibraleon, who approached the pope for him, for instance to get
a favour for Linacre, the King's physician.   A certain John
Clifton wrote him, while he was with the Swiss, that Burbank
was looking after his interests in London.   As an officer of the
court, Mr. Secretary Pace was supplied with livery or uniform.
' Ordinary ' breakfasts were served daily in the Counting House
for the officials of the court.   He had a house and servants in
London in May 1518, before he was dean of St. Paul's,[2] and payments were made to Thomas Cotton and his other servants by
the King.   Even in February 1518 Giglis still had gold cloth
and tapestry in Rome, belonging to Bainbridge's estate, and
some of his clothes, which were to be sent home by ship as the
cheapest way.   There are entries of payments to Mr. Secretary
for the French herald, who proclaimed the jousts at Greenwich,

[1] *Rogeri Aschami Epistolarum Libri Quatuor*, 1703, iii. No. 13, and
Allen, *Opus Epist.*, 277.
[2] *L. and P.*, ii. 47, Appendix.

in 1520, as if he had been in charge of expenses. Although he followed John Colet in being an abstemious man, he preferred good lodging to lean kitchen. At Reading, the King was ' contented ' with the abbot where he lodged, ' and all we courtiers have cause to praise him for his kind and loving cheer.'

Now he was principal secretary to the King, and only Wolsey and Ruthal were more important in the privy council. He was dean of St. Paul's, vicar of Stepney, and of Llangwrig ; he was a prebend of Southwell, of St. Paul's, and Salisbury ; he was archdeacon of Dorset, and treasurer of Lichfield. He resigned the treasurership of Lichfield before he came home again, but became dean of Exeter, dean of Salisbury, vicar of Bangor, and vicar of South Molton in the diocese of Exeter.

A few months after he had left England, Anne Boleyn returned to court to upset everything.

CHAPTER IX

A POPELESS ROME

EIGHT years enjoyment of the papacy had wrought a change in Leo. Viewing war with less dislike, he had come round to the anti-French policy of Julius, Wolsey, Bainbridge, and Pace. He was at his hunting-lodge, the villa Malliana, six miles down the Tiber, when he heard that the allies had captured Milan from the French. He rode into Rome in the evening, in a great state of excitement, and caught what appeared to be a slight chill, but fever supervened, and he died on the morning of 2nd December.

The emperor had told Wolsey, at Bruges, that he could rely on his doing his best to get him elected pope, should the great office become vacant ; and he renewed his promise at this moment.[1] King and cardinal turned again to the emissary who had gone for them on three missions of great importance. Pace was ordered to start for Rome, and was provided with bills of exchange, and with two sets of letters to the cardinals ; one in favour of the candidate whom the English ambassadors in Rome should decide to support ; and the other in favour of Cardinal Giulio de' Medici. If the King could not get his candidate elected, it would be well that he should appear among the supporters of the winner. At all costs the papacy must not go to a supporter of Francis. Pace was to promise the cardinals anything they wanted, if Wolsey's election seemed possible. Henry, in selecting Pace for this mission, said he sent him ' as if he had sent his very heart.' With him was to go Richmond Herald. If he found he could not bring about Wolsey's election—and it would be so unless the emperor helped him—he was to join the emperor's

[1] *L. and P.*, iii. 1877.

ambassador in persuading the new pope, whoever he might be, to take Leo's place in the league against France. So important was the emperor's co-operation, not only to the securing of the vote but to the preservation of the alliance against France, that Pace was to see him at Ghent and talk over plans. Wolsey did not intend to compete unless assured of the emperor's support, and Pace was left to judge of the emperor's intentions from his manner at the interview. The English ambassadors at Rome, whom Pace was to join, were John Clerk, lately dean of the chapel royal, and now bishop of Bath and Wells, and Thomas Hannibal, a doctor of law, an older man, whom Wolsey had been employing lately. Polydore Vergil says that Wolsey had, or pretended to have, hopes of being elected. And why should he not ? He was not always the best, nor the most popular, nor the most suitable candidate to whom the cardinals gave their voices. He was often one who would, at least, keep some other out of the papal throne—a stop-gap. If the alliance against France was to be kept together, and if the other allies wanted the pope to come in as a nominal head—and this they did want—and if they agreed that Wolsey would best complete this alliance, then Wolsey might well become pope ; although the cardinals pretended to think him too young, and although they feared electing an Englishman and a very able man. He was a little over fifty, but Leo had been younger at his election. If he was elected, the emperor and king might use the Holy See as if it was their own, unless, of course, after his election, he were suddenly to remember his duty to the church, as a temporal power. He himself professed not to desire the great office, unless the emperor and the King thought it to their advantage to put him in it. He knew he had no chance unless the emperor stood for him, and that his victory was very uncertain even then. It was very difficult to tell at any moment how great any influence among the cardinals would prove to be. News travelled so slowly that it was difficult to be prepared for an election, and keeping an agent in Rome primed with instructions, as to what he was to do in the event of the sudden death of a pope, was very expensive ; so chance after chance of getting a favourite elected might be missed. Henry and Wolsey, having started their political careers with a very full treasury, could not free themselves from the expectation that every one was to be bought—emperor, cardinals, Swiss—but the treasury was getting empty.   Probably Wolsey's exact feeling was that he did not despair of being elected, if Pace and the emperor's emissaries got to Rome in time, with the proper letters for the cardinals from the two sovereigns.   We are apt to think of a promise like this one, made by the emperor to the English chancellor, as being as valuable as would be one made to-day about some state affair by the prime minister to the president of the French republic ; but in fact it was of a very different nature.   It was in those days necessary to remind a pope, an emperor, or a king of his promises, which otherwise might prove to mean only that at a certain moment he had thought seriously of doing what he had appeared to plan.   Charles could influence the cardinals, but Wolsey's hope was that he would move his troops at Naples on Rome to overawe them.   Very likely Charles spoke the truth when he said that his ambassador had no orders—at the time the cardinals entered conclave—to influence them in any direction, except to the best choice.   This desire to call on electors to do their duty was proving a good excuse for sending agents to interfere with them—at Frankfort or Rome.   The emperor's ambassador in England dined at Richmond, and heard all that Henry and Wolsey had to say about the election. They seem to have dealt very honestly with him, and to have thought only of the good of the league, but he suspected the emperor was not going to act up to his promises.   So he wrote,[1] urging him to make a show of zeal and lively interest in Wolsey's pretensions, when he interviewed Pace at Ghent.   The emperor was to bluff Pace into speaking highly to his King of his goodwill and exertions.

Sir Richard Wingfield and Thomas Spinelli informed Wolsey that Pace had reached Ghent on the morning of 22nd, and had had an audience with the emperor in the evening.[2]   The emperor was even at this time only twenty-one years old.   Pace gave him letters from Henry and Wolsey, and laid before him all their desires and hopes and plans about the election.   Charles assured

[1] *L. and P.*, iii. 1884.   [2] *Ibid.* iii. 1890.

him of his support. Pace wandered to other subjects—the raising of Swiss infantry for service against France; Tournai was mentioned, and the possibility of bringing Venice into their league. Pace was anxious to go to the Swiss again—after his return from Rome. He did not like them, or their country, but he felt he could now do some more good work among them against France. The emperor had come to look upon it as natural that an alliance with England should lead to sending money by a emissary—Pace if possible—to hire Swiss infantry. He knew the French were making great exertions among them, and he urged that, if Pace could not go until he had been to Rome, they should be kept in hopes until then. Pace had the wit to tell him that Wolsey had been very pleased with his reception at Bruges, and had reported so to Henry. After the interview the emperor wrote to Henry and Wolsey, assuring them of his support of Wolsey's candidature—just as his ambassador in England had advised him to do. Pace had an interview with Margaret of Austria, for whom he had a letter from Wolsey, in which he gave her the name of ' mother.' She answered : ' I hope one day to be, therefore, mother of the pope. It will not be the emperor's fault if it is not so.' [1] He saw Sir Richard Wingfield and told him what he was going to do in Rome. On 24th December Gasparo Contarini, the Venetian ambassador with the emperor, whom he perhaps knew at Padua university, informed the Signory that at 9 o'clock at night, Pace had sent to his lodging asking to see his secretary, and had told him he was going to Rome by order of his King. He had asked for a passport through Venetian territory for one of his attendants, who was to be sent in advance, riding post. The secretary had a long chat with Pace, for they found they had known each other in Rome. Contarini gave the passport and called on Pace, who assured him of his continued affection for Venice, and asked him to let the Signory know at once that Henry desired the preservation of the Republic. Pace hoped the old alliance between France and Venice was at an end. Contarini told Pace the Turkish news, and tried to find out the exact object of his journey to Rome ; but all he could elicit was that

[1] L. and P., iii. 1904.

it concerned negotiations between his King and the new pope.[1] The Venetian concluded that this meant a new league of pope, emperor, and King, against France—and depended on who should become pope. It seems as if Pace asked for this passport in case he might be taken ill, and have to send his letters to Rome ; and, either at that moment or at a later stage of the journey, he did send on his servant Thomas Clerke, because he was ill. Pace left Ghent between five and six o'clock on the morning of 26th December, having omitted nothing during his stay there that might help him on his journey.

The weather was very rough, and the roads bad and dangerous. On 31st December he reached Spires ; and on 8th January he passed through Trent, where they did not know him, or had forgotten him, but talked about him at the inn. They said he was going to Rome ; that he was, if not the first in authority with the King of England, then at least the second. He went to see his old friend, Francesco Sforza, and had a long talk with him. The *proveditor* called him, ' one Richard Pace ' ; and he posted the news on to the Signory. Pace went on through Mantua, finding Italy in a lawless state, in consequence of the pope's death ; and the winter was one of the severest remembered there. Francesco Maria della Rovere, whom Leo had driven from Urbino, had got back again ; and was leading his army against Florence, Siena, and the Medici family. The Duke of Ferrara had recovered several cities in the Romagna ; the Baglioni had got back Perugia ; and if Lautrec had been sent money he could have led the French to a great victory.

Meanwhile in Rome thirty-nine cardinals entered conclave on 27th December. Pace reached Florence on 12th January 1522, and heard there, or just before he got there, that a pope had been elected on 9th, before his messenger had arrived with his letters. Few of the cardinals had ever seen the cardinal of Tortosa, the new pope, a Dutchman, the Viceroy of Spain, and Charles' old tutor, who was at Burgos. He took the title of Adrian VI. Letters had been dispatched by Wolsey to Campeggio in Rome, as soon as the news of Leo's death reached England, and they were delivered sooner than could have been

[1] *Cal. Ven. St. Paps.*, iii. 379.

expected, but after the election was over. Campeggio and de'
Medici had put forward Wolsey's name, and he received a few
votes. Outside the conclave his interests were looked after by
John Clerk. Campeggio assured Wolsey that he had left no
stone unturned to get him elected ; had disposed of the suggestion that he was too young, by assuring the cardinals that he
was nearly sixty, but they would not believe him. Like everything else in Europe the conclave was divided into French and
imperialist factions, and only part of the imperialist faction
favoured de' Medici, who most unfortunately was in a hurry to
get back to Florence to prevent a revolt against his family,
which would be supported by Francesco Maria. Therefore he
had to propose Adrian as a compromise, but the cardinals could
hardly say how they came to elect him, and afterwards tried to
blame the Holy Ghost. According to Clerk, if proper efforts
had been made in time, and the king and cardinal's pleasure
had been known, Wolsey might have been elected ; but when he
had left England to be ambassador at Rome, Wolsey had told
him that he had no intention of meddling in the matter.[1] The
English agents were not likely to admit they could not have
brought about his election ; they were more likely to speak
of lack of instructions than lack of influence. After the election
Clerk told de' Medici that Henry had sent Pace post with letters
to the cardinals ; and that these letters had been sent on to
himself, as Pace, through feebleness, was unable to continue
the journey. This is the only intimation that he was ill again.[1]
The sick man was sent time after time on journeys he was unfit
for. De' Medici told Clerk that, if they had come in time, the
King's letters would have had great weight with the cardinals ;
but that they were obstinate about the election of Wolsey. His
youth was the objection they talked most about, but there were
others more potent : they did not want a strong English statesman in Rome, nor a pope in London.

Pace was told that de' Medici would be in Florence in three
days' time, so he waited to see him ; but he was delayed by
having to make the journey from Rome by sea, and by ' strange
ways,' to avoid the army of Francesco Maria, which was

[1] *L. and P.*, iii. 1960.

besieging Siena. The cardinal's presence would keep order in Florence, though the French had a considerable following in the city, especially—Pace was told—among those to whom Francis was in debt. Pace's experiences had not brought him in touch with Florentine politics, and he now saw a danger that not only Florence but Bologna, and other cities, might fall to Francis, and that from them might be drawn much money. Pace sent Richmond Herald to the governor of Siena, and to Francesco Maria, to ask for passports to Rome. Richmond had only forty miles to ride, but he took such a long time about it that Pace was anxious. People in Florence told him that, even if he got the passports, he would not be able to travel, for the soldiers in the armies of Francesco Maria and of Siena were very undisciplined and robbed on the highroads. There was no need to hasten to Rome, now that the election was over ; and he moved about Florence, waiting for Richmond's return, and any further instructions from Wolsey, whom he kept posted up in his progress. People said that Adrian was ill, and Pace found Florentines betting he was dead ; he was interested, for if the news was true, there would be another election.

The astonishing news of the election reached the emperor at Brussels on 18th January—more certain news on 21st—and he wrote to his ambassador in Rome. Anxious as he had been that Pace should arrive in time to forward Wolsey's candidature, he was thankful, he wrote, that the choice had fallen on Adrian, whose election next to Wolsey's was most for the good of Christendom. Many historians have come to the conclusion that he really wished Cardinal de' Medici to be elected ; he sent the news on to London on 21st.

By 13th January Pace was expected hourly by Clerk in Rome. One of them would probably have to join Adrian in Spain as ambassador. Clerk hoped it would not be he, for it was a dangerous journey by sea or land, and he had no money, and his diets were in arrear. It might be a long time before the new pope got to Rome, for he had to hand over the government of Spain. Pace's fears for the safety of Richmond Herald, in the troubled country, were justified. He had been received politely by the governor of Siena, and told that the king of

England's subjects needed no passports in that territory ; but as he was proceeding to Francesco Maria's camp, he was taken by some thirty of his horsemen and robbed of all he had, even his herald's coat, on the pretext that it bore the arms of Florence, in which there was a fleur-de-lis and a lion. An ' honest gentleman ' of Mantua got him released, and he went before Francesco Maria with Pace's credentials. Francesco apologized for such treatment, explaining that his soldiers were without pay ; and he restored to him what had been taken from him. The duke granted the safe-conducts in the fullest manner, saying ' he did know me (Pace) for his friend, for pope July's sake.' They had met in Rome and in camps. The Florentines had been unable to ascertain the strength of Francesco Maria's army, but Richmond Herald had been into the camp, and had seen its feebleness, and the scarcity of victuals. So within two days the Florentines attacked and drove it off.

If Pace was ill it did not lessen his activity ; he thought he saw the Florentines wavering in their loyalty to de' Medici ; and managed to confirm them in it, for that meant a continued hostility to his old enemy Francis. Richmond had seen French officers in Francesco Maria's army. Cardinal de' Medici reached Florence late on the night of 22nd January, and at once sent the bishop of Capua, ' otherwise Fra Nicolas,' to welcome Pace to Florence, and to arrange an interview for the morning. Pace waited on the cardinal, and was received with great honour in the presence of the magistrates. De' Medici took him into a secret chamber, and told him he knew how much he owed to Henry and Wolsey, from the letters brought him by Pace's servant, and from what he had been told by the ambassadors in Rome. Pace told him more of Henry's and Wolsey's plans and intentions, and he said he would send his most trusted secretary to thank them. He declared that he would live and die the faithful servant of the King and the emperor. He said Francis had made him great offers since Leo's death, but he had rejected them all. He declared that he had given his vote for Wolsey at every scrutiny in the conclave, and had persuaded seventeen or eighteen of his party to do the same ; but, as he could not command more votes, he had thought it best to bring about

the election of one who would be friendly to the emperor and
Henry. Pace had no doubt he was a friend to Wolsey in all
his private causes. By way of present the cardinal sent
Richmond Herald a gown of the finest damask that could
be found in Florence.

The retreat of Francesco Maria enabled Pace to proceed to
Rome. On his arrival at Siena he went to an inn, but the
cardinal of Siena fetched him to his own house, and kept him
the night in as honourable a manner as could be desired, for
Henry's sake, ' whose name in these part now is of greater
estimation than ever was the name of any of his predecessors.'
Pace thought his coming had put an end to many things which
might have caused annoyance to the King and the emperor.
His host told him that the cardinals in the conclave had been
afraid that Wolsey would never come to Rome, if they made him
pope, ' and that ye (Wolsey) were *nimis potens.*' Pace felt
that, if he could have got to Rome in time, he could have removed those objections ; he hoped Wolsey would send a loving
letter to the cardinal, who had entertained him so honourably
and had admitted Wolsey's qualifications for the tiara. Pace
found a rumour in Siena that Adrian would be kept in Spain ;
or would go to Rome by way of England, Flanders, and Germany,
for fear of capture by pirates in the Mediterranean or by the
French in France. He thought that, whatever happened, some
Englishmen should be constantly near him to keep him in hand.
He should be met if he landed in Italy. Pace was willing to
undertake the task himself. On 26th January Pace wrote to
Wolsey from Palpa, and on 28th from Rome, which he had
reached on the 27th. There were just then heavy falls of snow
and rain, unlike anything seen in Italy for many years ; and he
had been delayed on the road.

He found the cardinals afraid to go out of their houses, ' for
fear of the people, which hourly crieth out against them, to
their great rebuke and shame, by reason of the said election.'
It was a shame to see the verses made against them—especially
Pietro Aretino's lampoons. The French cardinals were speaking
against the emperor and his allies, but they were very short of
money. The emperor's ambassador moved troops from Naples.

It was imperative that the new pope should come soon, to restore order, but ' a strong rumour ' had reached Rome that he was dead. At best he was in Spain and difficult to get at. There were terrible storms at sea, hordes of Moorish pirates, and the hire of a ship to Spain was very great. Meanwhile the cardinals, and lesser people, helped themselves to the treasures of the Vatican. Every one now saw the necessity for a pope of some reputation and substance to help the church. Pace made the acquaintance of Don Juan Manuel, the emperor's ambassador, whom he thought ' a singular wise man.' He suggested to him what had been mooted at Siena, namely, that the new pope should be taken to England, to confer there with Henry and the emperor, and that then the emperor should take him to Rome, leaving the King to protect the Netherlands, Germany, and Spain as well as he could. By this means the emperor might turn all Italy to the side of the allies, be crowned in Rome, and return to Spain by Naples, and all things be concluded ' *comme il faut.*' [1] This was a bad suggestion on Pace's part, from the English point of view, and he had at one time hoped that Julius would clear both Frenchman and Spaniard out of Italy. He was too late in appreciating that, if Habsburg dominated Italy, he might be a worse menace to England than the French King was. He was not entirely to blame for this shortness of sight, for Wolsey suffered from it too. Don Juan found this English ambassador a frank-spoken man, and greatly dévoted to the anti-French cause ; but he found he had got to know more about recent disorders in Naples than was desirable. He thought him very little inclined towards any plan which might give peace to France.[2] Pace found Cardinal Schiner in Rome, and heard from him that the Swiss were being worked up again to serve Francis. Pace had been sent out to bring the pope, Venice, and the Swiss into league against Francis ; and he was with none of them, at the moment, but at Rome, where there was no prospective ally with whom he could negotiate. Leo had left so many debts that it would be a long time before a

[1] *L. and P.*, iii. A great number of letters at this point deal with affairs under Pace's notice.
[2] *Cal. Span. St. Paps.*, ii. 383.

pope could equip an army. At any moment Francis might come down on Milan, and Pace was very anxious. While he had been at the King's elbow, and Wolsey at Calais, England had begun to prepare for war, and the preparations ought by this time to have reached an advanced stage ; but they might not prevent the French getting into Italy when the good weather came.

At Leo's death Baldassare Castiglione, whom Pace had probably known in Rome, was again resident as representative of the Duke of Mantua. Lascaris was still teaching Greek and, according to information given to Erasmus, Bombasius had returned from Switzerland and was in Cardinal Pucci's service. Raphael was dead, but Pace could have seen the tapestries he had designed in the Sistine Chapel and his work in the Loggia. While he had been away Piombo had painted the *Raising of Lazarus*, now in the National Gallery. A large part of old St. Peter's remained, but the new dome looked as if it would never be finished — too large for man to build. Agostino Chigi had been dead two years ; Silvester Giglis for less than one. Pace and Cardinal Campeggio were always on the most friendly terms. They had known each other in England, and they read each others letters from Erasmus, who at one time, knowing they were on the move, addressed one letter to both of them. There is evidence of Pace's buying books and manuscripts in Rome, for he had come back a rich man. There was not enough business to occupy his mind, and he turned back to literary work, but, adopting Erasmus' advice, confined himself to translating Greek into Latin, and abandoned attempts at original composition. He translated books of Plutarch, one edition of which was dedicated to Bainbridge and printed by Jacob Mazochisi at Rome. His servants must have gone out after him, and he probably recruited some fresh ones in Italy, for he soon had a considerable household. He always lived in a style befitting the King of England's representative, but he rarely mentions it in his letters. Occasionally he had to remind Wolsey of the great cost at which he stood. We hear of Thomas Cotton and Thomas Clerke, both of whom travelled with his letters, and of Hippolytus who was at one

time with Pole. His secretary was usually an Italian, engaged
when wanted, though Lupset seems to have worked with him
for a time.

Pending Adrian's arrival, the cardinals ruled in turns, but
they were at loggerheads. Pace thought most of them were
' French ' ; and he was pleased to find Mathew Schiner again
declaiming against that nation. There was a considerable
anti-Medici movement in Rome as soon as that cardinal went
to Florence. Pace and Clerk thought it would be best for them
both to stay in Rome till the pope came, for not even the legates,
who were to confer his dignities on him, could reach him. Clerk
followed up Pace's suggestion made to Manuel. If Wolsey
could induce the pope to go to England, ' there might great
chance arise thereby, for the pope is aged and sickly, and might
fortune to die in those quarters ; and if he so did, your grace,
by the reason thereof, might be present at the next election,
and these men here should be too far off to come thither, for ye
should not be bound to tarry *pro absentibus*, but ten days *post
mortem* ; and your grace, having only with you such cardinals
as be in those quarters, should then more easily attain your
purpose.' [1] Pace and Clerk had been thinking things out
and making plans for their master. They realized that the
Romans were indignant with the cardinals for electing a Dutchman, and that at the next election in Rome an Englishman
would not stand a chance. Wolsey had better capture the
conclave in England. They seem never to have asked themselves
what the effect of a schism might be. Neither of them wanted
to cross the sea to Spain, for pirates and tempests had driven
travellers back to port. Pace was afraid to go by France, even
with a safe-conduct, for he had little confidence in the promise of
a Frenchman. Of five messengers sent from Rome to the new
pope in Spain, three who went by land were reported captured
by the French, one who went by sea was driven back into
Civita Vecchia by storms and then into Nice by the Moors,
and the fifth disappeared.

It soon got known in Rome that Pace had brought great
sums of money with him, or could call on the bankers for it ;

[1] *L. and P.*, iii. 2017.

and now that it was not to be spent on bribing cardinals to tell Christendom who God wished to be His vicar, it appeared to lie idle, which seemed wasteful to Don Manuel. Pace had sent Richmond Herald to draw some money from Antonio Vivaldi at Florence, presumably in order that he should not be known to have any. He had brought it on to Rome, where the balance was to be paid him by bankers with whom Vivaldi was making arrangements. Don Manuel and Pace had a mutual friend, Augustino Folleta, on whose counsel Leo had often depended ; and Manuel asked him to speak to Pace about a loan to the emperor of 50,000 ducats, on good security, re-payable within six months, to pay the imperialist troops at Naples and near Rome. Charles was already following in his grandfather's footsteps, but he was never so impecunious and his credit was better. Pace, however, answered that, even if he had the money, he would not dare to lend it without his King's order. He would not part with a penny beyond paying his daily charges. He had started, as before, at a moment's notice, and had not been able to make any arrangements of a private nature, and £100, which Wolsey had given him at the last moment, had gone on posts along the road, and with it some of his own money hastily got together. He had had to buy proper clothes, and other things, when he got to Rome. One could not post with heavy luggage, and merchants took months bringing it. He had to borrow from the King's money in his hands to meet this expense. It was his wise intention to charge the King only for his diets, as was agreed before he started ; and he told Wolsey he would punctually account for what he was forced to borrow. He was afraid history might repeat itself, as it so often did, and that Wolsey might refuse to repay Vivaldi when he had drawn on him ; and, if he did, Vivaldi would pro-duce nothing more and he might starve in Rome. It would not be possible to borrow from Clerk, who had ventured to remind Wolsey that his own diets had not been paid; owing—as he tactfully put it—to his agent having neglected to sue to Wolsey for them at convenient times. Pace and Clerk, like the other ambassadors to the papal court, were in a curious position ; the pope to whom they were accredited was far away,

and Rome was nothing without him. They considered and
talked over the likelihood of the Duke of Ferrara, the Duke of
Urbino, and Venice coming into the league ; but all three
seemed to be set ' good French.' The two dukes were at the
moment plundering the estates of the church, and of Leo's
family, and they would not stop until the new pope, or the
emperor, had restored order. The only alternative would be the
descent of Francis into Italy, where many would prefer French
domination to anarchy. Don Manuel wrote a short letter to the
emperor, saying that Pace had sent to tell him that in his
opinion a war between England and France was inevitable. It
was what Pace hoped for, and he knew it was what was being
prepared at home ; but he wanted Swiss infantry to strengthen
the English attack by invading Burgundy. Prosper Colonna
and the Marquis of Pescara, the imperialist commanders of the
allied armies, were in Milan and Pavia. The French had
returned to Lombardy, under Lautrec, and had joined the
Venetians, and had been joined by some Swiss, of whom Clerk
and Pace had not heard a good account. ' The Swecys be not
elect persons, but rascal, and very evil appointed.' About
Easter-time the French were defeated at Bicocca, the truth
being that Lautrec was forced by his rascal Swiss to fight.
They demanded pay, leave to depart, or battle, and as Louise
of Savoy, Francis' mother, had stuck to their pay it was a
choice between battle and retreat. After this the French were
again driven out of Italy, and the rest of the fighting took place
on the frontiers of the Netherlands and Spain. In June the
sultan declared war on Rhodes. The result of Bicocca was
a great relief to Pace, who had feared that Francis was in a
position to overrun Italy. Any sign of his success would lead a
lot of minor states and princes over to his side, and the imperialists were terribly short of pay. Pace thought that if the French
had then taken Milan a million of gold would not have sufficed
to recover it. He spared no pains to let it be known in Rome
that Henry would shortly invade France—a thing doubted there
since Leo's death. He deplored the fact that Henry did not
well understand the affairs of Italy, and therefore did not realize
what a tremendous effect on the allies' cause the presence of the

emperor in Italy would have.[1] Pace was right ; half Italy would side with either Charles or Francis if he came as a conqueror. A long time elapsed before Pace and Clerk were instructed as to whether they should stay in Rome until the pope came, or hunt for him in Spain. Serving one's king abroad was not the easiest task, and travelling had many dangers. On his way home Richmond Herald had a nasty fall from his horse near Brussels, and had to send Pace's cipher-letters, which told Wolsey of some ' strange attempts lately begun here,' [in Rome], by another messenger. Pace had heard of the defeat of the French at Bicocca in time to put the news as a postscript to a letter dated the 30th April.

In May Henry and Charles met again in England and talked over plans and signed the treaty of Windsor. It set out the usual rigmarole, that it was time for Christian princes to arm against the Turk, but that it was impossible for them to do so until Francis' ambition had been curbed and universal peace established within Christendom. They hoped Adrian and Venice would join the league, which they confirmed on 16th June. Next day the Master of Rhodes wrote to report that the Turkish Fleet was in sight. The way for Venice to peace with the emperor was to be smoothed by Wolsey, who was to temper the terms to suit her. Gasparo Contarini, who had been in attendance on Charles, and had met Pace at Ghent, reminded the Signory that it was desirable to give cordial and honourable greeting to him, if he was sent to assist in making a treaty between Venice and the emperor—for he was the staunchest partisan of Venice, and, next to the cardinal, the most influential person about the King.[2] Francis had been stirring up trouble for England in Scotland and Ireland, and on 29th May, while Charles was still in England, an English herald appeared before him at Lyons and declared war. Charles sailed to Spain from Southampton.

Pace's instructions to go to Venice are dated Bishop's Waltham, 29th June 1522. The emperor's ambassador in Venice, Alonso Sanchez, had for some time been working to get Venice to desert France and join a league with the emperor ;

[1] *Cal. Span. St. Paps.*, ii. 406.   [2] *Cal. Ven. St. Paps.*, iii. 475.

but the Signory would come to no decision until Pace arrived.[1] The Venetians undoubtedly liked and trusted him, still associating him in their minds with Bainbridge ; but they used his coming as an excuse for further delay in answering the imperial ambassador. They were in grave doubt as to what was best for them to do, and, since their troubles over the League of Cambrai, it had been imperative that they should be on the strongest side. Suffolk with an English army, and the Count of Buren with a Netherland one, invaded France in June, and helped to draw the French out of Italy. The second part of the great war between Charles and Francis came to an end in the autumn 1522. Venice, Ferrara, and Urbino were now Francis' only important allies in Italy, and it was Pace's business to tempt them out of that alliance into one with the emperor. It was useless to try to get an Italian state into an alliance with England, unless the emperor was already in it, for the land routes which let Germans and Swiss into Italy could be cut by him. The Swiss still stood by France, as did the Scots and some lordings at the foot of the Alps.

The summer in Rome was always terrible for an Englishman, and was worse than usual in 1522 in that a destructive form of plague appeared. Cardinals, ambassadors, and magistrates fled, and it was thought Adrian's advent would be still further delayed. Rome lost all gaiety, and Pace longed to leave it. In an address in his Plutarch he referred to the pestilence which, he says, was growing worse every day when he left. A Greek led through the city a bull which, he said, he had cast under a spell, and he sacrificed it in the Colosseum to appease hostile demons who had sent the plague. Such heathenish rites so shocked the clergy that they instituted a procession of penitents to atone for them. Hundreds marched through the streets scourging themselves and crying ' *misericordia.*' Cardinal Schiner was among those who died. Pace's departure was delayed until 4th August, by illness—liver trouble—which appeared on the day he was to have started. Nine days after his departure the new pope reached Rome, and soon Clerk returned to England.

Pace's instructions were to repair to Venice with all possible

[1] *Cal. Span. St. Paps.*, ii. 447.

13

speed, and he rode post for two days and two nights, by which time he had reached Siena. Then he had to give up such an arduous method of travelling, for he was ill and it was terribly hot. From Siena he rode quietly on to Bologna, arriving there on 14th August. He was honourably received by the servants of Cardinal de' Medici, who was the papal legate, and the nobles of the city ; and he wrote to Wolsey that de' Medici wanted to know to what he was bound by the new league, concluded between Henry and Charles, in which he and the Florentines were included. Pace had told him it was Henry's intention to make it the prelude to another universal peace, but he knew very little about it. He went on by way of Ferrara. The Venetians looked forward to the coming of so great a friend of Venice as Pace was known to be, and arrangements for his welcome were ordered, and made, in Venetian towns. Alvise Foscari, the *podestà* of Crema, received him with honour, and entertained him in his house. The Venetians knew that there were two ways of getting them into the league ; by such negotiation as Pace would conduct, and by the seizing of their towns— Verona, Crema, Brescia—by the imperialists, as was suggested in another quarter. They preferred Pace's intervention. He had had discussions in Rome with the emperor's ambassador about the prospect of getting the Duke of Ferrara to join the allies, along with Venice ; and Juan Manuel had told him that, if he could thus convert the duke, he might settle other disputes about Ferrara as he liked. He seems to have been in the duke's favour, perhaps since his stay in Ferrara in 1508, and the result of their meeting there now was, if anything, favourable to the emperor's cause. He had had some thoughts of going to Padua to see his friend, Reginald Pole. The Signory wrote to Francesco Donato, the Captain of Padua, telling him to show every sign of honour to him if he arrived, and to tell Pole that Pace's coming was agreeable to Venice, by reason of his eminent qualities and rare endowments, and because their ambassadors in England had always found him to bear affection towards Venice, and the Signory were pleased their affairs were to pass through his hands. They instructed Donato to tell Leonicus, Pace's old master, who was now Pole's tutor, of the

Signory's good disposition towards Pace, so that he might bear witness to it, as of himself. Donato was to meet Pace, give him welcome, and tell him Venice looked upon him as a native Venetian. Donato was to render him as well disposed as possible, and to pay for his lodging and that of his retinue. If Pace lodged with Pole, Donato was to provide victuals for his board and that of his attendants, and fodder for his horses. Leonicus was to accompany Pace to Venice, letting it appear as if he did so of his own thought and wish.[1] But Pace missed out Padua, and from Ferrara went down the Po to Venice, which he reached on 20th August.

[1] *Cal. Ven. St. Paps.*, iii. 519.

CHAPTER X

VENICE

TWENTY-FOUR senators with nobles, doctors of law, and other Venetians, ' in the most pompous array,' were rowed out to meet Pace, at the island of San Spirito. They welcomed him most heartily, and took him to the monastery for rest and refreshment, and then to Venice, to Cà Dandolo in the Calle delle Rasse, on the Riva c̀' Schiavoni, a good house decorated to welcome him. We know it as Danieli's Hotel. Cardinal Adrian had been living in it, since he had fled from Rome, on being accused of complicity in the plot to murder Leo, and had vacated it, and left Venice, on hearing of Leo's death. Pace's slower journey had enabled his household to overtake him. He appreciated an honourable welcome, and never failed to report them to his King; but he was always in a hurry to get to work. Before his hosts had finished their complimentary references to Henry, he told them his business required haste, and asked for an audience with the doge. One was promised for next morning. It was not the custom at Venice for foreigners to join in an official welcome, so the emperor's ambassador, Alonso Sanchez, who was to be to some extent his colleague, had not gone to San Spirito on his entry, but afterwards had sent a servant to make his excuses and to tell Pace that he was waiting for him at his house. Pace asked to be taken to see Sanchez, who was at Cà Zorzi, at San Severo, and there he dismissed the Venetians, who were welcoming him, and sat down for a talk. Sanchez, at all events in his own opinion, gave him some useful hints. He explained the position of the negotiations and warned him against the

delays and tergiversations of the Venetians.[1] The copy of
the treaty between Charles and Henry had not yet arrived,
and Pace had to borrow Sanchez' copy and make a
transcript.[2]

In Venice were the papal legate (Tommasso Campeggio,
Bishop of Feltre, the brother of the cardinal) and ambassadors
from France, Mantua, and Ferrara. A Turkish ambassador
arrived soon after Pace and lodged at Cà Gixi.

The position of Venice was interesting. She had been
taught by the wars following the League of Cambrai that she
had as much to fear from Christian states as from pagan. She
saw she could not, after all, become a great power on the
mainland of Italy, and loss of trade with the East was diminish-
ing her shipping and would ruin her sea-power. She had never
loved the pope. She wanted to be on good terms with England
and with either the emperor or the King of France ; but which
would be her best friend was very hard to determine ; to be
against the emperor had almost become a tradition with her.
She was a city of business, a city of pleasure, and a city of
beauty—one of the sights of the world, and had the most cosmopolitan and picturesque crowds in Europe. There were usually
sightseers waiting about the piazza and piazzetta to see processions round S. Marco and notable personages arriving by
water at the Molo. There were inns on the Piazzetta, past
which Pace went to Mass in S. Marco, or to be received by the
doge and college. The old Procuratorie was just completed.
The Piazza di Rialto was still the business heart of the city ;
the Merceria, a street of shops, joined the Piazza of S. Marco
and the Rialto bridge. Giovanni Bellini had been dead six
years, Cima five, and Carpaccio a few weeks. Palma Vecchio
had five more years to live, and Pace could have seen his
St. Barbara in Sta. Maria Formosa, near which he lived for
some time. Basaiti had painted *The Sons of Zebedee*, seven
years before. Titian was painting in his house at S. Samuele,
close to the Grand Canal, between S. Marco and Rialto. He

---

[1] The *Cal. Ven. St. Paps.* has much interesting information about
Pace's mission to Venice.

[2] *Cal. Span. St. Paps.*, ii. 470.

had painted *The Assumption* five years before.   Aldus Manutius
was at work in his printing-house.   Pace described himself as
a Venetian by inclination, though not by birth ; [1] but no one
who cared as little as he did for beautiful buildings and paintings
could be any kind of a Venetian.   Nine days before he reached
Venice, the Council of Ten resolved to commission Titian to
go on with work in the hall of the great council ; and while he
was there Titian painted *The Madonna de S. Niccolo de Frari*,
now in the Vatican, and *The Madonna de Casa Pesaro*, still in
the Frari Church.   During this sojourn in Venice Pace obtained,
' con molto calore,' from the Signory, for Nicolas Leonicus, the
privilege, for ten years, to print his translation from Greek to
Latin of *In Parvis naturalibus* ; and Leonicus dedicated the
volume to him.   Pace himself put in Bernardino de Vitali's
press another edition of the translation he had made, while in
Rome, of Plutarch's works.   It was dedicated to Campeggio
and Tunstal.   Leonicus said that one need not learn Greek
while such a translation lived ; it was the stock thing to say
about translations.   During his last days at Venice he was
engaged in translating S. Chrysostom and S. Paul.[2]   He kept
up a correspondence with Tunstal, who had become Bishop of
London, and with Sir Henry Marney, of the English council.
Reginald Pole, Henry's cousin, came over from Padua to meet
him, and stayed with him till the scholar Longolius was taken
ill at Padua, when he went back to see him.   While Pace was
in Venetian territory, Leonicus wrote from Padua to William
Latimer, wishing that Lupset was with him and Pole at Padua ;
but he was much away with Pace, who did not like to have to
do without him.[3]   Perhaps the letter should be dated 1523,
when Pace was in Venice.   The doge wrote to thank Wolsey
for sending a man so famous for learning and virtue as Richard
Pace was.   Scandalmongers said that he had for some years
been receiving a pension of 1000 ducats from Venice, which
might have made the emperor's ambassador, who had heard
the story, suspicious of him ; but he found him reliable.   He

[1] *Cal. Ven. St. Paps.*, iii. 890.
[2] Gasquet, *Cardinal Pole and his Early Friends*, p. 45.
[3] *Ibid.* p. 35.

determined, however, to watch him.[1]   The ambassador reported
this scandal to the emperor—was actually writing the letter when
Pace was shown into his study.   The Venetians expected Pace
would rather favour their cause ; for so they thought he had done
in the past, since his days in Rome with Bainbridge.   His
instructions from Wolsey were to remind the Signory of the
ancient amity with England, and to point out the dishonourable
conduct of their ally Francis, towards Henry and Charles.   To
remind them that the treaty, which they had signed in London,
called on the parties to assist any signatory who had been
invaded by another of them, and that Wolsey at Calais had
decided that the emperor had with justice so complained about
Francis' invasion of Navarre and the Netherlands.   Also that
Francis had been guilty of hostile acts towards Henry in Scotland.   So it was their duty to stop assisting Francis and join
against him in a treaty with the emperor.   But although the
French had been driven out of Italy, they had a way of getting
back very quickly.   If they did so again they might take a
fearful revenge on a Venice which had gone over to their enemies.
After the League of Cambrai there was no state Venice would
trust.   She had at the moment a truce with the emperor, which
Pace was to urge them to turn into a peace before it expired.

In order to hasten Venice to a decision, Henry had arrested
the three Venetian trade galleys in England.   Pace was to
excuse this by saying that Charles, when in England, had wanted
them to take him to Spain, and that Henry, not liking to see
Venice treated in this way, and hearing that Francis intended
to capture them with their cargoes on their way home, the
wicked Francis being capable of robbing his own ally, had
arrested them to keep them out of danger and to prevent their
being used in the war against himself.   Pace was also to hint
that there was a rumour in England that Venice was at the
moment preparing to assist Francis.   If this was true Henry
had done what he was entitled to do, and what he would do
again.   He seized them as a friend, and as an enemy, of Venice.
Anyway he was going to keep them for a time, and they were
valued at some 200,000 ducats.   He was going to keep some of

[1] *Cal. Span. St .Paps.*, ii. 473.

their bronze guns altogether. He had longed for them ever since he had first watched their shooting at Southampton. The detention of the galleys had caused a scarcity of English wool in Venice, and, at the time of Pace's arrival, there was only enough to give the weavers a month's work.

On the morning after his arrival Pace had audience with the doge, Antonio Grimani, in the College of Savii (Council of Ten), who received ambassadors, and presented the King's letters. The doge, whom he thought exceedingly old, received him ' reverently,' and desired amity between England and Venice. A secretary read his credentials, and the requisition calling on Venice to carry out her undertaking in the Treaty of London (3rd October 1518), and they asked Pace to come back next morning. The Venetians who had been deputed to escort him were dismissed, and he remained in the college with a few of his own followers for an informal talk. That evening he went to Sanchez' house, and told him what had happened in the college.

Next morning he revealed his instructions rather more fully, and caused Henry's letter to be read twice, but would not leave it with the college. The doge told him the procedure was such that it would be three days before he would receive an answer. He verified this statement and found it correct. At the end of that time the doge sent for him, and ordered a secretary to read their answer ; but they would not give him a copy, saying it would be contrary to custom to do so, but he could have it read over as often as he liked, and they would send a copy to their ambassador in England. After the usual compliments they said they would welcome a peace between the Republic and the emperor, made by Henry's intervention, on the basis of articles drawn up by the emperor's chancellor, when in England, and modified by Wolsey. They would take time to deliberate as to whether Francis' conduct had been such that their duty under the treaty of October 1518 was to make war on him. So Pace began concerted action with Alonso Sanchez, who, knowing the Venetians well, said their natures led them to withdraw when courted. These two agreed to act with caution, sometimes approaching the Signory singly to coax them, sometimes together to demand compliance with the treaty. Sanchez formed a high opinion of Pace, but was afraid the flatteries of the Venetians might put him too quickly in hopes that they were coming to terms with the emperor. By flatteries he meant their soft words rather than compliments. Pace said he supposed the Venetians had been helping the French King for no other reason than because they wished to keep their promises to him. He urged what he considered stronger reasons for siding with England, their constant friend. He trotted out again the revelation that he had made to Giustinian in London, that Francis had been willing to betray the Republic to Maximilian, when Pace and his Swiss were in the field with him, on condition he would give up his attempt to seize Milan. One or two of the college confessed he had made a good point over this, and the rest ' appeared to be as sore abashed as they were with Pope Julie's ex-communication.' When Pace insisted on a promise that they would not help Francis if he invaded Italy, they said he ought to be able to judge of them from their having refused to allow the French captains, who had been turned out of Milan in the recent fighting, to enter Venetian territory. He said he could not be expected to guess what they meant if they used obscure words, he being ' Davus et non Œdipus ' ; and he finished by warning them that, if they assisted Francis, Henry would treat them with open hostility. ' This upset the whole assembly and they rose in their place, and came to me.' They begged him to believe they desired Henry's friendship ; but they intended to take plenty of time. Sanchez thought that Pace was doing well ; but Gattinara, Charles' chancellor, ignorant of Pace's reputation, was offended, because Venice had waited for his arrival, and had not made peace through Sanchez. The modifications, made by Wolsey to the suggested treaty between the emperor and the Signory, had not reached Pace by the end of August ; but at his coming to Venice the mediation, between the emperor and the Signory, really passed into his hands. He was entrusted with the task of bringing them to terms, and was given a very free hand. He feared that Henry and Wolsey were threatening the Venetian ambassador

in England too much, and that Venice might be driven into
Francis' arms. He soon discovered that the Signory thought
the emperor ought to have sent a special ambassador about
this treaty, and he communicated with him, and Charles
ordered Jeronimo Adorno to go to Venice. Adorno was brother
of the Duke of Genoa, and a very capable middle-aged man.
The Venetians sent copies of the replies they had made to Pace
to their ambassador in England to show to Henry and Wolsey ;
but every move they made was to gain time, to see who was
strongest in Italy, Francis or Charles. Even if they had found
that out it remained to be determined which was most inclined
to protect their interests.

In September Pace left Cà Dandolo and moved into Cà
Grimani, the doge's private house, near Sta. Maria Formosa ;
the doge and his family being resident in the ducal palace during
his term of office. Perhaps his move was connected with illness,
which troubled him in the autumn. From time to time the
Signory granted him permission to import wine into Venice,
free of duty, and it was a substantial privilege, for he had a
large household. In February of the next year he told the
Signory that, during the seven months he had been in Venice,
he had had licence to import twelve kilderkins (amphore) of
wine, duty free, for his own use and that of his household ;
but so much did not suffice, and he had obtained at his own
expense, and consumed, eight additional kilderkins, giving
a bond for the payment of the duties, in case the Signory declined to remit them. He applied for the cancellation of this
bond and for licence to import seven more kilderkins. The
Signory found that, ' owing to the quality of the present times,'
it was expedient to grant his request.

There was a good deal of ill-feeling in Venice against Henry
for seizing the galleys ; important Venetians had shares in
them. Henry and Wolsey began to go a little farther than at
first, and talked about keeping them until Venice had actually
declared war on Francis, which it would be unwise for her to do,
unless the emperor had previously undertaken to protect her.
Venice might be left bare before the French invader. Some
senators told Pace secretly that they no longer regarded them-

selves as bound by treaty to France, but that on the other hand
great lawyers had advised them that neither were they bound
by treaty to declare war on France. They had confidential
talks with Pace ; and he and Sanchez laid secret plans for
coercing the Signory. He brought forward the threatening
suggestion that the emperor and Ferdinand, their other neigh-
bour, might attack them from different sides. It was desirable
to get Venice to enter two treaties : one with the emperor and
Ferdinand, the other with the emperor, Henry, the pope, and
a group of other Italian states. The object of both would be to
keep France out of Italy. Those senators who had no share in
the three arrested galleys declared that no coercion would
persuade Venice to alter her foreign policy or to dissociate
herself from France. On the whole, the Venetian people favoured
the French alliance ; they hated any emperor, and had no great
love for Henry. Pace complained of the strong language used
by the Venetians against his King, who, he said, would be very
angry if he heard of it. The college said they could not prevent
people speaking as they pleased, but they promised to appoint
some persons to punish those who calumniated Henry. Pace
took the opportunity to complain that he had heard it said that
the Signory would call in the Turks, as an ally against their
Christian enemies. This suggestion they repudiated, and they
promised to punish any one heard saying such a thing. Pace
did not approve of coercing Venice by arresting galleys which
had come to England under a safe-conduct. He did not think
it fair to threaten that they would not be released until Venice
declared war on France. Venice had not arrested English
ships in her harbours. He thought the galleys ought to be
released, and that Henry ought to be satisfied with Venice's
promise that she would not help Francis if he invaded Italy.
He thought that much of this policy might be Wolsey's, and
not the King's.[1] He and Sanchez kept their ears open for every
bit of gossip, and went constantly before the college, throughout
the autumn, to complain that they had heard of secret negotiations with Francis or of preparations to help him.

It was hoped that Jeronimo Adorno would bring about an

[1] *Cal. Ven. St. Paps.* iii. 567.

agreement speedily. He arrived on 2nd December to be Sanchez' colleague, or rather a special ambassador; but illness delayed his first appearance before the college till the morning of 4th, when he went with Sanchez, Pace, and the Duke of Mantua's ambassador, and many Venetian noblemen. He was lame from gout, and had a red beard. He was finely dressed, and was followed by forty attendants. He presented his letters of credence, and the doge welcomed him. He said he had come to urge Venice to desert France and league herself with the emperor; the agreement she was asked to accept being that drawn up in May in England, when Henry and Charles met, and which Wolsey had undertaken to modify. The college demanded four days for deliberation, and then asked for four more, and then gave no definite answer. Adorno, when the gout permitted, went into the college with Sanchez and Pace. He grasped that the Venetians anticipated that Francis would soon be in Italy again, and did not dare to leave their alliance with him until the emperor provided for their protection.

On Christmas eve thirty-two silver tankards were stolen from Pace's house at Sta. Maria Formosa. He did not go that day with the doge to Mass in S. Marco; he had received an invitation, but it was etiquette that the ambassador of the King of France should precede the King of England's ambassador, and he could not bring himself to such a thing.[1] After Mass he sent his secretary to request Francesco Bragadin, one of the college, to come to his house to speak to him there; but Bragadin and his colleagues agreed it would be better to send the secretary of the college to hear what he had to say. This seems to have offended Pace, who would not make any statement to an underling. When the secretary told the college, they sent a great friend of Pace's, Daniel di Renier, to hear what he had to say, but he could not persuade him to give place to his rival.

Before Christmas Pace had heard he had been made dean of Exeter and dean of Salisbury, which shows that he was in high favour in England.

The doge was to hold a great banquet on Sunday, 28th

[1] *Cal. Ven. St. Paps*, iii. 604.

December, but first went to Mass, clad in crimson velvet, lined with lynx's fur, and a satin cap. He was accompanied by Adorno and Sanchez; the French ambassador, Angelo di Fiorenza; and by the ambassadors of Ferrara and Mantua. The English ambassador, we read, would not go because he would not be placed below the French ambassador.

About Christmas-time the Signory appointed three commissioners, Alvise Mocenigo, Giorgio Cornaro, and Marco Antonio Venier, to treat daily with the emperor's ambassadors, both parties agreeing that Pace should act as mediator. But fresh difficulties arose,[1] and Venice went on wasting time. There were too many negotiators to bring the matter ott expeditiously. The pope was interfering from Rome, Henry from England, and the Venetian envoys everywhere were putting their spokes in the wheel. Pace thought at first that in appointing these commissioners the Venetians had laid aside all ' craft and dissimulation,' and were ready to come to some agreement, but it was not so. They wanted to wait until it became more obvious which side it would be politic to be on. Pace sent home secret messages, by his own courier, so that Henry and Wolsey could write letters as if on their own initiative on certain points, for he found their views had much weight in Venice. Also they could influence Surian in England in his advice to the Signory. This was one of those conferences at which the parties could agree at any moment, but which could be protracted indefinitely so long as one of them was uncertain what the next few turns in the affairs of nations would produce.

Again, on 1st January 1523, Pace absented himself when the doge, in a mantle of crimson satin lined with ermine, with cape, and robe of crimson satin beneath it, went to Mass in S. Marco. On the day of the Epiphany, there was Mass in S. Marco, at which attended the vice-doge, Marco Antonio Loredano, in black velvet; the papal legate; Sanchez; the French ambassador; the ambassadors from Ferrara and Mantua. The great cold kept the doge away, the gout kept Adorno, and Pace did not go because he did not want to give place to the Frenchman. The legate and the ambassadors discussed the pope's attitude towards the

[1] *L. and P.*, iii. 2755.

league.[1] On 19th January it was proposed in the Council that Giorgio Cornaro should confer privately and alone with Pace, and assure him that the Signory relied on him to conclude the peace as advantageously for Venice as if the interests of his own King were concerned ; and to tell him that, if he—with his usual address—could get the imperial ambassadors to accept the replies the senate had made to them that day, as he had offered to try to do, the Signory would mark the love she bore him by making him a present of 4000 ducats. The motion was lost. On one occasion Piero Capello, in a discussion about the arrested galleys, used certain expressions, which made Pace very angry and cooled him a little in dealing between Venice and the emperor. At the end of January an entertainment was given by the Signory in honour of the emperor's ambassadors and Pace. A few days later the Mantuan ambassador, Juan Batista di Mala-testa, invited them to his house, Cà Mocenigo on the Grand Canal, and twenty-five Venetian gentlewomen to meet them— the only ladies, other than Queen Catherine, with whom Pace is recorded as having conversed up to this time. The host meant to do things well, and tried unsuccessfully to get leave for the ladies to dress in cloth of gold and ornaments, in spite of a recent sumptuary law. Sanchez was ill and could not go, but Pace and Adorno were there. The doge's nieces were among the twenty-five ladies, and could wear cloth of gold, the others silk. The husbands of the ladies and some of the ambassadors' suites completed the company. There was a long supper— pheasants, partridges, peacocks, and other things, which had been sent by the Marquis of Mantua, to honour Pace and his colleagues. There was masking, dancing, games of ball, and a comedy ; it was the talk of Venice for some time.

After dinner, on 1st February, it being the vigil of Madonna, the Signory went, according to custom, to vespers at Sta. Maria Formosa, close to Pace's house. That morning Adorno and Sanchez had received letters from the Viceroy of Naples saying that Rhodes was on the point of surrender to the Turk—news which had greatly upset the senators. The doge was not at the service ; he was old, and it was cold weather, and he was upset

[1] Many entries in Sanuto's *Diary* refer to Pace at this time.

by the bad news ; his place was taken by the vice-doge. Neither
of the emperor's ambassadors nor Pace turned up, because the
French ambassador was there ; but the ambassadors from
Mantua and Ferrara were present. Then came reports from
Corfu, Rome, Naples, Candia. Rhodes had fallen on 20th
December. Venice was full of tales of treason among the besieged knights and of delay in sending succour. Pace apparently
heard the news a little before 21st February, on which day he
wrote to Wolsey, ' I pray God send us better tidings, for this is
very sorrowful.'

Pace left no diary and there is little enough to tell us about
his private life. He went to Murano, to see glass made ; and
to the arsenal, to see the damage done by a recent fire. Jeronimo
Adorno, unlike Pace, was a lover of the Arts ; and hearing the
friars did not appreciate the great *Assumption* which Titian had
painted for them, he wisely, but unsuccessfully, offered to take
it off their hands. Titian became his friend and painted his
portrait, but it seems to be lost. They were near neighbours,
the ambassador being in Cà Corner, at S. Samuele.

On 13th February, in the afternoon, bulls were baited in the
Piazza of S. Marco, before the doge in gold brocade and cap, in
honour of his grandson's wedding. Many were there—the legate,
Adorno, the ambassadors of France, Ferrara, and Mantua, but
neither Sanchez nor Pace, for the Frenchman would not give
place to them.

The three commissioners and the emperor's two ambassadors,
with Pace as go-between, met sometimes at Adorno's house,
sometimes at Sanchez', and agreement was arrived at, up to a
point, by 21st February, on which day Pace wrote a long letter
to Wolsey. The Venetians were ready to enter an alliance with
the emperor for the defence of Milan and Naples, but the difficulty was to get them to agree to a sufficient contribution. Pace
thought letters from Henry might induce them to behave rather
more generously than they would otherwise do, and he assured
Henry that it was to his interest to break in at this point.
Adorno had told him that any money that could be got out of
Venice would be spent in the next summer on an invasion of
Provence. What more could Henry, Wolsey, and Pace desire

against the old enemy ? This cooling off by the Signory towards France had caused the French ambassador to fall into a frenzy. Pace, in hopes of detaching the Duke of Ferrara from Francis, wanted to go to Ferrara when his work at Venice was done. Francis would then have no friends in Italy ' *nulla penna qua volet Gallo relinquetur.*' The senate sent a humbugging message to Henry that nothing was so much inducing them to agree with the emperor as their wish to please him. It was difficult for the two imperial ambassadors to communicate with the emperor in Spain. Ships were constantly being taken by the French and the Turks ; no couriers could go by land ; and the emperor's new ambassadors at Rome, like others who had recently come from Spain, were reluctant to take upon themselves any responsibility which was not theirs. So it was difficult to lay the emperor's wishes before the Signory. Pace was little better off. He told Sanchez that up to the end of February he had not received a single letter from his master, since he had been in Venice, and Sanchez gave it as his opinion that this negligence of the English government was exercising a very bad influence on the negotiations.[1] This neglect has been thought to show that Pace was out of Wolsey's favour. When Wolsey was first on the English council, he feared Fox would take it amiss that he had not written for a long time. He knew how such an omission was considered. The fall of Rhodes produced certain good fruit. Naples was threatened by the Turks, and Adrian advised Venice to agree with the emperor. At the end of February Henry released the galleys, hearing the Republic was going to abandon the French alliance. Pace sent his secretary to tell the doge about it, for he was not well. Wolsey had seized the guns on the ships.

Henry and Wolsey felt that the negotiations were going well, if slowly, and that Pace's work was almost done. They had determined in March to send him to Milan, to confer with John Clerk, who was going out to Rome again—for Henry thought there would soon be a new pope. After seeing Clerk, Pace was to go to the Swiss to persuade them not to join Francis against the emperor's league. A commission was issued on 12th March,

[1] *Cal. Span. St. Paps.*, ii. 531.

authorizing him to sign as mediator between the emperor and the Venetians, and it seemed as if he would soon leave Venice ; but in the middle of March Adorno fell seriously ill, and he died on the night of 19th. On the next afternoon the bell of S. Marco tolled double peals six times, and stately obsequies were ordered at S. Stefano. Pace himself was ill, and for that reason was not present at the obsequies. March was a very bad month, very windy and unusually cold.

The pope sent Ennius, Bishop of Veroli, to the Swiss, on what the bishop regarded as the almost hopeless task of keeping them from joining Francis ; he thought it a great mistake that Pace had not been sent. But Pace was ill and Adorno's death had prevented the completion of the treaty. Surian told the Signory that Henry wanted to call Pace home to England ; but that Wolsey did not choose it, and so Henry was sending him to the Swiss.[1] Neither the pope nor the emperor had enough money to hire the Swiss, and for the first time Henry was so short of it that he had to summon parliament. As for Pace's recall, Ruthal had died in February, and it is possible that Henry wanted to make him privy seal, an office to which Wolsey would have wished to make the appointment. Sir Henry Marney, who was appointed, only survived a few weeks. Pace had already followed Ruthal as the King's secretary ; and this fresh step would have made him second to none in the kingdom but Wolsey. That he was still in the King's favour is shown by the fact that in April Henry conferred on ' Richard Pace his chief secretary ' the living of Bangor.

Two ambassadors arrived from Ferdinand, and made fresh demands on Venice, and a new ambassador, Renzo da Ceri, came from France. The Venetians themselves had demanded that Ferdinand should become a party to any treaty, but now that his ambassadors had come, they used his demands as a further excuse for delay. Pace went into the college on 20th April, and urged them to enter the agreement with the emperor ; the new French ambassador followed him and spoke to the contrary. Still further delay was caused by one of the commissioners, Alvise Mocenigo, being sent as ambas-

---

[1] *Cal. Ven. St. Paps.*, iii. 651.

14

sador to Rome, and by Giorgio Cornaro falling ill. Then on
7th May the doge, Antonio Grimani, died. This might be
used for further and indefinite delay, so Sanchez and Pace
went to the college and begged that body to remember that
affairs of State in Venice need not come to a standstill through
such an event. They asked for a definite answer about the
proposed alliance, but they could get nothing done until a new
doge was elected. The bells were tolling for the doge—double
peals at S. Marco, and at all the churches ; the corpse clad in
the ducal mantle lay in the '*portego.*' The doge's family had
to leave the palace, and Pace was occupying their home near
Sta. Maria Formosa, so they had to find temporary lodging.
The doge's obsequies took place at SS. Giovanni e Paolo ; Pace
would not attend them ; he would have had to walk below the
French ambassador. Sanchez thought that it was consistent
with his dignity, and that of his master, to attend on such an
occasion.

John Clerk was expected at Innsbruck. Pace was to meet
him at Milan, to hear what instructions Wolsey had sent, and
then go to the Swiss. He and Sanchez went before the college
and asked if the Signory had anything to negotiate before he
left, and it was determined that the commissioners should
that day meet Sanchez. The election of the new doge took
place on 20th May, and resulted in favour of Andrea Gritti.
On the same day came before the college the ambassador of the
Marquis of Mantua, to say that the old Marchesa, Isabella
d'Este, had arrived in Venice, and was at Cà Barbaro near
S. Vitali. Her brother, the Duke of Ferrara, and Baldassare
Castiglione were at Cà Foscari, a little farther along the Grand
Canal. The Duke and the Marquis of Mantua, like other Italian
states and princes, were anxious as to which side to join in
the coming contest. The bell of S. Marco was rung for the new
doge, but Pace was not present at the ceremonies which brought
him in, nor at the reception of the duke and Isabella. Andrea
Gritti was said to be pro-French,[1] and the French ambassador
was so satisfied with the result of the election that he made
fireworks. But the negotiations had gone too far to be stopped,

[1] Sanuto, v. 34, col. 157.

and nothing remained but to get Ferdinand's adherence to the treaty.

On the day of the doge's election came news of fighting between the English and Scots, and it was thought Henry might be prevented from invading France. In that case Francis would probably be in Lombardy by the autumn, so Venice wanted further time for consideration, and the delays of Ferdinand in sending instructions to his ambassadors unfortunately gave the excuse. Pace chafed at Ferdinand's neglect, ' for the said archduke is very obstinate in this cause, greatly to his dishonour, as all wise men do judge, knowing the importance of the matter. And it is to me a very strange thing, thus to be troubled with the said emperor's brother, after that we have in effect obtained all our purposes here against his enemies.' [1]

On 22nd May the doge issued invitations to accompany him to a splendid Mass in S. Marco, and all Venice was there, but not Pace. His instructions for his mission to the Swiss had been drawn up by Wolsey in March, and Clerk took them out with him, as well as his commission under the great seal.[2] He was to tell the Swiss the usual story about the French, and advocate an offensive and defensive alliance between the pope, the emperor, Henry, the Duke of Milan, the Swiss, and certain smaller Italian states, with the object of protecting each other against France, and of invading Provence in the coming year. Later there was to be a crusade. Pace was empowered to conclude such a treaty, but Henry was not prepared at this time to bear the charge of maintaining Swiss—if others could be induced to do it. On 29th Henry counter-ordered his going to Milan and the Swiss, and told him to stay at Venice and continue the negotiations ; he sent Knight to the Swiss instead. On Sunday, 31st May, the doge went out in the Bucentaur ; the ambassadors from the pope, the emperor, the King of France, Ferdinand of Austria, the Duke of Ferrara, and the Marquis of Mantua are mentioned as being there, but nothing is said about Pace. Before his fresh instructions arrived, he and Sanchez

---

[1] State Papers, *King Henry VIII*, vol. vi. Pt. V, lii.
[2] *L. and P.*, iii. 2901.

were able to tell the college that Ferdinand's mandate had been received by his ambassador. They asked that the matter might be brought to speedy conclusion, because Pace was obliged to depart, but the Signory did not think the mandate sufficient to bring Ferdinand into the proposed treaty. They were still playing for time, and Gritti would have been glad to get away from what had so nearly reached completion.

When Clerk heard Pace would not be at Milan, he sent his letters down to Venice from Trent, and went on to Rome. He had a commission to get the pope into the league against Francis. On 16th June Marin Caracciolo, protonotary, a Neopolitan, arrived at Venice to take Adorno's place, and went to live at Cà Pasqualigo, at Sta. Giustina. Sanchez and Pace introduced him to the Signory. He immediately suggested to Cornaro that his illness was delaying the negotiations, and that the three ambassadors should therefore resume direct negotiation with the college. It seemed as if negotiations would be broken off, when Pace and the legate went to the college, and urged the doge to the treaty. Pace undertook that Henry would persuade the emperor to be content with something less than his ambassadors had demanded. The doge unconstitutionally granted Pace a private audience, in view of the vast importance of the matter, and in conclusion Pace persuaded the imperial ambassador to be content with his modifications. The doge swore the senate to secrecy, before disclosing how near they were to agreement, and asking for ratification ; for the galleys were passing the French coast. So in the end it was Pace, and not Wolsey, who had modified the terms of the suggested agreement in favour of the Venetians. Final discussions began on 29th June, at Cà Pasqualigo, and went on far into the nights, while the French ambassadors did their best to persuade the college to stand by their master. At last Mocenigo brought the proposed treaty before the senate (9th July). The legate and Ferdinand's ambassador joined the others before the college to urge them to agreement ; and the French ambassadors to urge them to reject it. Fortunately for Pace, who was getting worn out by the anxiety and the heat, the emperor threatened to coerce the Venetians, and prepared Prosper Colonna to attack Venice. A final demand to the Signory was drawn up by Pace, and presented by him, by Caracciolo, and Sanchez on 16th.

The treaty was signed on 29th July, at Caracciolo's house, by the three commissioners, by Caracciolo, Sanchez, Pace, the legate, and the ambassadors of Ferdinand and Francesco Sforza, the latter having come secretly to Venice. The pope and Henry became conservators of the treaty, and room in it was left for the Duke of Ferrara. Early on the morning after the treaty was signed, the French ambassadors, Angelo di Fiorenza and Renzo da Ceri, went into the college to protest.

Francis and his mother regarded this breaking away from him by Venice as a disaster, and so it proved. Put very shortly, Venice was to pay the emperor 200,000 ducats ; all exiles, who had adhered to the emperor, were to be restored ; Venice was to provide fifteen galleys for the defence of Naples and five hundred lances for the defence of Milan. The emperor was to protect Venice from the French.

Pace was in high spirits ; he wrote to the doge that this agreement seemed ' mute,' and there should be rejoicings. Dominego Venier wanted to move in the senate for bells and bonfires ; but the doge was afraid of offending the French and the Turks, for the treaty might be regarded as against both.

It was the custom to compliment a prince on the manner in which his ambassador had conducted his business, and too much importance must not be attached to what was said about Pace, but there was a chorus of praise. The doge, by unanimous direction of the senate, informed Surian in England that throughout the negotiations Pace had displayed so much diligence, address, and prudence, and performed such good offices on both sides, that they deservedly commended him, as he had laboured incessantly until the conclusion.[1] On the same day the doge thanked Henry for his intervention in favour of peace, and referred to Pace's strenuous co-operation for the attainment of his majesty's friendly and loving desire for the treaty.[2] The doge wrote to Wolsey speaking highly of Pace ; and Caracciolo and Sanchez jointly commended him

[1] *Cal. Ven. St. Paps.*, iii. 715, 717.   [2] *Ibid.* iii. 712.

to Wolsey, and suggested a reward when occasion offered.[1] Caracciolo wrote to the emperor saying it would be ' sacrilege ' if he did not mention Richard Pace, who had shown the utmost sagacity, prudence, and dexterity in bringing the negotiations to a satisfactory conclusion. He could not have shown more zeal for the emperor if he had been all his life in his service.[2] Pace congratulated the emperor on the conclusion of the peace. He did not think the Venetians could have done his imperial majesty much harm ; but this treaty went to show that he had been elected by God to punish the disturbers of peace, and to secure tranquillity to the Christian world ; as Augustus did, during whose reign the temple of Janus was closed. He told the emperor that, while he had been in Venice, Francis had sent a great number of ambassadors, envoys, and confidential agents to try to dissuade the Republic from making this peace. But he, Pace, being an Englishman, and being persuaded that he was predestined to be the cause of ruin to the King of France, had not been afraid of the French machinations.[3] Venice powerful at sea would be the emperor's most valuable ally, when the time came to fight the Turks. Perhaps he could see, in his mind's eye, the Adriatic strewn with the wrecks of Turkish vessels, after Lepanto, and hear the cheers of the victorious Spaniards and Venetians. In October the emperor thanked Pace for his valuable services, and asked what kind of reward would be most acceptable.[4] There was one dissentient in the vote of praise passed in Pace's favour, and that was before the splendid result of his work had appeared. After Adorno's death the Duke of Sessa, the emperor's ambassador newly come to Rome, wrote to the emperor about the negotiations which were entrusted to Pace and Sanchez. He spoke of these two as faithful servants of the emperor, but gave it as his opinion that they had neither the authority nor the mental qualities necessary for so difficult a task.[5] He thought little of Pace at any time.

On the last day of the month Pace informed the Signory that he was about to leave Venice ; and it was moved in the

[1] *Cal. Span. St. Paps.*, ii. 577. [2] *Ibid.* ii. 579.
[3] *Ibid.* ii. 581. [4] *Ibid.* ii. 603. [5] *Ibid.* ii. 557.

Council of Ten that a thousand golden ducats should be spent on a gold collar for him, to do him honour for the trouble he had taken in the negotiations, and, as it was stated, to keep him well disposed towards the Signory. But an amendment was carried to reduce the sum to eight hundred. His secretary was voted fifty golden ducats in money, plate, and other effects —gold and silver coins were always difficult to come by. This secretary must remain anonymous, but Thomas Lupset is said to have served him in this capacity at some time. Pace's destination was not known for certain, some said it was Switzerland, others Naples. On Sunday morning, 2nd August, there was High Mass in S. Marco for the league, to which went the doge in his robes, the legate, the emperor's ambassadors, Pace (knowing he would not meet the Frenchman), and the ambassadors of Ferdinand, of the Dukes of Milan and Ferrara, of the Marquis of Mantua, and of the King of Poland, all splendidly dressed. Altogether nine ambassadors were there, and many procurators, patricians, and senators. Pace left Venice on 5th August, before the gold collar had been provided, going by way of Padua, where he seems to have been Pole's guest.[1] The Signory ordered the rectors of the university to do him honour. He went on to the Swiss, but found that not even the going over of Venice to the emperor had changed their minds, and that they stood by Francis. So he returned to Italy. He went to Ferrara to see the duke, Alfonso, about joining the league, but found he could not make up his mind between the order of St. Louis and that of the Garter. From Ferrara he passed through Mantua, where he was honourably received, and lodged at the castle. The marquis visited him in the morning, and carried him off to dinner to a palace of his, four miles distant—perhaps Marmirolo. As they went, he kept on expressing his desire to serve Henry with 2000 light horse. From Mantua Pace went to Milan, and the duke, Francesco Sforza, sent a gentleman to welcome him outside the town. Pace had letters for Sforza from Henry and Wolsey, and they discussed a possible invasion of France. On the 2nd September were read to the Signory letters from Pace dated at Milan [date

---

[1] Gasquet, *Cardinal Pole and his Early Friends*, p. 54.

obliterated], saying that he had found the Swiss diet pledged to France, and so he had come down again to Milan. He went on to Cremona and Brescia, and perhaps Padua again. The imperial army, composed of Spaniards and Italians under Prosper Colonna, lay at Pavia, Milan, Cremona, and Lodi. The French were coming into Italy again, and crossed the Ticino in September. There was some fighting round Milan, and Pace was still at Crema on the 20th. A few days later news came which made him hurry to Rome. Adrian had died on 14th.

CHAPTER XI

BOURBON

A S long before the event as April Henry had been expecting Adrian's death. He had sent Clerk to Rome to smooth the way for Wolsey's election, but there was much less chance for a non-Italian candidate than before ; for the Dutchman had not been a success. The city had never been so glad of a pope's death ; for he had kept no state, and little money had been spent. Rome had been very ' empty.' Some light-brained fellows decorated the house of his physician with garlands, and the inscription ' *Liberatori Patriae* S.P.Q.R.' He had cared nothing for Greek or Roman antiquities, architecture, painting, sculpture, or literature ; but he had been one of the few to stay in Rome with the poor during the plague, and he was a pious man. He had tried to remain neutral between Charles and Francis, but Cardinal Giulio de' Medici, who managed everything at the Vatican, proved to him that his friend, Cardinal Soderini, was conspiring to help the French in Sicily and Naples. This discovery threw Soderini into the castle of S. Angelo, and Adrian into the league with the emperor. He signed the treaty on 4th August, with the emperor, Henry, Ferdinand, Francesco Sforza, Cardinal de' Medici (for Florence), Genoa, Siena, and Lucca, to keep the French out of Lombardy. After this de' Medici was the greatest man in Rome and sure to be the next pope, who would have to be the emperor's man. Wolsey might prove otherwise ; so might de' Medici, but Charles thought he could rely on him, and in July had instructed his ambassador in Rome to procure his election. The league, defensive though it was, and the agreement made at Venice, by Pace's help, had seemed to change the face of affairs. Mild

celebrations had continued in Rome for some days. The
weather was very hot, and the pope sat through a long sermon,
preached against the French, in the notoriously cold church of
Sta. Maria Maggiore, and caught a fatal chill. So the future
of the new league was rendered uncertain. Francis would
have invaded Italy at once in person, but the treachery of
Bourbon, Constable of France, had come to light, and he was
in doubt about his position.

Wolsey at once informed Henry that he was preparing
fresh instructions, similar to those given to Pace at the last
election. He probably did not know where Pace was at the
moment, but he was arranging promotion for him. On 30th
October he was presented to the living of Southmolton in the
diocese of Exeter. Wolsey's instructions, signed by Henry,
were sent to Clerk, Pace, and Hannibal. They were to do all in
their power to bring about his election, and if that proved impossible they were to work for the election of Cardinal de' Medici.
Wolsey asked Henry to write a letter in his own hand to the
emperor, to remind him of his promises. He told these agents
to say, if he was made pope, he, the emperor, and Henry would
set up a great alliance against France, and restore peace to
Christendom. Only that thought, he said, made the idea of
election bearable to him ; he wished to please the emperor and
the King. He had some sort of promise of support from
Cardinal de' Medici and from Cardinal Campeggio. He supposed
that de' Medici would take it for himself, but something might
turn up to hinder his doing so. The agents were sent two
commissions : one in recommendation of Wolsey, the other in
general terms. They were armed with alternative sets of
letters to the cardinals : one in favour of Wolsey, the other of
de' Medici. They were to approach de' Medici, and tell him
they had instructions to favour him. They were to judge
from his manner whether he expected, and intended, to be
elected. If so, Wolsey would have no chance, and they were
to present the letters in favour of de' Medici. If de' Medici felt
he was unable to win, they were to get his voice for Wolsey.
They were then to ' practise ' with the cardinals, praising
Wolsey, and promising rewards. Henry would no doubt visit

Rome, if his minister was pope, and Wolsey himself would be
there within three months. Clerk was treated as the leading
agent, and he was to make handsome promises, especially to
the young cardinals, who were generally the most in need of
money.

Pace reached Rome before the end of September, and the
cardinals entered conclave in the Sistine chapel on 1st October,
before Wolsey's instructions had arrived, and were shut in next
day. All business ceased in Rome, but there was no disorder
until the people began to complain of the long delay. They
were quieted by the threat to elect a foreigner. If the conclave
found it impossible to agree on a prominent cardinal, who was
present, they might again resort to the expedient of electing an
absentee, who might be Wolsey. ' Give us a Roman even if
he is a log of wood,' agreed the Romans. The cardinals in the
conclave were as anxious to await the turn of military events
in Lombardy as the doge and senate had been. On 3rd came
news that the Duke of Ferrara had seized Reggio and was
threatening Modena, papal towns, and the cardinals sent for
some bankers, to be brought to the door of the conclave, to
have money borrowed from them to be sent to pay troops.
Three French cardinals arrived late, and hurried into conclave,
wearing laymen's riding dress, ' short weeds ' with boots and
spurs, which were thought very dissolute but amused the
people. Pace was afraid that the French section of the cardinals
might win the election, and the coming of these three rather
threatened de' Medici's chance. At the last election Clerk had
managed to get news from the conclave daily, by secret means ;
but he could not arrange it this time. It was only on 19th October
that the English agents received Wolsey's final instructions
(dated 4th), but they could scarcely have acted differently if
they had received them earlier. They told de' Medici's agents
in the city frankly that Wolsey only expected to win if their
master stood aside for him, and that Henry and Wolsey had
written to the cardinals on de' Medici's behalf. De' Medici's
agents said they would try to get word of this to their master
in the conclave. The English ambassadors knew they could
not deliver Henry's letters in favour of Wolsey to the cardinals

in conclave. So the best thing they could do was to approach
de' Medici's friends, who might be in touch with him, and
persuade them that Henry favoured de' Medici, with Wolsey
as a second choice. They hoped to influence the de' Medici
faction if some event put them in a difficulty. It was to be a
long conclave—fifty days. Cardinal Colonna and Cardinal
Soderini were leading the French party in opposition to de'Medici.
It was purely a struggle between imperialists and French for
the election of one who seemed likely to become an important
ally on one side or the other. Farnese had some chance,
because he was a Roman and neutral between imperialist and
Frenchman. Alberto Pio had come to Rome as Francis'
ambassador, and managed, apparently quite easily, to communicate with the cardinals. He urged the election of de' Medici
with good results, for this cardinal was elected on 17th November after he had struck a bargain with Colonna.

The election was popular in Rome, for it promised a return
to the days of Leo. The new Medici pope took the title of
Clement VII, and could claim to have been the imperialist
candidate and, after Alberto Pio's coming, that of Francis as
well. Not even the King of England could find much fault.
The three English ambassadors advised Wolsey of the election
of the new pope on 19th November, and in this letter they make
a statement which shows that Wolsey, in their experience, had
had very little chance. The cardinals would not hear of his
candidature, and even abused those who spoke of it.[1] Leonicus
fancied that Pace would be specially pleased at the result, for
he had long regarded Clement as his friend.[2]

The new pope was crowned on 26th November. He was
personally popular, and it was thought he might save Italy
from anarchy. He loved music, art, and literature. He was
aged forty-six—younger than Wolsey—and lived a decent life.
People flocked to Rome in spite of plague and famine.

Pace and his colleagues were not slow to congratulate the
pope on his election, and as soon as he was enthroned invited
him to join the league into which Adrian had entered, largely

[1] *L. and P.*, iii. 3592.
[2] Gasquet, *Cardinal Pole and his Early Friends*, p. 44.

on his advice. But Clement was afraid the emperor would
have exhausted his money by the spring, and that to join him
would mean being left in the lurch. He referred also to the
possibility of the failure of the conspiracy which was being
hatched round Charles of Bourbon. The French army, now
under de Bonnivet, was entering Italy at the moment of Adrian's
death, but did not seem very formidable. The English army,
which had been sent to Flanders, was being disbanded by the
time Clement was elected, and—as Clement said—the emperor
was short of money. Wolsey ordered the three English ambassadors to impress on the pope that if the French conquered
Italy he would be no more than Francis' chaplain, and that
Lutheranism would penetrate France, Spain, and Italy. They
were to find out if the Venetians, and the Duke of Milan, were
standing to the league, and then, if all seemed to be going well,
Pace and Hannibal might come home. Pace was to see Bourbon and the imperialists' army on the way, and would have
been in England by the end of January 1524 if Wolsey had not
changed his plans. Prosper Colonna died at the end of 1523,
and was succeeded in the command of the imperialists by
Charles de Lannoy, the new Viceroy of Naples.

The three English agents soon found that the cardinals,
almost to a man, were opposed to a league with the emperor ;
and they worked as hard as they could to carry Rome in the
opposite direction. The pope wanted to know precisely what
the emperor and Henry proposed to do against France in the
spring, and the three ambassadors were not kept primed with
their plans. There was too much talk of a secret expedition,
just when the new pope wanted no secrets. It seemed as if
Charles and Henry intended to invade France in the spring, but
would either of them have any money by that time ? Pace and
his colleagues urged Wolsey to delay in offering England's
Obedientia to him until he declared himself, ' *quia Judas non
dormit.*'

There were a few outstanding matters to be mentioned to the
new pope, notably two. One concerned the King and the other
the cardinal. Leo had received Henry's book against Luther
' lovingly,' and there had for some time been thoughts among

the cardinals of conferring some title on him, such as Apostolicus, or Protector, and, at one time, of transferring to him the French King's title of Most Christian King. Leo's bull conferring the title of Fidei Defensor is dated 11th October 1521. Pace expressed himself as marvellously glad that by God's help, and Wolsey's wisdom, Henry had obtained the most excellent title he could have. Henry himself was delighted to find ' the great honour, laud, and commendation ' he had earned by writing the book (the words quoted are Pace's) against the detestable heresies of Martin Luther. At Leo's death the bull confirming the new title was ' under lead,' and signed by all the cardinals, but not dispatched. With the bull confirming and approving Henry's book it was in the hands of the then Cardinal de' Medici, who had said he held them for the King. Pace now asked for and obtained the dispatch of the bulls. As for Wolsey's ambition, Adrian had lengthened his legateship, and now Pace procured from Clement a confirmation of this authority for his life : a thing never before heard of ; and in addition a bull to suppress the monastery of St. Frideswide in Oxford, and apply the endowments to his college.[1]

On 8th February the three ambassadors wrote to the Duke of Bourbon, assuring him that Henry was determined to persevere in the enterprise against the common enemy—the French King. Henry, besides other plans, intended to make a secret enterprise by the aid of Bourbon, and desired him to go to England to talk it over. Bourbon received this letter at the imperialists' camp in Lombardy. Long. before this Jeronimo Adorno had broached a plan to Henry, and had sent Giovannino Centurio to Venice to explain it to Pace, who talked it over with Sanchez at Venice before Adorno had joined them there. It had been talked over in secret chambers in Milan and Venice. Sanchez asked Pace, long before this, to advise Henry to provide the money ; for the King knew little about the plan. Pace knew the difficulty Wolsey was having at the moment in getting money in England, but he laid the scheme before Henry as a cheap and easy way of conquering France.[2] Cavendish,

[1] Strype's *Memorials*, i. Pt. I. p. 79.
[2] *Cal. Span. St. Paps.*, ii. 491.

Wolsey's biographer, says it was the cardinal who first thought of making use of Bourbon against Francis, and that he laid this plan before the King and the council, and that it went from them to the emperor.

Charles of Bourbon had been made Constable of France by Francis. He was about thirty-five at this time; the most powerful noble in France, and a small king; the last of the great vassals. His domains comprised the Bourbonnais, half Auvergne, La Marche, Beaujolais, Le Forez, La Dombe, Clermont, Beauvoisis, and other fiefs. He had fought at Agnadello, Marignano, and Ravenna and was at the Field of the Cloth of Gold. He had held Milan while Maximilian and Pace were marching lansquenets and Swiss up and down Lombardy. But Francis had been foolish enough to deprive him of part of his possessions. Some may hold that, faced with so great a loss, he was entitled and wise to declare war on his King and country, and to ally himself with their enemies—that is what he decided to do. Others might agree with Bayard that he was a villainous traitor. He opened secret negotiations with Charles in the summer of 1522. In June 1523, while Pace was converting the Venetians to the league, and Clerk was travelling to Rome to convert the old pope and take care that a new one should be imperialist, Henry and Wolsey sent William Knight to find Bourbon at his home and induce him to join the league. But at the last minute, when it appeared that a hitch had occurred in the negotiations at Venice, and that Pace must stay there, the plans were changed, and Knight was diverted to the Swiss in Pace's place. The emperor and the pope had agents among the Swiss, but they were not bribing them well enough; Knight knew the Swiss, who at that moment were under orders from Francis to be ready to march at fifteen days' notice. So Wolsey sent Sir John Russell to Bourbon in disguise. Matters were to begin with a rising in France led by Bourbon; but Francis learnt all about his treason in August, and he fled just when his rising should have co-operated with the invasions of Charles and Henry. This put an end to the old schemes, and new ones had to be devised, with a fresh fate for France; but Francis had to postpone his invasion of Italy until the spring

or summer of 1524. Nothing would happen till then. The
new treaty was on these lines. Bourbon was to invade Provence ; Henry was to be recognized as King of France ; until
he invaded Picardy Henry was to subsidize Bourbon ; Charles
was to subsidize Bourbon and invade France from Spain. Charles
was to have Burgundy, and Bourbon was to have a separate
kingdom and receive one of Charles' sisters in marriage. Bourbon joined the imperialist army in North Italy, and was given
command of the expedition ; and we find Clerk, Pace, and
Hannibal corresponding with him about the enterprise intended
to trample the French under foot. The secret enterprise was
the invasion of Provence by Bourbon and the Marquis of
Pescara. Of course great reliance was placed on a revolution,
to break out in France as soon as this army had entered it ; and
it was of the utmost importance that Henry should invade
from the north at the same time, or send plenty of money to the
imperialist army ; and that Charles should break in from Spain,
and send money. Provence had not long been annexed to
France and was not expected to be very loyal to Francis. It
seems as if at one moment Henry intended to send a second
army, actually to join Bourbon, and that this was the real
secret enterprise. It would have been much more surprising
to Francis than anything else to see English soldiers coming
over the Alps. De Bonnivet did not take Milan in the early
spring of 1524, as he should have done ; and the Venetians,
seeing their new allies so strong, advanced to join them, and the
imperialist cause seemed to shine brightly. The emperor
always maintained that he must hold Genoa and Milan, to
connect Spain, Flanders, and Naples. Now he might get
Marseilles as well. De Bonnivet having failed to establish himself in the great towns and castles, the French were driven out
of Italy in May—a retreat famous for the death of Bayard.

Henry had recalled Pace from Rome, and ordered him to
the imperialist army in Lombardy to see Bourbon and the
leaders on the way home.[1] There exists a copy of the commission, which had been given to Sir John Russell, dated 2nd
August 1523, to negotiate with Bourbon, in which Pace's name

[1] *L. and P.*, iv. 362.

has been substituted for Russell's, and the date changed to
7th May 1524. On 4th March the pope indited a complimentary
letter to Henry [1] and confirmed on the following day the new
title of Defender of the Faith. On 10th the Venetian ambassador at Rome reported to the Signory that Pace was on the point
of leaving for England, and would pass through the imperialists'
camp.[2] But on 25th Wolsey was addressing letters to him, as
if he expected them to find him still in Rome ; a curious point,
for an ambassador could not have started home without his
leave. Wolsey had half a mind he should stay in Rome and
conduct the negotiations with the pope, for the treaty of peace.[3]
Wolsey only caught him at Malines, near Brussels. Before
leaving Italy he had been to Lannoy's camp, at Camaria, and
left it on 11th April, taking with him a satisfactory answer from
Bourbon.[4] Thence he went to see the imperial army at Alessandria and other places and thought well of it. This would be
just before this army drove the French from Italy—they were
retreating on Novara while he was with the army. On the
evening of 16th April he reached Bergamo from Milan. He
went next morning on his way to Brescia and Trent.[5] He
reached Brescia on 17th April, and was honourably received by
the podestà, Antonio Sanudo, and continued his journey early
next morning.[6] On his way through Germany he may well
have been alarmed at the growing menace of Luther's changes,
for Ferdinand of Austria had just found it well to ask the pope's
help in the matter, and the pope was sending Cardinal Campeggio to Nuremberg. Both Campeggio and Pace had written
to Eramus before starting, and their letters reached him together
at Basel.[7] From a letter written by Leonicus, at Padua, it
looks as if his friends there had heard of Pace's departure from
Rome and from Italy, but expected he would be in some other
country for some time before going to England.[8] Leonicus
had heard the rumour that the Bishop of Veroli expected to
meet him somewhere in Germany or Switzerland. Several

---

[1] *L. and P.*, iv. 143.   [2] *Cal. Ven. St. Paps.*, iii. 809.
[3] *L. and P.*, iv. 252.   [4] *Cal. Span. St. Paps.*, ii. 632, 645.
[5] Sanuto, xxxvi. col. 230.   [6] *Ibid.* xxxvi. col. 235.
[7] Allen, *Opus Epist.*, v. 407.
[8] Gasquet, *Cardinal Pole and his Early Friends*, p. 59.

15

letter-writers thought he went to the Swiss, but he seems to have gone straight down the Rhine, and he dated a letter from Malines to Wolsey in the middle of May.[1]

His commission and instructions had been sent by the post to Bourbon's camp, and had missed him on his way. He received the letters sending him back at Malines ; he did not reach England. He was to go back to Bourbon, in North Italy, and act for the King. In the letter to Wolsey, written at Malines, he expressed his willingness, notwithstanding his desire to get home and the length of the journey he had just taken, to turn round and go back. He had just seen Bourbon, and was confident of success. He trusted and hoped that he would soon be on the way home again, this time going with a victorious army through France.[2] Wolsey did not hide that it was doubtful if Henry would invade France that year, unless some exceptionally favourable opportunity arose ; but Pace seems to have brushed the doubt aside, and dreamt that he was sure to embark on such a glorious expedition. Henry was to send 100,000 crowns, and Charles the same, to maintain Bourbon's army as soon as it entered France. Sir John Russell had left England to collect the English money at Antwerp. If Henry invaded France he need no longer pay his contribution, and, before Pace handed over any money, Bourbon was to do homage and take oath to Henry, as King of France. Pace was so often being put in charge of money which he was to deny to those expecting it. Bourbon was not to get any money if he refused to cross the Alps, and invade France. Wolsey seems to have had no doubt that Russell would easily raise the money and waft it across Europe. Apparently the decision as to whether Bourbon's oath was sufficient to earn the subsidies was to rest with Pace. Above all, Pace was to keep Wolsey posted up in how things were going, so that he would know how to act. Pace was to be very careful to send accurate information ; for it would decide whether or not it was wise to invade France. A few weeks later Pace regretted that he had not at this moment known about the money being sent out by Russell ; for if he

---

[1] *L. and P.*, iv. 374.

[2] *State Papers King Henry VIII*, vi. Pt. V, p. 288.

had he would have taken charge of it at Antwerp. He thought
he would have had to have guides as far as Namur, but once
past the domains of the Wild Boar of the Ardennes he would
have travelled quickly without them. He too seems to have
forgotten how difficult it was to carry gold. But he knew
nothing about the money when he started back to Lombardy.
As a matter of fact the Antwerp merchants had a good deal of
difficulty in collecting it, and he would have been delayed.
On or about 24th May he passed through Stuttgart, and he
might have seen a Lutheran burnt there. He went through
Trent and wrote to Wolsey. On 9th June Sanchez wrote to
the emperor, from Venice, that he had reached Lombardy, and
on the margin of this letter Gattinara, in Spain, wrote: ' Very
well. Good results are expected from the journey.'[1] He
reached Brescia riding post on or before 10th June ; and the
new podestà, Antonio Surian, who had arrived since his last
visit, and whom he had known well in London, went to call on
him at his inn, before dinner, and Pace gave him some misleading information.[2] After dinner he rode on. He wrote to
Wolsey from Milan on 11th June. He held credentials to
Francesco Sforza, Duke of Milan, and he told him that Henry
intended to invade France, which he knew to be by no means
certain. The duke said he felt he owed his restoration to his
dukedom more to Henry than to any other prince, and he
would do all he could to help Bourbon. With Sforza he found
the Marquis of Pescara, who held a high command in the army.
Pace went on to the imperialist camp at Moncalieri, near Turin,
on 13th, where he found Bourbon, Charles de Lannoy, the viceroy, and Adrian de Croy, Seigneur de Beaurain, who had acted
between Charles and Bourbon.

His journey had been an arduous one, and Wolsey called
Henry's attention to ' all the great travailles, labours, and pains '
he had sustained on it. He told Pace that he must act with the
very greatest sagacity and discretion ' whereby ye may be sure
to do a thing that shall . . . redound to your honour, weale,
and promotion.' Pace did not write a long account of his
honourable reception at the hands of these men in camp because,

[1] *Cal. Span. St. Paps.*, ii. 657.   [2] *Cal. Ven. St. Paps.*, iii. 835.

he said, arms and not ceremonies were the business in hand. He was going to be particularly careful what information he sent home, knowing its importance. Wolsey had supplied the money he had promised to Bourbon. Sir John Russell was in Antwerp about it—£20,000—but it might arrive late ; it was almost certain to be late, but perhaps not too late. Wolsey did not intend to invade France until the fight was already won. Henry might go over to beat a conquered France. We must leave Russell in Antwerp, and, until he reached Pace, Bourbon's army would have to look to the emperor for pay, which would come in ' parcels,' and never a sum large enough to pay up all arrears.

Pace formed an extraordinarily high opinion of Bourbon : ' I do see in the Duke of Bourbon so faithful and so steadfast a mind, without vacillation, to help the king to his crown of France, that, if he be assuredly entertained, the king shall assuredly obtain his crown of France ; considering his intelligences [his adherents in France], and the favour he hath universally in that realm, like as the French king is universally hated.' [1] Pace realized that efforts were being made, and would be made, to tempt this royal traitor back to allegiance ; and it was essential that Henry should keep him attached to himself by favours and assurances. With Bourbon as an active ally, Pace thought Henry had the best chance he had ever had of conquering France. He felt that a letter written by the king's own hand did wonders in such cases. So much was left to his discretion, when he could judge of the way things were going, that there were few letters of preliminary instruction from Wolsey ; and he had not seen a copy of the treaty between Henry and Bourbon. As soon as he felt he had been long enough in the camp to make his information of value, he wrote his general opinion of what he saw around him. He found Bourbon had a high opinion of Beaurain ; important nobles were already coming to Bourbon out of France. If Henry would not go to fetch the French crown, this great and valiant army would bring it to him. Francis and Bourbon resembled two great champions, who meet man to man. Pace reminded Henry that, if Bourbon

[1] *State Papers King Henry VIII*, vi. Pt. V, p. 313.

was left to fight alone, Francis could turn his whole strength on
him. He thought Bourbon would stand by his promises.
Bourbon's invading army could go either along the coast of
Provence, or make straight for Lyons ; and Bourbon preferred
the former course, because he could get supplies from the fleet,
which would sail from Genoa. Marseilles alone would offer
strong resistance, but that might mean a siege. After taking
Marseilles, he would certainly march on Lyons, which was badly
fortified, and to Paris, where he would meet Henry's army.
Francis had no army ready at the moment, but any force he
collected must be brought to a battle at once. Bourbon's army
consisted of 6500 Spaniards, 5400 German lansquenets, and
3000 Italians ; 5000 more lansquenets were expected : there
were in all 20,000 foot. There were 800 men-at-arms, provided
by the emperor, and 300 provided by Bourbon : in all 1100
men-at-arms. There were 1800 light horse, 16 pieces of artillery,
with gunstones and powder, and 1000 pioneers. At sea there
were 18 galleys, a carrack, 4 ships, 4 galleons with 4000 sailors,
under Hugo de Moncada, who would sail round from Genoa and
meet the army on the coast of Provence. Most of the infantry,
whether Spaniards, Italians, or Germans, were veterans, and
had been with the colours throughout this war, and had driven
the French from Italy. The German lansquenets were thought
to be proving almost as good as Swiss. The viceroy was to stay
at Asti with a small army, for either French or Swiss might come
over the Alps.

On 16th June some Spaniards and some German lansquenets
were moved forward to seize the Alpine passes. Wolsey had
drawn up a list of questions as to the military preparations and
plans ; and Pace went about pumping nobles and officers, and
watching. He pumped Bourbon's private secretary as to how
much money his master had in hand, and what jewels. What
would happen if the Swiss invaded Italy while Bourbon was
away ? Answered : that there were enough troops in Italy,
and Bourbon would not have to rush back. Pace was wrongly
persuaded ; for, if Italy was invaded, Bourbon would have to
rush back to defend Milan and Pavia and towns and camps.
Wolsey wanted to know Bourbon's proposed route. Was Lyons

well fortified ?   What would be the attitude of the Duke of
Savoy ?   Would he supply the army with victuals, and allow
messengers to pass ?   Pace thought Savoy would be friendly ;
for the duchess had visited Bourbon and they had danced and
made high cheer together for three days.   Bourbon reckoned
that he had four months left to make war before winter came—
July to October—which Pace thought quite long enough to
enable him to do great things.   Pace heard Bourbon say in
open audience, that if Henry would but invade Picardy at once
in person, he might pluck out his eyes if he were not in Paris
by All Hallows.   Then all the realm would be his, and at Paris
he would take 200,000 or 300,000 crowns.   Pace was to consult
Bourbon as to the route which the invading English army should
take in France ; he advocated the same as that taken by Suffolk
in the previous year, but the plan must depend on the strength
of the opposing army, which in its turn would depend on what
force was sent south to oppose Bourbon.   If Henry found he was
feebly opposed, he should go straight for Paris, and when Paris
was taken so was all France, just as Lombardy went with Milan.
If Pace had received instructions personally from Wolsey, he
would at least have been certain what Wolsey agreed Henry was
bound by treaty to do.   As it was he took it from Bourbon, and
offended Wolsey by urging in a letter, written before starting,
that Henry should cross the sea at once.   At Moncalieri Pace
was finding that, just as Maximilian in days of old was ever
fearing that Henry was going to fail him, so did Bourbon now,
when he demanded his oath to Henry as King of France.   Bourbon was naturally reluctant to commit himself to that extent,
while there was ' perplexity ' in his mind.   He referred Pace to
Beaurain—the go-between,—who explained that Bourbon had
heard certain things that made him wonder if Henry and the
pope were slipping away.   There was always room for such a
suspicion in any of the alliances of those days, personal as they
were to the sovereigns ; and, if put up, proved a good excuse
for vacillating conduct.   Was there a friar in England, sent by
Francis' mother, Louise of Savoy, holding secret communication
with Wolsey ?   Pace told him he should not give credence to
friars and fools in the King's matters, but to ambassadors like

himself (Pace), who was in possession of the facts ; and that Bourbon's security was not going to be less considered in England than that of the pope or the emperor. Pace was not in possession of the facts ; there had been a friar in England, sent by the French court. Beaurain seemed satisfied, and said Bourbon would take the oath to Henry, as King of France, as he had promised to do, but reserving the liberty of his duchy and Provence. He asked that the matter should be kept very secret, for taking the oath would displease many of Bourbon's adherents in France, who wished him to take the crown himself. Bourbon claimed that he had not even done homage to Francis, and would do it to none. Pace had to be contented with this, not wishing to waste valuable time in demanding more ; and received the oath, feeling sure, in spite of this limitation, that Bourbon was to be trusted to stand loyally by all treaties, for he thought him free from subtlety and craft. Bourbon took oath, in the most serious manner, that he would go straight to Rheims to crown Henry King of France.[1] Pace felt that this oath should be regarded as sufficient, and he found the duke ' good, noble, and faithful.' His efforts were rather hampered by the action of the ubiquitous Archbishop of Capua, who had been sent by the pope to Charles, Francis, and Henry to suggest peace, and on his way back to Rome had passed through the camp, at Moncalieri, three days before Pace's arrival. He had told Bourbon and the viceroy that, from what he had seen and heard in England, he thought there was little good in looking in that direction for aid or co-operation. Pace could only say that he and not Capua had been sent to describe what Henry intended to do, and he stated that he had full powers to treat about such co-operation, if he judged that any good order was being taken for the invasion of France by Bourbon. But it was Capua and not Pace who had been in England, and he knew more than Pace did about the military preparations there, which were not sufficiently advanced for an army to cross the Channel that year. Capua was a German named Nicholas Schomberg, a great favourite of Clement's, who turned him into a touring angel of peace,

[1] L. and P., iv. 589.

but he was imperialist in politics. Pace met him several times.

Later on Pace had to admit that he had taken rather too optimistic a view of Bourbon's prospects, but at the time secret partisans in France were daily promising victory if he came soon. They would rise as soon as he was across the Rhone ; and he might be across in a few days. Pace was shown letters in which the emperor told the viceroy to obey Bourbon in all things, and to pledge the crown of Naples rather than run short of money. He saw bills of exchange which satisfied him that Charles had plenty of money in Genoa. At that moment he thought that Wolsey's preparations for the invasion of France were much further advanced than they were, and that Henry could do at once what he could hardly do until the spring. This over-zealous attitude and his vehement call to do what Wolsey regarded as unwise, or impossible, somewhat angered Wolsey ; but even he felt a really good opportunity for bursting into France ought not to be missed. After all it only took two months to collect an English army. The camp-talk was that Bourbon was the most popular man in France, and Francis the most unpopular, and that the persecution of Bourbon was one of his maddest acts ; but camp-talk is not a good foundation for an English war. Pace could only inquire, listen, and guess what would be attempted, and how much of it could be achieved. Wolsey at home knew less than he did—and might do too much or too little. His plans might have to be changed in the twinkling of an eye ; they were indeed in such a fluid state that they were scarcely plans at all.

Wolsey's letter of 18th May, containing his instructions, had been handed to Pace, when he reached the camp. This letter contained the news that Sir John Russell was on his way with £20,000, but no one knew where Russell was ; and Pace, remembering the old days, begged Wolsey to take care that any money sent should not reach him too late, ' as the lack of it makes the soldiers murmur and hinders enterprise.' If he did not take Russell's money over the mountains with him, he would probably never get it ; but he arranged with the Duke of Milan to do his best to send it on if it came through Trent after they had started. It would be a pity if the enterprise failed for lack of money ; for there never was seen a more valiant army, or one better disposed. Pace must have thought of those days, eight years before, when he, Schiner, and Galeazzo were enrolling men at Constance ; for he used almost the same words. He wrote to certain bankers to get them to advance money until Russell's money came ; but the results were disappointing, mainly because there was pestilence at Genoa and Milan. Antonio Vivaldi again proved his faithful friend. Pace and the viceroy wrote to the pope and the emperor to send money; but they had little hope of any coming from Rome, and the emperor was sending what he could. The Duke of Milan's treasury was getting empty ; Genoa's burden was the cost of the imperialists' fleet. Pace's instructions were not complete. It was a pity that Wolsey had not let him come from Malines to Dover and talk the matter over with him ; but he realized what he had to do—he could fill the blanks in his instructions. In 1515 he had gone to Switzerland to induce the Swiss to enrol under Maximilian. He had received their pay; it had been his duty to prevent Maximilian purloining it. He had made promises to the mercenaries in Henry's name, and at great personal inconvenience had marched with the mercenaries as a hostage for the carrying out of the King's promises. He had at first gone willingly as a hostage. Now, just as he had been nearing home to rest, he had been sent back to join Bourbon. Wolsey hardly knew what might arise ; he sent Pace as the most reliable servant of the crown to deal with the situation. He was, of course, to hold all the allies in the league against France. He was to receive the money promised by Henry to Bourbon, and he was to help on in every way this great expedition—this murderous thrust, this raid on England's hereditary foe. But he had a special and more important duty. He was to be in Bourbon's camp as a spy, a reporter, to keep Henry and Wolsey perfectly informed how things were going ; so that they could invade France if Bourbon's success promised English arms an easy victory in the north of France ; or break away from the alliance if a complete fiasco in Provence should let loose an infuriated

French King to wreak vengeance on the English coast. His knowledge of history must have taught him that, whether Henry invaded France or not, would depend on his own advantage. Anyway, Wolsey must be supplied with news. Pace therefore arranged with the Duke of Milan to lay posts behind the army, through Savoy and Italy to Trent; and Henry arranged with the imperial postmaster to lay them from Trent to Calais. The Duke of Genoa, Antonioto Adorno, was to send his dispatches by sea to Henry when the army had crossed the Alps; for the Genoese fleet would maintain communications with the army in Provence. Pace left little to chance; he could take responsibility, and act on his own initiative when alone. That is why Henry and Wolsey employed him on these missions abroad, and praised him. Wolsey had given him instructions to reside with Bourbon, and he saw that the object of his residence was to glean news, which could not be done if he was not with the army. So he determined to march with it, ' and thus by chance become a soldier,' a terrible task for this elderly ecclesiastic in poor health—he was now about forty-two, which was quite old in those days. He told Wolsey he would go without fear, for the army was able to fight all the power of France, and was determined to do so. It was, he thought, high time to assert Henry's right to the French throne, and if this army of Bourbon's was obliged by lack of support to retreat, such another would never be got together.[1] Eight years before he had hoped that Maximilian and the Swiss would invade Provence by the same road, after taking Milan, and here was his dream coming true.

The viceroy had been informed that Francis contemplated an invasion of Italy by some other pass, while Bourbon was going into Provence, a likely enough manœuvre (although Wolsey pretended to regard his alarm as groundless), and the men-at-arms were kept back for the defence of Italy. This Pace regarded as a ' shameful act ' on the part of the viceroy : he would have staked everything on Bourbon's invasion. He never forgave the viceroy for this, or for what he called the ' embezzling ' of part of the emperor's promised contribution ;

[1] *L. and P.*, iv. 422.

by which he meant that the viceroy had used some of the money sent for the expedition on Italian affairs. He did not trust the viceroy, imputing to him jealousy of Bourbon's position in the emperor's favour. He had a brave heart, but he was dispirited for a time, just before he marched over the Alps. He sent letters by a trusted courier, and asked Wolsey to send him back again with ' comfortable ' tidings. He was troubled to find that Henry and Wolsey left so much to his decision ; for he was alone, and such a matter required many councillors.

Bourbon and Pace started with the vanguard on 24th June, preceded by Beaurain with the light horse. On the next day they were at Savigliano, and Pace wrote enthusiastically to Henry and Wolsey about the army and the enterprise. Having no goods to give he would spend his life in the King's service following the army. The music of drum and trumpet always went to his head. He might never see the King again, so he told him a few things. The pope was not to be trusted nor were some of the lesser Italian states—Wolsey knew as much as that. He had some fear that back-biters had been telling Wolsey that he had some ' affection ' for Italian affairs ; for Wolsey had ordered him, when making his reports, to set aside all ' affection,' meaning biased feeling. He declared his affection was to see Henry recover his rights in France, though he admitted he had some affection for Italian affairs. He denied that he ever had any affection for the interest of any prince but Henry, and he declared he had never made reports for lucre or promotion ; and if he were to die on this expedition he would do so contentedly, thinking that no subject ever served his prince more faithfully than he had done.[1] Excitement stirred him to sit down and write another letter before the courier had started from the camp. Wolsey would sometimes receive half a dozen from him in the same batch. Nice had already been offered to Bourbon by the Duke of Savoy, and there were great hopes of other towns rising in their favour. Bourbon's chief hope rested on such risings in his favour, as is always the case when a rebel invades his fatherland. These letters which Pace wrote, just before the army marched, were

[1] *L. and P.*, iv. 440.

those which seemed to Wolsey to be too optimistic and too likely to urge a policy really adverse to Henry's interest. Some ' fine man,' whom Pace mentions, had perhaps tried to influence Wolsey against him.[1] When Pace in due course learnt Wolsey's mind, from his replies, he pointed out that he had merely intended to lay the facts before him, and meant that Henry should take a risk only when Bourbon's successes made it seem worth while. At Savigliano Bourbon confessed, and communicated very religiously, before setting out to war, and then sent for Pace, and promised that, with the help of his friends, he would put the crown of France upon ' our common master's head.' He said his attachment to Henry arose mainly from the virtues which ' I did diligently mark at my being with him at Guisnes and Arde.'

On 27th June the army was at Borgo, at the foot of Colle de Tenda, and next day the enemy were driven back in a skirmish in a mountain pass. From Borgo Pace ascended the Alps with the soldiers. He described the passes in the Colle de Tenda as so steep that in places he had to creep on all fours.[2] Those who had not seen it would not believe how dangerous the road was, and he was surprised there were so few accidents. They went thirsty in the heat, and hungry. Pace himself was in the saddle or on foot continuously from midnight to midnight, scarcely daring to cast his eyes on the precipice on his left. They were the highest and most terrible mountains he had ever seen, although he had supposed he had already travelled through the worst in the world. Antonio de Leyva was carried all the way on men's shoulders. By the evening of the next day they had passed the great mountains and reached Tenda, ' and thus everything, thanked be God, succeedeth prosperously, and is like so to continue.' Next day they descended into Provence, crossed the Var, and entered France on 1st July, by which time Pace had sent three special couriers to Wolsey since he had left Milan.

While Pace was painfully making his way through the Alpine passes Wolsey was dictating a letter to him to say that at the end of the month English troops would cross to Calais

[1] *L. and P*., iv. 589.   [2] Strype, *Memorials*, i. Pt. II. p. 27.

to join the Burgundians in an invasion of France. Pace wrote
to Wolsey from St. Laurent du Var in Provence. The imperialist fleet had already taken the town and castle of Antibes ;
and on the previous day the town and castle of Villeneuve had
surrendered to Bourbon ; and he had summoned Grasse, which
surrendered. Bourbon could not sleep for joy, and was anxious
to push on with part of the army, and leave Pescara and Pace
behind with the rest ; which Pace did not like. Pace had hurt
his hand in crossing the Alps, and his secretaries had to write
his dispatches ; but he seems otherwise none the worse. There
was a rumour in the army that Francis would soon have a body
of Swiss in the field ; but Pace was so enchanted with Bourbon's
army that he entirely forgot his old opinion of the mountaineers,
and reported to Wolsey that his present comrades did not think
much of six or even twelve thousand of them. Some Frenchmen had come to Bourbon to tell him that Marseilles was not
so strong but that he could take it by assault. The army
rested at St. Laurent for five days, and expected the men-at-
arms, whom the viceroy had kept in Italy, and there they met
the Genoese fleet. Rations in plenty were supplied from the
fleet and brought in from the country ; and they did some
looting. Pace was amazed to see the spoils. Nothing escaped
the Spaniards ; they searched for valuables buried or hidden
in holes in walls. But there was no news of Russell and his
money, or of the money which the emperor had promised to
pay Bourbon on his arrival at St. Laurent—100,000 crowns.
There were several small fights between the fleets, in one of
which the Prince of Orange was captured by the French. They
witnessed a naval action from the shore, although it rained gunstones. Bourbon's artillery had been brought from Genoa by
sea ; and the French fleet, under Andrea Doria, trying to
prevent its being landed, was driven off with difficulty. The
artillery was safely put on shore. At this moment Bourbon
received a letter, dated 19th June, stating that Russell was
still at Antwerp, unable to arrange for the transfer of the
money, which should have arrived by the time the army entered
France. Pace, mindful of earlier adventures, requested
Bourbon to keep him in pledge for the money. Not only had

Charles and Henry promised that Bourbon should have the money when he entered Provence, but the former had promised to be invading France by Perpignan at that same moment. Bourbon was in Provence, and it remained to be seen whether the others would come up to their promises. Henry was either to place his money with Bourbon or to invade France.

Francis was collecting an army at Avignon and would be free to move against Bourbon as soon as he was sure he would not have to face either Charles or Henry. Bourbon met little opposition on land until the army reached Fréjus, where there was another skirmish, in which some French men-at-arms, arquebusiers, and archers were driven back. Pace waited for the money at St. Laurent, after the army had passed on, and some arrived from the emperor; but it was all in driblets, only just enough to keep the army going, never enough to satisfy their just demands, which only Russell's £20,000 would do. The army went on to Draguignan. The roads and mountain passes in their rear were beset by villains and robbers, and it was unsafe to send dispatches; so Pace got Sir Robert Curson's nephew to take a letter and a message to Wolsey. The nephew seemed to him an honest young man, not without cleverness, though not with as much of it as he could have wished. On this day (16th July), Wolsey's letters of the 28th June, already described, reached him, and comforted him more than news of promotion for him in England could have done, since they promised an English invasion of France. Pace left St. Laurent on 17th July, by which time there was a growing anxiety about the money. Bourbon, whenever he saw Pace, boasted that France was theirs if Henry moved in time; but Pace was watching the roads anxiously for Russell. If Henry would not embark on military operations that summer, he and the emperor ought to pay Bourbon's army all the winter and invade France in the spring.

It has been said that Wolsey at this time, or within the next few months, held Pace in hatred, was jealous of him, was keeping him out of England, because he was afraid he was too much in Henry's favour. So attention should be paid to the letter which Wolsey wrote him on 17th July—that is to say when Pace was leaving St. Laurent—in answer to his letters written before the expedition started. Wolsey had not received the latest news from Provence, but that makes little difference. The greater part of the letter consists of a recital of the contents of Pace's last letters to him ; which seems superfluous, as Pace methodically kept a record of the dates of his letters, and perhaps copies, and could describe them afterwards as ' my melancholic letter ' of such and such a date, or as it might be. Wolsey refers to a private letter to himself, which he describes as ' concluding last of all, that, to speak unto me (Wolsey) boldly, if I do not regard the premises, you will impute unto me the loss of the crown of France.' This Wolsey had laid before the King and some of the council ; he took no offence, but sent Pace the King's thanks for his zeal. The King and Wolsey might differ from Pace's opinions on some points, he being, as he himself wrote, alone, and necessarily ignorant of many things which he would know if he were in England.[1] But Pace seems to have thought Wolsey was offended, and explained that he had only wished to ' stir ' Wolsey; and afterwards he did impute the ill-success of the expedition to Wolsey's hesitation. Wolsey set out the matters which Pace might have been unable to observe, but which might be good reason for Henry's being slow to invade France, personally or by his lieutenant. For instance Bourbon was (might be) making war on Francis for his own ends. He might have agreed secretly to hand over part of Henry's kingdom of France —such as Provence or Marseilles—to the emperor, who might get more out of a defeat of France than Henry would. It might be that neither the emperor nor Bourbon intended Henry to get the crown of France. Anyway Henry had not intended to invade France that summer unless Bourbon's successes warranted it. Wolsey was sure Francis was not as generally hated, nor Bourbon as generally loved in France, as Pace had been told ; and there was not likely to be a revolution. Pace had exaggerated Bourbon's chances of success ; it was too late in the year for Henry to begin a campaign; and there was great scarcity across the channel, so Margaret of Austria might

[1] *L. and P.*, iv. 510.

not be able to collect supplies. Pace's suggestion that Henry should go over himself to Calais, to make it appear that he was going to do something, would be unwise ; because it would be said he had gone over to treat secretly for peace with Francis. Next year was the time agreed with the Emperor for their joint invasion of France. Henry had only intended to invade in 1524, if Bourbon's success secured him a walk-over to Paris. The best thing would be for Henry to keep Bourbon supplied with money. By his treaty with the emperor he need not do that if his own army invaded France. Wolsey wanted Bourbon to go by Lyons straight for Paris, and he saw that the taking of Marseilles, for the emperor, was likely to be Bourbon's object ; and this would bring no gain to Henry. Admitting that Henry had to provide money for Bourbon, as soon as he entered France, he said Russell was bringing £20,000. He did not excuse himself for the delay in the money's arrival. He probably thought it had arrived. If the expedition was only for the benefit of the emperor and Bourbon, Henry would be unwise to finance it. Put shortly, Wolsey's policy was this : no English invasion of France that year, unless Bourbon met with some extraordinary success ; perhaps an invasion next year ; certainly £20,000 (though it might be late), even if Henry got nothing for it ; possibly quite a lot more money next winter if it appeared that some advantage would be derived from such an outlay. It was a wise policy. Did Wolsey really want to recover the French crown for Henry ? He did not think Bourbon would meet with much success unless he was helped by a revolution. Pace was to assure Bourbon that Henry would get money ready, whatever happened ; and that, if he marched triumphantly into the heart of France, Henry in person, or by his lieutenant, would lead an English army to meet him, whatever time of year it might be.

On 20th July Pace was with the army at Fayence, twelve miles beyond Grasse, and next day at Draguignan, fifteen miles farther on. They were meeting with no opposition. If they went forward three miles, said Pace, the French ran away ten. He wrote from Tourves to Wolsey, speaking in enthusiastic terms of Bourbon's successes. God had evidently taken him into His keeping, and he had already conquered more than half Provence. Pace sent a list of the towns he had taken. The enemy were retreating beyond Rhone, ten or twelve thousand of them ; and the Spaniards and lansquenets counted their infantry but as so many fleas. If the enemy did not wait for battle on his side the Rhone, Bourbon would go for Marseilles. Pace did not see that the French were illuding battle and letting Bourbon consume his resources. The imperialists had just taken Vergin, and Pace spoke of the theatre and other Roman remains—his only published reference to classical ruins. He had heard nothing of Russell since 8th July, and pay sent bit by bit by the emperor was being doled out to the Spaniards and lansquenets. The list of towns taken comprised Grasse, Vergin, Antibes, Villeneuve (where they found four hundred large casks of the best wine), Cagnes, Cannes, Draguignan, Fayence, Lorgues, Trets, Brignoles, Hyères, and Tourves. The Spanish captains, Pace said, had no doubt about taking Marseilles.

The reader of Pace's letters may complain that it is difficult to tell from them what his real opinion was, as to the success with which Bourbon was meeting. He had, no doubt, over-estimated the value of easy successes, won in open country against little resistance ; and he got dejected whenever he felt that he was doomed, by lack of money, to see the utter defeat of the French slip from Bourbon. The Duke of Sessa, the emperor's ambassador at Rome, who was never an admirer of Pace, told his master (24th August) that he wrote from the army ' in a thousand colours ' ; in one letter he would say that the imperialists were prospering beyond all expectation, having already conquered the whole of France, and in another he would pretend that all was ruined and the army lost.[1] This trait in his character has been noticed already.

Aix surrendered on Bourbon's approach, and he entered it on 9th August, and on 12th Pace received letters from Henry and Wolsey to hand to Bourbon, the viceroy, and Beaurain. The covering letter was that of 17th July, in which Wolsey informed him that there would be no English invasion of France. When Pace gave Bourbon his letters and told him

[1] *Cal. Span. St. Paps.*, ii. 675.

that Henry would not lead or send his army across the Channel by reason of lack of victuals, etc., he was ' somewhat abashed.' He sent for Beaurain, who knew, or was supposed to know, the emperor's mind, and told him and Pace that he had been sent into France by their masters, trusting that they would invade France in co-operation with him. Now he saw he could not rely on their coming themselves, or even sending their armies ; and so he bade them write to find out what their masters would do—continue the war, make peace, or truce ; it was all the same to him. Pace assured him Henry would do all he had promised, and pointed out that, when the letters in his hand were written, Henry and Wolsey had not heard of his successes in France, which would make a difference. Pace went further : he assured Bourbon, in spite of the letters, that Henry was making great preparations for war ; and that it would not be long before Russell arrived with the money. Bourbon said providing the army with money was Pace's and Beaurain's business, and that he would continue the war as long as they had a crown to give him. If Henry's money came, he hoped to cross the Rhone and stir up all his friends to provide money in his own country. Then on to Lyons. But thinking it over at Aix he realized that he could not penetrate to Lyons, if his allies did not co-operate with him. To get possession of Marseilles, therefore, seemed the best thing to do. It would be a good place to winter in, if that had to be done, for it could be supplied by the fleet. Its possession would satisfy the emperor, even if the campaign produced no other fruit. It would serve as a splendid base for an invasion of France in the following year. Wolsey was not opposed to the taking of Marseilles, or indeed of Arles. In fact he saw that Bourbon should not leave these two strongholds in his rear, if he marched into Central France ; but he feared that Henry was being decoyed into an invasion, which would draw off part of the French army, and so enable Bourbon to capture Marseilles for the emperor, who would then withdraw from the allies. It is difficult, when reading an account of Bourbon's campaign at this distance of time, to realize that—outside his own promised kingdom—he was taking towns and receiving friends, not for himself, or for

the emperor, but for Henry, as King of France. Wolsey's
demand that this should be made clear comes as a shock.
Richard Pace, the Dean of St. Paul's, seems, but for a few
servants, to have been the only Englishman in the armies
which were attempting to conquer France and set the crown
of it on his King's head.

On the night of 14th August Bourbon and Pescara
reconnoitred the defences of Marseilles and found them very
strong, but some troops were sent up next day and the siege
was laid on 19th. The town had been prepared and provisioned
by Francis in the summer, but there was a weak bit of wall.
On 23rd Bourbon attempted to make a breach by cannonade
for the Spanish infantry—who constituted the best part of the
army—to go through, but after four hours it was realized that
—as Pace puts it—the powder was not good enough. A mine
was then begun, and the army waited for fresh powder. The
capture of Marseilles would be of no advantage to Henry, unless
it were a step in the campaign and not the sole result of it ; but
for the emperor it would link up Barcelona and Genoa. It
must be taken quickly, or else money must arrive to maintain
the army, which would then go on, and find the enemy across
the Rhone. The longer the battle was postponed the better
for Francis. Pescara told the Duke of Sessa that it was Bourbon
and Pace who urged the commanders to attack Marseilles,
Arles, and Avignon. He said these two were always in a
passion, ' thus the captains are placed between two passions.' [1]
Others said it was Pescara who urged an attempt on Marseilles,
having been ordered to do so by the emperor, and that Bourbon
wanted to march on Lyons. Anyway, a council of war decided
on it. Pace's view was the same as Wolsey's : that Bourbon
could not leave Marseilles in French hands, in his rear, and that
the news of its capture would result in the surrender of other
towns. The captains, he thought, laid the siege more by
necessity than will, and simply wished it would fall, so that
they could continue their march, and had no thought of the
emperor's getting possession of it. They wished, said Pace, it
were a pie's nest to be thrown down easily with a bird-bolt.

[1] *Cal. Span. St. Paps.*, ii. 673.

The French might try to relieve it and be drawn into battle. Pace thought the French had the larger army, but not the best men. So bad was the intelligence department that at the end of August Bourbon did not know whether the emperor had an army co-operating with him on the Spanish frontier or not. He only had news that an army had marched towards Perpignan, and, he said, if this was true he would be able to cross the Rhone. Then twelve thousand French gentlemen would rise for him, and there would be the revolution Wolsey looked for.

Pace wrote to Wolsey on 26th August as enthusiastically as ever about victory, after having been a week before Marseilles. Even half the money Henry had promised would enable the army to achieve some notable victory, if it arrived in time. If it did not come he did not know what would happen to them all, but they would rather die in battle than retreat with shame. The Spaniards could be relied on to fight their way home ; but the lansquenets were less to be trusted, and might go over to the enemy. If the army broke up all might be slain. At the moment Francis was reported to be at Lyons. The season was advancing, and, if Bourbon did not get money to win a great victory soon, he would have to end the campaign by retreating ; or by going into winter quarters, which meant paying the army 40,000 or 50,000 crowns a month until the spring. Who was to pay the army ? Francis was scarcely likely to grant a truce while the enemy was in his kingdom getting ready to beat him in the spring. The emperor's ' parcels ' of money still just kept the troops going, and many Spanish officers were rich enough to advance their men's pay—a surprising circumstance.

At last—on 26th August—Russell reached the camp with his £20,000, which might last until the end of September.[1] He had been coming by way of Geneva, in great fear of being robbed by Swiss and German lansquenets going to join the French. At Geneva he packed the money in bales with oats and old clothes, and put a merchant's mark on them. When he left the town the Duke of Savoy sent friends to meet him and bring him down to Chambéry, where he hired fresh mules, and put

[1] *L. and P.*, iv. 608.

bales on them which seemed to be those in which the money
had been. He took these mules out of Chambéry while others
took the money by Mont Cenis to Turin, packed in coffers
used by the Duke of Savoy to take the furniture of his chapel.
He was almost too late, as Pace said. Beaurain was at once
sent to the emperor to get more money, and it was hoped he
would be back with it before Russell's was exhausted. He
could be back in three weeks. Wolsey dispatched another
£10,000 in crowns-of-the-sun to Pace and Russell,·in August,
by Mr. Weston, the Turcopolier of the Order of St. John, who
was going to Viterbo, travelling as Christopher Barber, with
some score of Englishmen. Wolsey's calculation was that, if
the emperor had sent his money according to agreement, Henry's
money—Russell's £20,000—would not have been needed until
30th July, and it should have lasted until 27th August : that
the emperor's next contribution should have kept the army
going until 24th September.[1] But ' like as in all other proceedings, the emperor's folks make great avaunts and promises
for payment of money, but when it cometh to the point nothing
is observed.' He did not realize that the money he was sending
was late too. Russell was with Pace before Marseilles on
30th August and Pace knew all about the Turcopolier. Towards
the end of August Wolsey received the letters Pace had written
from Tourves, well into France, showing a measure of success,
and they rekindled his ardour. It began to seem to him more
possible for the English to invade France. With them were
letters from Bourbon and Pescara, urging Henry to invade
quickly. Wolsey wrote—one may think chaffingly to Pace—of
this expedition ' for the helping whereof ye desire me to lay my
cardinal's hat, crosses, maces, and myself in pledge at this
time.' Surely this is a dig at Pace by one who had poured cold
water on his enthusiasm, but contemplated returning to the
plan. There is nothing in the whole letter to indicate he was
displeased with him. The King held a council on the matter, and
it was decided to send (Sir) Gregory de Casale to Bourbon with
the King's reply, that they held Pace's information in no small
estimation, and that their action would be determined by it.

[1] *L. and P.*, iv. 590.

If Bourbon could cross the Rhone and get 'into the bowels of France' towards Lyons, then it would really be a pity if the King missed the opportunity to strike a blow for himself, even though the season was rather far advanced. Indeed Wolsey was sufficiently moved to order musters and collect wagons and supplies in Flanders. He ordered Pace definitely in this letter (31st August) to urge Bourbon to go on into France, and promised that, on receipt of news of his determination to do so, Henry's army would cross to Valenciennes, join the imperialists, and march on Paris, or effect a junction with Bourbon on the Rhone, as might be thought best. Wolsey was pretty well supplied with information, and dealt with the matter as a statesman should. He could not tell whether Pace knew more or less than he did. He could not determine what to do, and so he laid all he knew, and could think of, before him, so that he might let him know what was happening in the south ; he indicated on what points he was to report. When Wolsey wrote this letter he seemed to hold Pace in the highest esteem, but he was not to give such advice as would lead Henry into allowing himself to be made use of by the emperor. Pace received this letter on 15th September, and afterwards spoke of it as bringing news too late that English troops were ready to cross the Channel whenever he (Pace) said the word. He afterwards blamed Wolsey for so much delay which spoilt the enterprise.[1] The delay before Marseilles spoilt Bourbon's chance of pushing on towards Paris before the bad weather came, and the difficulties in the way of keeping the army together until the spring had induced the emperor to open negotiations for peace with Francis at Rome. Wolsey instructed John Clerk to stand in the way of the negotiations, but about the end of September Clerk received a letter from Pace, dated 16th, showing he had little hope of Bourbon's taking Marseilles. It could be supplied by the French fleet, and the townsmen hated the Spaniards. Rome had been inclined towards the French side for some time, and when the news from the army grew worse, the pope came forward to suggest peace between the emperor and Francis. Thereupon Wolsey told Clerk to open similar negotiations, in the

---

[1] *Cal. Ven. St. Paps.*, iii. 388.

event of news coming of the total ruin of Bourbon's army, or of news of conclusion of peace between Charles and Francis. By the end of September the army would be in dire need of more money.

A council of war decided to assault the town, and if that failed, to march against the French army at Avignon. Next day Russell sailed from Toulon to Genoa and posted to Milan to find the Turcopolier, who reached Viterbo, near Rome, on 6th October, Russell being then at Mantua looking for him. The Turcopolier was travelling on the business of his order, and there was no reason why he should go out of his way to deliver the money. Even when Russell got to Viterbo he preferred to go on to Rome to ask Clerk what he had better do with the money. While he was in Rome news came that the army was retreating to Italy. The siege had lasted forty days, and it had been a case of smash the enemy or run home. The French vanguard, under La Palice, was approaching from Avignon. Bourbon and Pace [1] were for giving battle. Pescara, Beaurain, and other captains were for withdrawing to Piedmont to defend Italy. They made one more assault on Marseilles, on 24th September, and commenced the retreat on 28th, for the troops would not meet the French in the field without pay. History had again repeated itself. Bourbon's retreat from Marseilles was brought about in the same way as Maximilian's from Milan. Again Henry was subsidizing the expedition ; again the money was punctually dispatched ; again it arrived too late ; again Pace was with the army to be responsible for the money ; again he had the mortification of retreating before the French in the midst of a finer army than theirs.

Pescara commanded the rearguard, a day's march behind Bourbon, and covered himself with glory in the Alps, fighting night and day against the French van under de Montmorency. Pace rode with the main body. They marched across to Grasse, where they stopped for food ; to St. Laurent ; across the Var again ; to Nice, where they enjoyed their first long rest since leaving Marseilles. The unsympathetic Clerk in Rome, who trusted to reports, told Wolsey, ' If they had made

[1] *L. and P.*, iv. 780.

as good speed onwards as they have made homewards, they might have been at Calais long afore this time.' From Nice they went by Monaco, Villeneuve, Albenga, Finale, then across the Ligurian Alps to Alba. From Alba they retreated on Pavia, leaving Asti and Alessandria behind, and covering as much as forty miles in one day. Francis with the main body of the French army was at Aix on 1st October, and went by forced marches up the valley of the Durance and over the Cottian Alps, hoping to reach Italy by a short cut before the imperialists, and so find Milan undefended. He came down into Italy between Turin and Vercelli. On 8th October the viceroy was at Asti, where he hoped to rally the imperialists and make a stand for Milan ; but the army was broken and streamed past him. He fell back with the garrison on Alessandria, and then Pavia, hoping to decoy Francis from Milan. Bourbon and Pescara went on to Pavia. Francis reached Turin on 17th October, and Pace was at Milan on 20th. The suddenness of the change of events made Milan entirely unprepared for defence. On the day of Pace's arrival the governor discovered that so many citizens were sick of the plague that even a show of resistance was impossible. The Duke of Milan was already in Cremona Castle, where he would have a chance of putting up a good fight. The viceroy arrived at Pavia on the night of 21st, with men-at-arms and infantry, and marched at once to Milan. Francis should have left the towns and caught the retreating army in the field and cut it to pieces, but he wanted Milan and Pavia. He and his army had performed another splendid feat of arms, and another victory in the field like Marignano might have given him Italy for ever ; if he could have consolidated his successes before the imperialists got more pay. But he delayed and lost his opportunity.

CHAPTER XII

PAVIA

FROM Milan Pace retired behind the Adda. The Venetians had kept up a fine army, under the Duke of Urbino ; but would they stand loyally with the emperor in his adversity ? Pace, with all his love of Venice, was often impatient that she should pick her way so carefully—' I may reasonably compare (her) to the bat, deplumed for her inconstancy of part-taking now here, now there, giving aid where she saw victory incline, as a condign punishment for her defection from her natural lord and capitain—as referrith the wise fable of Æsop.' [1] These men of the Renaissance, of necessity so changeable themselves from lack of news, despised the same weakness, or fickleness, in others. Pace's first surviving letter after the terrible experience of the retreat is addressed to Wolsey (22nd October) from Brescia, which he had reached a day or two previously. He lodged with Antonio Surian, the *podestà*. All who were with him were in great fear of the French. Russell was sending back the Turcopolier's money to Wolsey, who intended to spend it in fitting out an expedition against France in the following year ; but Pace thought he still had it under his own control. He was being asked for it by the imperialists, and he said he had no commission to pay it to them. He did not think it could be spent to Henry's advantage, and it was not sufficient to sustain the imperialist army long enough to bring forth any good. From Brescia he went to Mantua to see the marquis, by which time the imperialists were falling back on the Adda. [2]

[1] Strype, *Mems.*, i. Pt. II, p. 30.
[2] Several reports recorded in Sanuto's *Diary* refer to Pace as he went across Italy.

Francis entered the west gate of Milan on 26th October, as the imperialists were leaving by the east gate ; but the castle held out for Charles. On 28th Francis was before Pavia, which was held by Antonio de Leyva. The safety of every town in Italy seemed threatened, and on 2nd November Pace wrote to Henry telling him of Francis' approach to Pavia, which he regarded as the key to the Milanese. It was likely to hold out. He thought Bourbon would stand firm, and he had appealed to the pope for aid. The Venetians seemed to be coming up to the scratch, but all Italy was inclined to favour the winning side. There was peace talk. Francis was sounding Bourbon, and the pope was sounding Charles and Francis. Pace was still at Mantua with the marquis on 19th November, but he did not hear much good reliable news of interest. While he was there he stated that he had not received any letters from England since the retreat, but writing to the emperor this Francophobe still cried out the necessity for all states to combine against the common enemy, the French. On the way to Verona he stayed again with his friend the *podestà* of Brescia on 22nd and 23rd, and on the night of 22nd the house was perhaps an unquiet lodging, for Surian's wife gave birth to a son. The father declared that he would have none but the Duke of Urbino (Francesco Maria), who had been given the command of the Venetian army, and the English ambassador for godfathers. He wrote to the Signory of Pace as his ' very great friend.' Pace rode at dawn on 23rd to Lograto, and dined with Bourbon, who had come over from Soncino, where the viceroy was forming a great camp on the Adda, and where the imperialist leaders had assembled. Bourbon arranged this interview because Pace was supposed to be on the point of departing to England, and he could describe the situation to Henry. Bourbon said the imperialist army was large and good—as no doubt it was. They held the castles and camps at Alessandria, Como, Pavia, Lodi, Pizzighettone, and Cremona. Venice was likely to come in with them. Francis had weakened his army by sending part of it, with the Duke of Albany, towards Naples. Bourbon told Pace of his intention to shut himself up in Lodi or Cremona ; but Pace tried to dissuade

him, and wrote to Wolsey to get him to change his plan. He
wanted him to keep a mobile army to relieve Pavia. After
the interview Bourbon rode back to Soncino, and Pace to the
podestà at Brescia, with whom he had a long talk on the situation. To Soncino the pope sent a legate with suggestions of
peace. Pace wanted to go to Innsbruck, to the Archduke
Ferdinand of Austria, to get reinforcements, and, after that, to
post to England to induce Henry to invade France, perhaps in
person, in the spring at the latest ; but he had to wait at Trent
till he got instructions from England. He wrote to Henry on
27th November from Verona setting out shortly Bourbon's
plans for a joint invasion of France. If Henry would not go,
Bourbon would go alone, and depend on a revolution, which
might tempt Henry to come in later. Bourbon warned Henry
that however good the imperialist army might be, want of
money might compel the viceroy to make peace, to save Milan
and Naples, and probably the pope would make peace if Francis
took Pavia. Pace had shrewdly formed the opinion that
Giovanni de' Medici, thec aptain of the Black Bands, took
bribes from the French. He thought him a very light
person, who regarded neither pope nor Christ, but followed
his own fancies. He thought the pope held the casting vote in
Italy.

At this moment, far away in Madrid, the Venetian ambassador, Gasparo Contarini, was discussing with the Archbishop
of Capua possible representatives of the powers at the peace
conference, which had been suggested. The names of Thomas
More and Pace were mentioned for England. Capua had
recently been in England and had heard the latest opinions—
such as that Wolsey was grasping too much power—and he
said of Pace that he himself thought him too ' vehement ' for
such a mission.[1]

Wolsey answered a whole batch of Pace's letters—from
Mantua, Verona, and Trent—at once, probably in December.
He did not know where Pace was or what he was doing—
thought he was with Clerk. He was to stir Venice against
Francis. At Trent Pace could get dispatches from England

[1] *Cal. Ven. St. Paps.*, iii. 899.

and hear all news. When he went there his secretary took his place as godfather to the *podestà's* son. Bourbon decided to go himself to Ferdinand for guns and men, and on his way to Innsbruck he saw Pace at Trent. In December a secret treaty was made between the pope, Venice, and Francis for the protection of the pope's towns,[1] but the Venetians were not bound to help France in the field. Clement had not proved as imperialist as Charles and his ambassadors at Rome had hoped he would do. He had soon shown signs of desiring to remain neutral—a good Christian wish in God's vicar, but not pleasing to a holy Roman emperor, who had brought about his election in his own interest. From a neutral attitude he veered to the laudable plan of joining Venice and the Duke of Milan in an attempt to kick both Charles and Francis out of Italy—which had been old Julius' policy. His holiness accounted for this breaking away from the alliance by saying that strange and unfortunate rumours had floated from England of peace-talk, and he was afraid of being left in the lurch. After the retreat from Marseilles Francis' mother, Louise of Savoy, fearing an invasion by the English in the spring, sent an agent to England —a Genoese, usually called John Joachim. He lay concealed at Blackfriars in London, and managed to have many secret interviews with Wolsey. The first gossip of his doings was enough to alienate the allies, for news of his presence went out of England, although Wolsey, on one occasion at least, seized the letters sent by the emperor's ambassador. Pace had told the *podestà* of Brescia that he was afraid something of this nature was going on, but that he did not believe there would be any treacherous falling away from the alliance by England. He suspected that Wolsey had had secret intelligences with Francis, because of his evil nature.[2] Never before do we catch Pace speaking ill of a patron. The historian Guicciardini, who was at this time soldiering in Lombardy with the imperialists, and may have known Pace at Padua university, and may have met him again now, wrote of Wolsey's ' Infirma condizione e sangue sordidissimo.' Pace had heard in October that Joachim,

---

[1] Pastor, *History of the Popes*, ix. 267.

[2] Sanuto, xxxvii. col. 94.

whom he knew, was in England, and he warned Henry that if he dealt truly with him, it would be what he had never done with any one, for he was one of the craftiest fellows, and associated with the French party in Genoa.[1]   The allies naturally thought that the holding back of Henry's money was Joachim's and Wolsey's work. Such a discovery made the Francophobe Pace hate the cardinal for undoing his work, while he was enduring the rigours of the campaign. He began to say— seriously this time—that Henry's failure to recover the French crown had been chiefly due to Wolsey's hesitation. All he could do in Italy was to assure the allies that Joachim had concluded nothing in the way of peace between Henry and Francis. He professed to have seen some of Joachim's letters, which had been intercepted, in which Henry's honour was ' not a little diminished.'

Pace spent Christmas at Trent; and on 16th January he reported to Wolsey that he had heard an assault on the enemy at Pavia had been planned for that day, which should end the war, either by a victory, or by cessation of hostilities through lack of money. Bourbon had reached Ferdinand at Innsbruck, and found him still favourable to the allies' cause ; so he was able to return to Lombardy with re-inforcements, and join Pescara at Lodi, on the line of the Adda.

On 16th January Wolsey ordered Pace to go to Venice to solicit the speedy dispatch of the Republic's army to join the imperialists. A few days before this (5th January) the pope had made a treaty with France, and it was feared Venice might join it.[2]   Pace was to point out to Venice what might happen to her if Francis captured Naples as well as Milan ; and he was to remind her of her sufferings through the League of Cambrai. He was to tell the doge and senate secretly that Henry had heard that the Spaniards had behaved with such cruelty in Italy that there was likely to be a movement to help in the French. Henry would try to put Francesco Sforza back in Milan, and get rid of both Spaniards and French. Wolsey had told the imperial ambassador in London that he would back

[1] *L. and P.*, iv. 760.   [2] Pastor, *History of the Popes*, ix. 267.

these entreaties by threats to break off trade with Venice.[1] Gregory de Casale was to go to the viceroy as Henry's representative in the imperialist camp ; Clerk was at Rome ; and Pace was to be at Venice. All the Italian states were watchful to be on the winning side, and the Florentines, the Duke of Ferrara, and the Marquis of Mantua were soon in the league with the pope and Francis, and were tempting Venice. In the middle of January it was known everywhere that Bourbon was ready to attempt to relieve Pavia, and a bloody battle was hourly expected.

Casale brought out Wolsey's orders, sending Pace to Venice, and handed them to him at Trent on 1st February, having come at top speed from England. Pace was to start at once, and he was off next day. Casale went on to the camp near Pavia. Pace had pledged Henry's credit to subsidize lansquenets, and to make provision for the imperialist army, and Casale brought the requisite orders on Clerk to redeem the pledge.

It was generally thought in Padua and Venice that Pace had been to the Archduke Ferdinand ; but he seems to have remained at Trent to receive orders from England, for all messengers came through Trent, and might be unable to find him when they had once got into Italy. Before leaving Trent he found time to write to Clerk in Rome, urging him to induce the pope to break away from his new amity with Francis and to stand in with the emperor and Henry. He did this because he was sure he could not keep Venice with the emperor and Henry while the pope was proving that he believed Francis to be stronger than they were. From Bassano he wrote to his old associates, Caracciolo and Sanchez, who were still at Venice, telling them he was on his way to aid them to influence the Signory. He begged them to tell him frankly what chance of success there seemed to be, for if there was none he felt he would be wiser not to go to Venice, as he could do better work for the imperialists in other parts of Italy. He was ready to disobey Wolsey's orders in that case. He awaited their answer in the house of Reginald Pole at Padua. He was riding post

[1] *L. and P.*, iv. 1015.

in front of his servants.[1] This letter was carried speedily and
the imperial ambassadors answered next day, begging him to
come to Venice as soon as possible, as his presence would
certainly be a great advantage to Charles and Henry; they
were expecting news of a battle at any moment. Venice was
full of rumours—perhaps spread by the French—of Henry's
secret negotiations with Francis, and Pace's presence would be
proof to the contrary. They did not know the rumours were
true.

With Reginald Pole at Padua was Lupset, and they all
went on to Venice on 7th. Pace was honourably received in
the customary manner, at Fusina, five miles out of Venice, by
a company of twenty gentlemen, and conducted to the lodging
in Cà di S. Marco at S. Giorgio Maggiore, which had been prepared for him. The house belonged to the Signory, and was
used to lodge ambassadors; perhaps it was that in the Bene-
dictine monastery which had been assigned to Philippe de
Commines, thirty years before. On the next day he went into
the college. We get so few descriptions of his appearance that
it is interesting to read in Sanuto's *Diary* that, on this occasion,
he was wearing a long gown of black satin lined with sables.
He was accompanied by some senators, doctors, and other
noble persons, dressed in scarlet. When he entered the college
of Savii the doge went forward to meet and embrace him at
the foot of the platform. He presented his King's letters, which
he had received from Casale, and declared his mission; he
exhorted the Signory to keep in league with the emperor, and
to send their army to join his. The doge answered that they
always intended to observe the treaty; and suggested that
their hasty preparations for war, when Francis suddenly chased
Bourbon back into Italy, had prevented his extending his conquests to the south. He showed that several matters had
disquieted the Signory—the pope and the Florentines had now
made a treaty with Francis; the pope had allowed the Duke
of Albany to march through his territory into Naples; Henry's
money brought by the Turcopolier had been recalled; the
French seemed very strong and the emperor had no money for

[1] *Cal. Span. St. Paps.*, ii. 714.

his troops ; they heard that Henry was thinking of peace. Apart from all this, they feared the battle might be over before their army joined the imperialists, and that they would get nothing but the vengeance dealt out to the defeated. Pace could not deny that the pope had made a treaty with Francis, but he represented that his holiness was not such a great peace-maker. It was not consistent with a desire for peace to cause his Florentines to lend Francis 100,000 ducats for war against the emperor, as he had done, or to allow his vassal, the Duke of Ferrara, to send Francis men and money, as he had done. He declared emphatically that, whatever they had heard, Henry would not make peace without the express consent of the emperor, although, for the good of Christendom, he was in favour of an honourable peace that would not prejudice his allies. With regard to the last part of their argument, he said the addition of their contingent to the imperialists might turn the scale, and induce Francis to go out of Italy without a fight. He left the Signory to consider these points.

The pope's ambassador called on Pace at his house, and told him he was too late to win the Venetians again without great difficulty, and the irate Pace answered that the difficulty was not as ' displeasant ' to him as was the author of it—namely, his master—the pope.[1] Everything depended on the news from Pavia, and he wrote home that affairs in Italy were not likely to turn much to Henry's advantage before a battle, as the Italian states cared little for him or the emperor, and would side with the strongest ; and Francis would seem to be the strongest, until the imperialists got some more pay, and perhaps even after that ; they would not know until the battle had been fought and won. He ended his first letter, written after his arrival at Venice, with the admission that he despaired of winning over the Venetians again, and he blamed the pope's treaty with Francis. At the most he thought he might prevent them sending troops to help Francis, which was what the emperor's ambassadors feared they would do. He kept this letter back two days expecting news of a battle ; false reports were constantly arriving. The French ambassador went before

[1] *L. and P.*, iv. 1072.

the college, and exhorted them to leave the league with the emperor and Henry. He was followed by Pace, who made answer. Pace, in coming down from Padua to Trent, had moved out of the chief post-road and his news was not so likely to be fresh; and there were three weeks of skirmishing between the two armies before the battle. The three friends—Pole, Pace, and Lupset—had been closely studying the military situation at Pavia—had been perusing maps. Perhaps it was the reunion with scholars after his experiences in camps that led Pace to seek solace in study. At Venice, and perhaps at Trent, perhaps even when he was with the imperialist army, he had been translating the Psalms. Leonicus admired him for thus keeping his soul in perfect peace amidst the terrible disturbances around him.[1] As a matter of fact poor Pace was sick in body and in mind. Leonicus' letters to Pole from Padua could move him to laughter, and the writer was glad of it; for he felt he could have little amusement while treating of affairs and business. His friends felt he wanted cheering up. He was in need of that holiday in England so long deferred that it might come too late.

Meanwhile, Henry and Wolsey were anxiously discussing Pace's letters on the Italian situation. Wolsey advised, or reminded the King, that, if the imperialists were defeated— which was not probable—' thanked be God, your affairs be, by your high wisdom, in more assured and substantial train, by such communications as be set forth with France apart, than others in outward places, would suppose.'[2] He refers to his negotiations with Joachim, and Pace was in two senses in an outward place. Pace's duties became somewhat monotonous, to go almost daily to the college, ask for the dispatch of troops to the imperialist army, and give assurances that Henry still stood by the emperor. On each occasion the doge would postpone a decision, hoping for some news which would make known the winning side. In the middle of the month Pace, Sanchez, and Caracciolo were joined by two ambassadors from the Duke of Milan; and they went in a body to urge the

---

[1] Gasquet, *Cardinal Pole and his Early Friends*, p. 84.
[2] *L. and P.*, iv. 1078.

17

Venetians to march, at least to the banks of the Adda, and assured them the allies would be victorious. We get, perhaps, the real views of the doge and senate from a letter of instruction to their ambassador at Rome. Venice wanted peace; and the imperialists wanted war, and were being urged on to it by Henry, through Casale. Venice was afraid Francis might be beaten, and she therefore wanted the pope to bring about a peace. Henry was right in thinking Venice wanted neither a victorious Francis nor a victorious Charles in Milan; but, if she must have one of them, she would rather it were Francis, because she hated the Spaniards—and because the Germans could come down on her easily, through Trent. As it was she had Charles' brother on the other side of her. The doge and senate thought they elicited information from Pace adroitly, and he flattered himself that he handled them with ' loving and dulcet ' words. On the night of Sunday 19th, letters reached the pope's ambassador from his master, and he took them to the Signory on the Monday morning. The pope desired Venice to assist him in making peace between the two armies, for which purpose he had sent the inevitable Archbishop of Capua to Lombardy. He asked the Signory to hold solemn processions in aid of that object, as he was doing in Rome. He told them they would disturb the peace, if they sent their army to join the imperialists. By the middle of the week Pace realized that the imperialists had the pope, Venice—' every one in Italy,' —against them, and only God for their protector ; but he was sure they would defeat the French.

After the college had adjourned, on the Saturday morning, 25th February, and while the doge was dining, a post arrived with news of a battle. It had come in a letter from the imperialists' camp and was not to be doubted. The French were routed; but the battle was not at an end when the letter was written. The news was true, the French were routed. Francis was wounded, and a prisoner. The doge sent word at once to Pace, Sanchez, Caracciolo, and the Milanese ambassadors ; and they all, and many of their attendants and many refugees from Milan, met hurriedly, with very great joy and gladness, and trooped to the church of the Madonna dei Miracoli. A very grand Te Deum was sung, with vocal and instrumental music, and the vesper service was performed in great state.[1] That evening a comedy was acted on the upper floor of Cà Dandolo, formerly occupied by Pace, but then rented by the Paduans. The actors were a company who called themselves *The Valorosi*. It was apparently only a rehearsal for a performance to be held at carnival three days later, but it was turned into an important occasion by the good news fresh come that day. It became a *répétition générale*, and to it came many old men of note, and the papal legate (in disguise) ; the ambassador from Mantua ; Reginald Pole, so well known to the Paduans ; and some aged noblemen, but not many ; and the diarist, Marino Sanuto himself, who describes the evening. It seems probable that, under the circumstances, Pace would have gone with Pole, who was his guest in Venice, perhaps like the legate, disguised.

Next day, Sunday, Pace, and the other victorious ambassadors went into the college ; all wearing doublets of cloth of gold, and gold chains. They were obviously in good spirits. They came with a number of Spaniards, and *émigrés* from Milan and Genoa—about one hundred altogether. When they were seated, Caracciolo spoke about the victory and capture of Francis, which would give peace and quiet to Italy ; and reminded them that the victory had come on St. Matthew's day, which was the emperor's birthday. The doge offered Venice's congratulations, and thanked God for so good a result. He tried to explain why the Venetian army had not been there. As they were departing the ambassadors asked for gunpowder to fire salutes, and pitch to make torches ; for they meant to rejoice at their houses—the imperialists at Cà Zorzi, at San Severo, Pace over at S. Giorgio Maggiore, and the Milanese in Cà Pasqualigo, at Sta. Giustina. These commodities were voted to them, and sent from the arsenal ; and they rejoiced for three evenings — firing cannon and displaying fireworks. When they had left the college the French ambassador came, obviously much upset.

The hostility and enmity of England towards France abated

[1] Sanuto.

after the battle of Pavia, and Pace's career was at an end. The Venetians were sorry enough they had not chosen to be on the winning side. They expected the wrath of the imperialists ; they feared that Charles would become as much their enemy as Maximilian had been. The question for Wolsey became whether Francis had not fallen too low—so low that Charles was too strong ; but with such matters Pace was in future to be little concerned. He was ill again, and, when the excitement over the issue of the battle passed from him, he collapsed. He seemed scarcely well enough to express his joy at the downfall of Francis. Sanuto recorded ' Be it known that Pace, the English ambassador, is sick and unwell. The Signory sent physicians to visit him.' [1]

The first news of Pavia reached London on 9th March, but no further certain news for another week. Pace's first surviving letter written to Wolsey after the battle is dated 12th March. He says he had been in continual fever for ten days and nights. He was better and the physicians had given him hope of his life, but he was so enfeebled that he did not expect ever to be able to ride up and down as before. He, therefore, asked Wolsey to obtain the King's leave for his return, ' after soo long travayles and paynes by me sustaynyd in outward parties ; which I wolde not refuse also now to do, if it were to me possible.' [2] He gave news of the captive Francis, of the whereabouts of the Duke of Albany, and of the death of Richard de la Pole in the battle.

On 10th March, that is to say the day after receiving the news, Wolsey instructed Pace to assure Venice that Henry intended to continue the war against France, and Pace informed the college on 5th April and told them English money was being sent to the imperialists.[3] Wolsey had not yet decided what to do. In the meanwhile Pace considered the payment of the imperialist army as Henry's business, to some extent. Sanuto observed of him on 5th April that he was well enough to go into the college to thank the doge for sending physicians to him, and for other help. He said that if he had been ill anywhere else

---

[1] *Cal. Ven. St. Paps.*, iii. 947.   [2] Ellis, *Letters*, Series II, i. p. 304.
[3] *Cal. Ven. St. Paps.*, iii. 972.

than in Venice he would have died ; he thanked the doge for
his house at S. Giorgio. On the same day, the Signory sent
instructions to their ambassador, Lorenzo Orio, who was on his
way to England, that at his first audience with the King and
cardinal, or as soon afterwards as possible, he was to bear ample
testimony to the adroit, loving, and prudent offices performed
at Venice by the Reverend Richard Pace, his majesty's ambassador, for the benefit of the Signory's affairs.¹ But a further
and separate instruction, on the same day, advised Orio to take
great care not to praise Pace to Henry so highly, if Wolsey was
present, as he might do in his absence ; for they understood that
Pace was not in great favour with the cardinal. They gave him
this hint, so that he might exercise his prudence in accordance
with the state of affairs, which he should discover at the English
court.² This is most important, as showing that the well-
informed Signory had heard of difficulties between cardinal and
secretary. Pole went over to Pace in April and corresponded
with Leonicus about his health ; he was then enduring a flux
which indeed soon passed away.³ On the vigil of S. Marco the
doge went to vespers with ducal ceremony, and Pace is mentioned
as being present, wearing a long black velvet robe. The ambassadors of the pope, emperor, Milan, Ferrara, and Mantua were
there too, but he is the only one mentioned by name, and no
clothes but his are described. With him was Reginald Pole,
White Rose, dressed ' as a gownsman.' On 27th Pace went into
the college, and asked permission to retire to Padua for some
days to recuperate ; the doge gave it him, and ordered the
rectors there to treat him with honour. In the middle of May
he seems to have returned to Venice to continue the business
negotiations, which were to produce money for the imperialists.
On 14th he again applied to Wolsey to be recalled ; his work
for Henry was at an end, his expenses in Venice were too great
for him, and the imperialist army was melting away.⁴ In June
he applied to the college for the reversion of a broker's patent
in the German warehouse, for a bastard born of a German father

¹ *Cal. Ven. St. Paps.*, iii. 974.   ² *Ibid.* iii. 975.
³ Gasquet, *Cardinal Pole and his Early Friends*, p. 87.
⁴ *L. and P.*, iv. 1, No. 1337.

and a Venetian mother, and it was agreed to put it to the ballot. These sinecures were given to such persons as the official painters —Bellini and Titian. Pole returned to Venice in June, and, like Pace and the other ambassadors, accompanied the doge in state to Mass in S. Marco, at Corpus Christi, and, according to custom, went in procession from the Scuola of S. Rocco. Pace did a good deal of ceremonial Mass-going at this time, being perhaps in better health. Francesco Maria, Duke of Urbino, and his duchess, Leonora, came to Venice, and an ambassador from the sultan ; the last, to spy out the land, Pace thought, for he took great interest in the Christian processions and services. The chronicler Hall narrates, in connexion with the defeat of the Christians by the Turks at Mohacz, that the Venetians gave proofs of friendship with the Turk, even in Pace's presence. At the end of June came the Bishop of Bayeux from Francis' mother, to win Venice over to mediate with the pope, the emperor and Henry for the liberation of Francis, assuring the Signory that France would meddle no more in Italy. The doge and college informed Lorenzo Orio that every day they were more satisfied with what Pace was doing.[1] On 1st July he went into the college to say he purposed going for a few days to Conegliano for change of air, and he had started by next day. During his absence news came to Venice, mostly from Lorenzo Orio, of John Joachim's negotiations in London ; and the imperialists everywhere began to fear this was the beginning of a league against their victorious emperor— made by the pope, England, France, and the Venetians. Pace was back in Venice before 12th July, when he wrote to Wolsey. The allies had good reason to fear that England was forsaking them ; and a treaty was signed between England and France on 30th August, but Venice was included in it. Venice might have something to fear from the unpaid army of imperialists, but nothing from France. Pace's work as England's representative was done, and he received little more in the way of instructions. This may have been the outcome of Wolsey's displeasure, but Lorenzo Orio had reached London and commended his wisdom, prudence, and address to Henry.[2] That Pace's efforts had been

[1] *Cal. Ven. St. Paps.*, iii. 1050. [2] *Ibid.* iii. 1037.

honest ones to keep faith with the emperor, is proved by the fact that, when Henry sent Tunstal and Sir Richard Wingfield to Spain, to drive from Charles' mind doubts as to England's attitude, they were provided with copies of the correspondence of Casale, Pace, and Russell. The old policy was to be reversed; but Pace was by then too ill to care about such changes, and he kept out of Venice as much as he could. On 4th August he was at Padua and complained in a letter to Wolsey of sleeplessness— 'disease of watching' (ἀγρυπνία)—saying he had come from Venice to consult a physician at Padua.[1] He regarded this as a fresh illness. Erasmus at Basel had heard of Pace's illness 'a plague on these embassies and counter-embassies! Pace was born for the Muses.' Erasmus was afraid, love affairs—sexual pleasures (τὰ ἀφροδίσια)—might have increased the evil. His letter is to Lupset, presumably at Padua.[2] If Erasmus was right Pace's friends at Padua must have known about it. Lupset was nursing him, and wrote to Erasmus from Padua on 23rd August, conveying Pace's best wishes, and referring to his insomnia, which, he says, came originally from too much care and anxiety; and he feared terribly for his future.

In the middle of the month Lorenzo Orio reported from London that Pace had received leave to return home, and made the surprising statement that, although others wrote to him in the King's name to go back, Henry himself had ordered him not to obey them, and to come straight home. He added that this letter of leave was written by the King's order, without the knowledge of the cardinal.[3] We have in the correspondence of these Venetians a reference to suggestions made by Polydore Vergil,[4] and followed by Holinshed and Shakespeare, that Wolsey was jealous of Pace's influence with the King, and kept him abroad. We have seen that instructions, based probably on Pace's own statements at Venice, were given to Orio, to refrain from praising Pace very much to Henry, if the cardinal

[1] L. and P., iv. 1546, and see iii. 2420.
[2] Ibid. iv. 1547.
[3] Cal. Ven. St. Paps., iii. 1097.
[4] Angl. Hist. (1651), Bk. xxvii. 65.

was present, as he seemed to look on him with disfavour. We see that in London in August 1525 the rumour was that Henry knew his chancellor was keeping his favourite secretary abroad, and was taking steps secretly to get him home. Two years before this Surian had written the same tale, actually blaming the cardinal.[1] Pace was looked for daily in London. Even Richard Sampson, who was doing his political work, thought he was on the way home early in September. His illness, which the doge and college described as a nervous (fastidiosa) disorder,[2] grew worse at Padua ; and he returned to Venice at the end of August, or in the first days of September, and chose again to reside in Cà di S. Marco, on the island of S. Giorgio Maggiore.[3] The Signory were very anxious for his welfare and health, both because he was Henry's ambassador, and for his own most worthy qualities ; and at Padua and at Venice they watched over him. He was better by 18th September, and they thought he might be completely restored to health. They ordered Orio to tell the King these things, and, should he think fit, the cardinal too—another suggestion that all was not well between the chancellor and the secretary ; and this part of the letter is in cipher. Orio was to report to the doge when he had seen the King on these matters. The doge, Andrea Gritti, whose portrait was painted by Titian, and whose features are well known to visitors to Venice, wrote a long letter to Wolsey, dated 1st October, on his final departure.[4] He said he had been ill almost all the time he had been in Venice, and had been sleepless for nights and days together. The best Venetian physicians had been unable to find a remedy, but agreed that the air of Venice did not suit him. The only thing for him was to go away. The college dispatched Francesco Donato and Zaccaria Bembo to Pace, who was too ill to go to the college to take leave of the doge, and, in accordance with a decree of the senate two years before, they presented him with a gold chain worth 800 ducats.[5] John Foxe[6] was told by the brother of a man who lived with Pace just before his return to England, who may have been

[1] Sanuto, xxxiv. col. 114.
[2] *Cal. Ven. St. Paps.*, iii. 1114.
[3] *Ibid.* iii. 1105.
[4] Rymer, *Foedare*, xiv. 96.
[5] *Cal. Ven. St. Paps.*, iii. 1127.
[6] *Acts and Mon.*, iv. 598.

Lupset, that the cardinal sent a letter to Pace, ' so powdered (with what spices I cannot tell) that at the reading thereof Pacy, being then in the fields, fell suddenly in such a mighty running for the space of two miles, that his servants had much ado to take him, and bring him home.'

CHAPTER XIII

THE END OF LIFE

PACE began his last journey home on the morning of 3rd (possibly 2nd) October. He went by way of Padua to Treviso, and the governors of the towns in Venetian territory were ordered to entertain and honour him. He reached Bassano on 10th, and departed next day for Primolano, at which place the landlord of the inn had been prepared to do him honour, and make no charge, as the Signory would pay for everything. At Trent he found troops out to encounter the peasants ; for the Bishop of Brixen had just executed two heretics ; had cut off the hands of others, and put out the eyes of a few more. Some hundred were in prison awaiting similar treatment. Coming through Flanders he may have heard the people curse the new peace between England and France, saying they had to victual the English army, and provide transport, and now England had gone over to their enemies. These cries came to the ears of the chronicler Hall. Pace arrived in London by 17th November, and the Venetian ambassador reported that he was still ill. Up to the end of the month no one was allowed to see him,[1] and then on 23rd December Orio wrote more openly—his brain was affected (*a mal nel zarvello*).[2] He was melancholy ; he thought the King had taken all his possessions, and that he was penniless. His friends tried to comfort him by assuring him that the King loved him. He was perhaps a shade better for a few days just before Christmas.

[1] Sanuto, xl. cols. 433, 555.
[2] *Cal. Ven. St. Paps.*, iii. 1187.

266

At this home-coming Leland wrote these verses to him :

IN REDITUM RICHARDI PACAEI, UTRIUSQUE LINGUAE ORNAMENTI CLARISSIMI

Jam sospes rediit noster ab inclytis
Pacaeus Venetis, Aonidum decus,
Et secum in patriam lumina rettulit,
Aut (verum ut fatear) numina rectus.
Ecquis lucidulis candidus unio
Conchis innitet ? Ecquis mihi fulgidus
Ramus concrepitat frondibus aureis ?
Cum quo pectoris ingentia gaudia
Plaudentis celibrem ? Quae mihi consonae
Musae clara ferent carmina, queis ego
Pacaeo reduci gratuler intime ?
Quem absentem miseris vocibus ambiit
Doctorum chorus, O sidera conquerens
Vel crudelia. Quem splendidus insuper
Nympharum numerus notus Apollini
Absentem indoluit mirificis modis.
Quem salvum ac reducem visere gestiens
Grex natus studiis, plausibus assonat
Quem Musae reducem denique splendidae
Vinctae purpureis tempora floribus
Certant carminibus vel ter ovantibus
Ad coeli nitidi tollere culmina.' [1]

Pace's biography has to be almost entirely based on his correspondence, and as soon as his illness prevented his writing we have nothing but glimpses of him for a period of ten years. Then a casual reference to his death. Dated June 1526 we have a letter from him to Lord Darcy, which contains mistakes such as might be made by a sick man. He sends a message to Lady Darcy, one of his few references to a woman. No acquaintance with women is recorded, except with Queen Catherine, with some ladies at a fête in Venice, and with his sister-in-law ; but we are set wondering by Erasmus' reference to τὰ ἀφροδίσια, and possibly by his application for a sinecure for a Venetian woman's bastard. It would be unfair, unpleasant, and ridiculous to found a theory on such trifles, but they remind us that we know little of his private life.

[1] Leland, *Collectanea* (1544), v. 99.

In November 1525 John Clerk was on his way home from Rome, recalled for other service in England and abroad. He was afterwards one of Catherine's counsel at her trial. We do not know what Henry had intended to do with Pace, if his health had improved ; we may presume Wolsey would not have suggested employment for him. Ruthal, Wolsey's right-hand man, had died in 1523, and was succeeded as privy seal by Sir Henry Marney, who died within a few weeks, and was followed by Tunstal. Pace in good health, and in the cardinal's favour, should have had this office. While he was in Italy the duties of Mr. Secretary had been discharged by Richard Sampson, archdeacon of Suffolk, dean of Windsor and of the chapel royal, by More, and Brian Tuke. It was kept open for Pace, but when he had been in England for some months, and it was obvious he could not return to duty, Dr. William Knight, who had become archdeacon of Chester and Huntingdon, was appointed in his place. It was Knight who had so often gone to the Swiss when it had proved impossible to send Pace.

In August 1526 the court was at Winchester, and Knight told Henry that Wolsey wanted Sampson, Richard Wolman, and himself (Knight) to be appointed coadjutors of such deaneries as Pace held, and Henry fell in with the suggestion. Wolman was archdeacon of Sudbury and dean of Wells. The fact that this matter came up at Winchester suggests Pace may have ʰ been in the neighbourhood.[1] The deaneries were St. Paul's, Exeter, and Salisbury.

On 16th December 1526 Knight wrote to Hennage, one of Wolsey's household, that he had been arranging an interview between Wolsey and Pace. Wolsey had appointed it at Hampton Court, and Pace asked that a day might be fixed, so that he might not find Wolsey too busy to see him, for he was still sick and sleepless. Knight gave it as his opinion that he would be relieved if he could secure this interview.[2] He intended to go up to London and bring Pace to Hampton Court.

A year's rest in England brought little improvement, and work on the council, or in the deanery, was still out of the

---

[1] *State Papers King Henry VIII*, i. 173.
[2] *L. and P.*, iv. 2712.

question. Pace feared the cardinal, but not the King. Had he
failed in his duty ? or was Wolsey displeased without cause with
this zealous servant of the crown ? Godwin's *Chronicle* suggests
that, while he was in Italy, he failed to grasp the change taking
place in Henry's mind, presumably with regard to the balance of
power between Francis and Charles.[1] Certainly he did not know
of this change ; nor was Wolsey sure there was to be a change,
nor was Henry himself, until after Pavia, and really not even then.
Godwin evidently considered that Henry had determined to
divorce Catherine before Pace started home, and that this
weighed English policy towards friendship with France. Pace
knew nothing of this trouble. Godwin thought that Pace,
finding money promised for the imperialists was slow in coming
to him in Italy, had pledged Henry's credit with merchants to
an extent unauthorized—a sum not large enough to be of much
use to the army, but too large for his own estate to meet, when
Henry repudiated liability, which repudiation was in part due
to Henry's alienation from the emperor, in consequence of the
overthrow of Francis, and of his intention to put away Catherine,
the emperor's aunt. It is difficult to say when he could have
heard of Henry's plans for Catherine, but not before he reached
home, by which time his mind was already deranged. The
common people—according to Hall—did not get the news until
the spring of 1527, when the bishop of Tarbes came to London
to talk of a marriage between a French prince and Princess Mary,
who might thereby be proved illegitimate.

Strype says that towards the end of his life the cardinal grew
morose, and as his greatness and wealth increased so did his
pride, which made him ' froward and uneasy ' to others, and apt
to revenge any supposed neglect, or want of respect, towards
himself ; and that this deficiency in him made him get Pace cast
into prison ; and that such treatment as he received from the
cardinal, after his great and faithful services to him, and to the
King in foreign embassies, put him out of his wits.[2] This we
know to be inaccurate ; for he was mentally distressed in Italy,
but even there some sensed the cardinal's displeasure, when he

[1] Godwin's *Chronicle* (1630), 61.
[2] *Ecclesiastical Mems.*, i. Pt. I, 190.

was left without instructions and money. In answer to this it may be said that in Germany and in Switzerland, when basking in Wolsey's favour, he had been no better supplied with either. It was a fault of the system and not necessarily evidence of a malicious design upon him. That Wolsey kept him abroad when he might have come home is suggested by letters, already referred to;[1] and Polydore Vergil says that Wolsey sent him abroad on foreign missions, and kept him away, because his music and personal charm won him a place too near to the King's heart.[2] Shakespeare took the idea from him:

> 1st *Gent*: And generally—whoever the King favours,
> The Cardinal instantly will find employment,
> And far enough from court too.
>
> *King Henry VIII*, ii. sc. 1, 47.

But public servants were not called home as soon as their work seemed completed. They were left for a time among people they knew—Romans, Venetians, Swiss—in case, as so often happened, a sudden change of fortune might offer further employment. A lot of guessing has been done about a possible quarrel between the cardinal and Pace, based on very meagre evidence. Beyond doubt the ambassadors and courtiers thought he was out of Wolsey's favour about the time of the battle of Pavia, and even two years before that. Some think churchmen who filled great offices of state—Wolsey, Richelieu, Mazarin—were little likely to have time or inclination, after a rigid schooling, to stoop to the promptings of spite and jealousy; but the contrary is the truth. No man's brain is too occupied to find room for cruel thoughts if his nature gives birth to them. They may come as a relaxation. When Wolsey was young, Sir Amyas Paulet put him in the stocks, and long afterwards, according to Cavendish, he took his revenge by confining his tormentor to the Middle Temple. Sir Gregory de Casale once fell ill on hearing he was displeased with him. But pride was nearing its fall, and Pace outlived the cardinal, whose arrogance was in full blast at the time of his return. Hall says the King

[1] Pp. 209, 263 *seq.*   [2] *Angl. Hist.* (1651), Bk. xxvii. 65.

kept few at court, for fear of the plague, in the winter after
Pavia, so that it was called the Still Christmas ; but Wolsey at
Richmond kept open house in royal manner, and the people
were ' sore grieved,' and his taxes were making him unpopular.
Even Warham, Archbishop of Canterbury, was in peril from the
cardinal. Buckingham, Polydore Vergil, the poet Skelton, and
Cardinal Adrian felt his displeasure.

Professor Pollard says Pace criticized Wolsey's policy, and
his change of policy.[1] Anthony à Wood and early writers
attribute the cardinal's displeasure to Pace's over-zealous
championship of Bourbon, and his failure to secure Wolsey's
election to the papacy, and say that Pace's friends in England
warned him secretly of his danger while he was at Venice.[2]
In point of fact every mission on which he was sent ended in
failure, but in each case because the initial enthusiasm of the
King and the cardinal had cooled, or because money had not
reached him, or because of some miscalculation by Wolsey of
the chances of success. Pace's ability, zeal, and energy were
never responsible for failure ; but sometimes he was sent on
missions which required a stronger physique and better health
than ever supported him. Wood repeats the story that the
Venetian ambassador in London went to the cardinal and asked
whether he would not send some instructions to Pace in Venice ;
whereupon Wolsey explained, ' Paceus decepit regem,' and that
Pace heard of this and became ill. Wolsey's biographer, Fiddes,
speaking of the doge's letter about Pace's health, and his return
to England, adds : ' Tho' soon after his return from Italy and
by some error or supposed error in his conduct there he was so
unhappy as to fall under the cardinal's great displeasure.' [3] The
compilers of old biographical dictionaries scented a quarrel of
some sort between these two men, from contemporary gossip,
and guessed at its origin, being content, as Shakespeare was, to
assume that the greater ill-treated the less. As long before this
as 1522, when he was talking over the plans for Bourbon's
campaign with Sanchez in Venice, Pace said he had a great many
enemies in England, and that he feared they might avail themselves of the opportunity to injure him, if he advised Henry to

[1] *Wolsey*, p. 107.   [2] *Athenae*, i.   [3] (1724), p. 378.

come into the league.[1] The enemies on the look-out to avail
themselves of such an opportunity could hardly include Wolsey,
who could have broken him any day he had wanted to. Some
time after all these events Robert Wakfeld wrote to the Earl of
Wiltshire—Anne Boleyn's father—referring to Pace who, he
says, like John Fisher, ' was treated unworthily, badly, and
unfairly by a friend of mine and yours—rather our enemy—
who forcibly shut him out of his own home. And Pace
had deserved well of him (this enemy) and of all scholars,
and was the glory of England.' [2] One would naturally suppose
that this enemy to Wakfeld, Boleyn, Fisher, and Pace, was
Wolsey.

The year 1527 is an end-point in the story of Pace's active
life, and it is the beginning of a new epoch in the history of
England, no longer called upon to take sides in the struggle
between Habsburg and Valois, though there was still much
talk and planning of alliances and wars. There was enough
to do at home, for the quarrel with Rome was in sight, and a
score of new matters were in men's minds. The next few years
saw the sack of Rome by Bourbon and the imperialists, the
defeat of the Christian army by the Turks at Mohacz, the amazing episode of the Nun of Kent, the dividing of Englishmen into
parties over the divorce of Catherine of Aragon, and the spread
of ' heresy ' in England. On Shrove Tuesday 1526 a number of
heretics did penance at St. Paul's in the presence of the cardinal,
and of a number of bishops, abbots, and priors ; and the Bishop
of Rochester preached a sermon, just as he had done in 1521, but
now Pace—the dean—was too ill to be present, or to translate
it into Latin. With reference to the defeat of the Christian
army at Mohacz, Hall records that the Great Turk wrote about
the victory to the Venetians, as if to friends who were not
Christians, and that the letter was read openly in Venice
when Pace was present. Pace had left Venice long before
the battle was fought ; but there is some truth in the story,
for he regarded Venice as too friendly with the enemies of
Christendom.

[1] *Cal. Span. St. Paps.*, ii. 491.
[2] R. Wakfeld, *Kotser Codicis*, folio P.

Richard Sampson was admitted vicar of Stepney on 18th June 1527 on the resignation of Pace,[1] who retired to the famous Brigettine cloister of Sion at Isleworth. Among the friars was Richard Reynolds, a friend of Pole's, a Latin, Greek, and Hebrew scholar, and afterwards a supporter of the Queen's cause. He went to the Tower and Tyburn over the quarrel between the pope and Henry ; and the vicar of Isleworth went too. This vale of rest was to be a scene of the Nun of Kent's activities. In 1534 the commissioners reported that the friars of Sion were minded to offer themselves in sacrifice to the great idol of Rome. After Pace had left the cloister More talked to the fathers at the grate, and they told him the Nun had been with them, and they did not seem entirely pleased with her. More had an interview with her in the chapel which cost him dear. It is possible that Pace was sent to Sion by the cardinal, for it was a place chosen by him, and Cromwell afterwards, for the confinement of mild offenders; and in those days a lunatic was regarded as little better than a criminal ; he was one possessed of the devil, and was treated accordingly ; but many were gentle with Pace.

On 30th July 1527 Gasparo Spinelli, the secretary of the Venetian ambassador in London, wrote to his brother, ' I went to Sion to visit the Reverend Richard Pace, who leads a blessed life in that beautiful place. He wears his clerical habit, and is surrounded by such a quantity of books, that for my part I never before saw so many in one mass. He has rendered himself an excellent Hebrew and Chaldean scholar, and now, through his knowledge of those languages, has commenced correcting the *Old Testament*, in which, as likewise in the *Psalms*, he found a stupendous amount of errors. He has also corrected the whole of *Ecclesiastes*, and in a few days will publish them. He is now occupied with the *Prophets*, and the book will assuredly prove most meritorious, and render him immortal. When the first part is printed I will endeavour to obtain it.' [2] Richard Wakfeld was a scholar and cánon-lawyer, and had been instructor in Hebrew to Reginald Pole,

---

[1] Anthony à Wood, *Fasti Oxon.*, p. 57.
[2] *Cal. Ven. St. Paps.*, iv. 144.

and chaplain to the King. He states [1] that he taught Pace Hebrew, Chaldee, and Arabic in three months, and it seems to have been at this time ; but Pace knew some Hebrew as long before as 1525, for he was translating the *Psalms* in Venice. Would we could leave Pace with the volumes he loved, and know that he would go only to a better resting place, but ' the king's matter ' had come up ; his conscience was troubling him ; he feared he had been living all those years in incest with his dead brother's wife, and such a friend of the King's and such a scholar as Pace could hardly escape giving an opinion. In May there had been a fictitious matrimonial application to the legatine court, so by midsummer the affair was no longer a secret, and Wolsey was consulting the bishops. From Sion Pace sent letters to the King (July 1527), and a book written by the counsel of Master Wakfeld, which he thought answered the objection to the King's contention about his matrimonial position, which had been raised by some of the counsel, that *Leviticus* was annulled by *Deuteronomy*. Pace told Henry that Wakfeld wanted to know whether he was willing to hear the truth in this great matter. Wakfeld offered to ' show unto your Highness such things as no man within your realm can attain unto or show the like, and as well for you as against you.' It seems as if Wakfeld, and perhaps Pace too, had already given the opinion on the case that Henry's marriage with Catherine, being by Dispensation, was lawful. After that Pace had been told by Henry, and several others, that Arthur's marriage with her had been consummated, which he had not previously suspected, and he was now of opinion that notwithstanding the Dispensation, Henry's marriage was bad. He had been with the King on the day before he wrote these letters and had come more fully to understand the King's contention, and had heard for the first time the councillors' opinion that *Deuteronomy* xxv. 5– 10 cured *Leviticus* xx. 21. He went back to the monastery and talked it over with Wakfeld, with the result that they were both of opinion that Catherine should be put away. Pace professed only to seek the truth ; Wakfeld was perhaps a little more inclined to be swayed by the King's wish, and, having already

---

[1] *Oratio de Laudibus*, etc., folio E2.

expressed himself as of opinion that Henry's marriage was good, he asked that none should know that he had changed his mind. Very likely a better understanding of the King's wishes had more weight with him than the information about Arthur's marriage, but Pace's honesty was never questioned by any one. The people sided with Catherine, which was in itself a good reason for Wakfeld's keeping quiet his change of sides. He and Pace argued with Fisher, who was the chief protagonist of the theory that *Deuteronomy* swept away *Leviticus*. Pace commended Wakfeld for his excellent learning and wonderful knowledge, but pointed out that he would not meddle in the matter without Henry's leave. He sent also a Hebrew alphabet (grammar), desiring that it might be delivered to Richard Fox, now old and blind, with orders to get it by heart ; for by so doing he would in a month be able to judge of the correctness of the Vulgate and *Leviticus* xx. 21, and to show the King the truth.[1] Wakfeld wrote to Henry offering to defend his cause in all the universities of Christendom ; so it is possible that Pace and he in their talks in the monastery forestalled Cranmer, who has been said to have owed his rise to fame and power to his suggestion of getting the universities' concurrence with the King's views. At what moment did these scholars realize that they were not being asked to soothe the King's conscience ? How many of them sought to quiet his scruples, and found suddenly they had incurred his anger ? A statement that a Hebrew scholar sought to please the King does not, in the early stages of the case, make it certain that he pronounced against his marriage. Pace, while he was at Sion, was giving the question his best consideration. He had not definitely decided that he ought to support or oppose the King's and Wolsey's contention, at a moment when the smooth and speedy gaining of Henry's ends was a matter of life and death to the cardinal. He seems only to have sought for what was lawful and right to do.

Pace wrote to his brother, John Pace, and it would be well to know the precise date, but he had fallen into the unbusiness-like habits of Sion, and did not date the letter. ' Whatever is spoken here of my lord cardinal's evil mind against me, it is

[1] *L. and P.*, iv. 3233, and *Kotser Codicis*, R. Wakfeld, i. folio P. iii. seq.

untrue ; for he hath nothing done against me but that is to my high contentation, and rather advancement than hindrance. And this I heartily pray you, and command you, to show to all my friends ; and to publish the same abroad. I wrote to his Grace this day to admit you to his service. Let me have knowledge what he will say thereunto.' [1]

What does this letter suggest and prove ? It certainly does not prove that the cardinal had not become Pace's enemy ; even the cardinal's own assertion to that effect might not be considered conclusive evidence. It proves that the general opinion in Sion, and out of it, was that Pace had incurred the cardinal's displeasure, which is just what the rumour had been in Venice. It proves that whatever Pace had hitherto thought about it, now—when his mental condition permitted him to study languages and the King's divorce business, and promised a return to public life—he wanted to prevent chatter of this sort among his relations and friends, which might come to the cardinal's ears and do him harm. Wolsey would not have taken him back into the council if he had felt him a potential enemy, a man with a grievance. This letter proves that Pace was still in the King's favour, or at least had reason to think he was. It proves that he knew people were saying the cardinal had injured him. He had by this time been three years home from Venice.

He was still at Sion in August 1527, and John Crucius of Bergen-op-Zoom, the tutor of Lord Mountjoy's children, was with him. He was then engaged in a discussion with the Bishop of Rochester over the translation of the *Septuagint* in its relation to the divorce. Crucius thought the rest at Sion had restored him to health.[2] Here is a strange letter, given again no place or time, but probably written at Sion. It is to his brother : ' Sir,—I command you immediately upon the sight hereof, to repair to me hither, with all my servants, as many [as] will come ; and bring with you also your wife and children, one maid to wait upon her, leaving the other to keep your house. And do you set written upon [the] door " God save the king, Amen." I know the king's mind. Do you as I command you,

---

[1] *L. and P.*, iv. 3235.   [2] Allen, *Opu Epist.*, vii. 296.

whatsoever any other man shall say.' [1] If Pace was still out of his mind this letter is of course valueless as evidence to establish anything else. It suggests he had suddenly felt himself capable of returning to public life, and intended to set up his household again—some of his old servants being still bound to him and some not—but he wanted the assistance of his brother and sister-in-law. It was a common practice to fasten a scroll on a house-door, but this ' God save the king, Amen,' may have had some special significance. What was on foot which might have reopened the way for him into affairs ? Wolsey went to France in July 1527. If Wakfeld taught Pace Hebrew, Chaldee, and Arabic in three months we may suppose Pace was with him at Sion in June, July, and August. It was thought that once, when Wolsey was absent, Pace's friends found means to bring him to Henry at Richmond, when they talked alone, for two hours or more, and Henry was pleased to see him better in health than he had been.[2] Pace's letter, written at Sion to the King about Wakfeld's views on the marriage question, shows that an interview took place in July. Wolsey was then in France. Sion was close to Richmond, and Pace's departure from Sion in September may have been the result of the interview. It seems to have been about this time, namely, 8th July 1527, that Pace resigned the deanery of Exeter. According to Haile, Pole who had just returned from Italy succeeded him in August. In September Pace would have heard that Wolsey's journey to France had resulted in a treaty with his old enemy, and that Henry had renounced his claim to the French crown.

By the autumn of 1527 Pace was living in his own house in London with his servants, and the cardinal was supposed to have spies in his household. With the exposure of the King's and cardinal's schemes about Catherine all eyes were turned on Don Inigo de Mendoça, the emperor's ambassador in London, who had arrived in January ; for Charles was Catherine's nephew. Before the battle of Pavia had checked Francis, Charles' friendship had unquestionably been necessary to Henry. Now he

---

[1] *L. and P.*, iv. 3236.
[2] J. Foxe, *Acts and Mon.*, iv. ; and Anthony à Wood, *Athenae*, i.

might be able to do without it, and it became possible to suggest
the divorce of Catherine. Unfortunately the matter was no
sooner broached than the pope fell into the hands of the imperialist troops, and Charles could make him do what he liked. So
the future of the marriage remained in doubt, even if Henry
could make out a very good case against its validity. Henry
and Francis were friends and the French were back in Italy.
Henry must wait and see Francis overcome Charles, or else the
pope compelled by Charles to refuse his request to free him from
Catherine. As a supporter of the imperial alliance, Pace was in
good company ; the queen, Norfolk, Suffolk, all London, and the
south and eastern counties. John Fisher opposed the King and
cardinal in the matter of the divorce, on the ground that
ecclesiastical law was with the queen ; but most Englishmen
who sided with her did so because they thought she was being
unjustly treated. Pace would have learnt what popular feeling
was if he left Sion about September and moved to the deanery
of St. Paul's ; but Sion itself, not long afterwards, became a
meeting-place of those who opposed the King in this matter.
Perhaps Wakfeld and Pace wrote with such secrecy to the King
because Sion even then favoured Catherine. Back in the
deanery, and free to go about the city of London, Pace must
have heard that Catherine denied that her marriage with Arthur
was complete, and he was soon convinced of the validity of her
marriage with Henry, which meant his being against the King
and the cardinal. The former might at first be tolerant, but
difficulties in the latter's path might cause his fall. Pace's
change of view seems extraordinary, but made honestly ; for it
was clean contrary to his self-interest, and put him at variance
with Wakfeld. Sir Gregory de Casale was entrusted with the
divorce matter at the papal court, and we may presume that,
if Pace had still been employed at Rome, it would have been
in his hands.

At Michaelmas 1527 John Pace presented an inventory of
his brother's plate, whom he described as dean of St. Paul's.
The weight of each piece is given. The gilt plate amounted to
332 ounces at 4s. an ounce, and the white and parcel-gilt to
366 ounces at 3s. 6d. an ounce ; the total value being £130, 12s. 9d.

Between Pace's home-coming and this Michaelmas John Pace had paid from the estate £135 to Vivaldi ; £13, 8s. 8d. to Mr. Russell, and £80 to Mr. Stokesley, presumably the Bishop of London, and owing in connexion with the deanery of St. Paul's ; £73, 6s. 8d. to Mr. Elys, executor of Mr. Ashton ; £50 to Mr. Langton's executors ; and £40 to the Bishop of Bangor, which seems not to have been incurred by his care of Pace, which did not begin till 1528. Besides this the administrator paid £67, 14s. 9d. due on the King's subsidy; also £26, 14s. 8d. due in the same direction on behalf of St. Paul's, £18 for Salisbury, and £17 for Exeter and Southmolton. John Pace was left with a balance of £80 less £20 owing to himself.[1] It seems as if John Pace was giving an account of his administration of the estate on his brother's return to the world.

About 12th October Richard Pace met some English merchants, who traded with Spain and Flanders, in the street. He asked them after de Mendoça, and requested one of them, Master Parmer, to tell him that, if he would send one of his servants to speak with him, the emperor's interests might be served.[2] De Mendoça knew Pace now favoured Catherine's cause, and thought he might be able to advise well upon her affairs, so he sent Juanin Corchiero, who understood English. Pace received him secretly, and told him it was very important, in the emperor's interest, that, before he (Pace) saw the King again, he should speak to de Mendoça. He suggested Paul's as a meeting-place not likely to arouse suspicion. Mendoça feared Pace was again not quite right in his mind. He knew that the cardinal and he did not stand well together, and that it was rumoured Pace was inciting people against the cardinal. So he did not see him. Also the ambassador knew the cardinal had spies everywhere. According to his statement, the cardinal did at once learn of Juanin's visit to Pace's house through spies in his household, and summoned Juanin to appear before him in the council, where he was charged with having taken the ambassador's cipher to Pace. Juanin related what had passed, and stated that Mendoça, doubting Pace's sanity, had not met

---

[1] L. and P., Addenda (1929), i. 185.
[2] Cal. Span. St. Paps., iii. Pt. II, 440.

him in Paul's. The cardinal dismissed him saying he was to come before the council again. The cardinal had made exhaustive inquiries as to whether Pace and the ambassador had met and talked, but they had not even corresponded. Probably Juanin went before the court of Star Chamber, presided over by Wolsey. According to de Mendoça, Pace and some of his servants were arrested on 25th October. It is difficult to see what offence there could have been in Juanin's taking the cipher to Pace, if the Spanish ambassador permitted it. It seems to have been no business of Star Chamber, unless the suggestion was that the ambassador had written some treason to Pace in cipher, and that Pace wanted to decode the message. Pace had been better in mind for the last three months. It was said he had spoken to the King about the divorce and the government of the cardinal, expressing himself like a good and loyal subject, which to the Spanish ambassador meant in favour of Catherine. What else he may have said Mendoça knew not. When the cardinal came back from France in September he had ordered a legal inquiry into Pace's conduct, and he advised the ambassador not to listen to what ' disloyal ' Englishmen said about the divorce or to any reports about Pace. The ambassador reassured the cardinal, who thereupon (this is entirely Mendoça's account of what occurred) uttered one of those monstrous lies, in which he was known occasionally to indulge : that Pace had confessed that a letter in cipher, found among his papers, was from the ambassador—though afterwards he had admitted it was not. The ambassador expressed to Wolsey his surprise at all this ; for he had never seen or spoken to Pace, and had not accepted his invitation to meet him at Paul's. With this the cardinal seemed satisfied. This suggestion that Pace was one of the first to get into trouble for espousing Catherine's cause can be appreciated by those who are conversant with the drama played during the next ten years. Such men as John Fisher, Thomas More, and Reginald Pole went to the scaffold or exile ; and several of them were Pace's intimate friends. Perhaps the cardinal heard that the King had granted a secret interview to Pace in his absence, and feared he might have said something to his prejudice. Perhaps

Pace actually made such charges. Anthony à Wood [1] says
that Pace did make charges which the King called on the
cardinal to refute, but that, instead of doing so, he and Norfolk
sat in judgment on Pace [probably in the Star Chamber], really
in Wolsey's own cause, and Pace did not get justice and went
to the Tower a prisoner. Later on (1534) Thomas Cromwell
reproved John Fisher for not having revealed the alleged
prophecies of the Nun of Kent, which were thought to be
detrimental to the King, and Fisher pleaded that others had
not reported treasonable sayings of Pace. To this Cromwell
answered : ' Concerning an imagination of Master Pacy. It
was known that he was beside himself, and, therefore, they
were not blamed that made no report thereof, but it was not
like in this case, for ye took not this nun for a mad woman, for
if ye had ye would not have given unto her so great credence
as ye did.' [2] This shows that Pace had spoken treason in his
madness ; it is Fisher, Pace's friend, who says so. But treason
is an ambiguous term, and its importance depends on the
mouth from which it proceeds. While Wolsey was in France,
planning to free Henry from Catherine and place a French
princess in her place, Henry at home had decided to marry
Anne Boleyn, to which Wolsey would not agree readily. If
Henry saw he might have to do without Wolsey, he would have
looked for the next most able man in the realm to help him.
Ruthal was dead. Did he send for Pace to come secretly from
Sion to Richmond, hoping Wolsey would never hear of it, to
see if his state of health permitted his becoming chancellor ?
It is pure guess work. He would have told Pace Catherine's
marriage with Arthur was complete. Pace would have promised
his support to the King, which he had previously refused ; he
would have decided to leave Sion ; he would have sent for his
servants to set up house ; he would have re-entered the world.
Then he would have heard from Catherine's friends that the
King had duped him, and that Arthur's marriage was bad and
Henry's good. Wolsey on his return would have discovered
the secret meeting and treated him as his enemy, saying he was

[1] *Athenæ*, i.
[2] R. B. Merriman, *Life and Letters of Thomas Cromwell*, i. 378.

disloyally opposing the King. Wolsey and Norfolk's sitting in
trial on him would have prevented any further chance of his
becoming Wolsey's successor. Wolsey's power lasted for a
short time longer, and he fell when he could not get what
Henry wanted from Rome. More succeeded Wolsey, and
Gardiner was secretary ; neither of them at all the kind of
minister Henry needed for his new plans, and Pace was of
unsound mind. If Pace's health had been good in 1527 all
might have been different, but these new troubles made him
worse. In October 1529, when Wolsey fell, many hoped to
see him chancellor. The failure of the old counsellors to go
further in the King's policy and Pace's incapacity brought up
such fellows as Cromwell and Cranmer.

Mendoça did not know much about Pace and described him
to the emperor, who knew him well. He knew him as the Dean
' of London,' and thought he had been in Rome when he fell
out with the cardinal. As he was out of any office most people
at the moment knew him as the Dean of St. Paul's, and they
were greatly aggrieved at his arrest, saying openly—according
to de Mendoça—that he had been imprisoned for speaking the
truth, which was the opinion of all impartial persons. Wolsey
spoke to de Mendoça about Pace in what the Spaniard described
as most abusive terms, and said he should never quit the Tower.
Pace's writings were examined, but nothing incriminating
was found, except, perhaps, one which he had written on the
irregularities of the pope and cardinals—perhaps de Mendoça
meant his book on dispensations. To the imperial ambassadors
any Englishman who became Catherine's partisan was a hero,
and too much reliance must not be placed on what de Mendoça
reported to his emperor about the quarrel between the cardinal
and Pace ; but it goes to show the rumour was that Pace was
offering resistance to Wolsey in two important affairs. People
said that he was proclaiming that Henry and Catherine were
well married, and that he had found fault with the pope and
cardinals. Most Englishmen were saying either that pope
and cardinals did nothing wrong or else that they did nothing
right, and here was Richard Pace speaking impartially. He
could say that all was not perfect at Rome, but that in this

matter, of marrying Henry to his brother's wife, Rome had done perfectly. Perhaps his mental condition prevented due attention to caution, but it probably saved him from the scaffold.

Erasmus wrote to him 20th February 1528, congratulating him on having been rescued from the troublesome waves of diplomacy and restored to his country, and the cultivation of the Muses, and on his studying Hebrew.[1] But he had left the frying-pan for the fire. Erasmus was in correspondence with Pace's companions in Italy and England, and he was always anxious for news of him ; but he may not have known the origin of his fall out with the cardinal—very likely Pace did not know it himself. In this respect there is a very important letter written by Erasmus to John Lasky on 27th August 1528, that is to say ten months after his arrest. He speaks of the illness of John Antoninus the physician and then :

' Richard Pace when he was on an embassy in Italy . . . became a prey to sleeplessness, which was followed by dotage (*deliratio*). The physicians found they could do nothing for him and so he was taken home to England, where he became his old self. But something worse was to follow. He wrote I don't know with how much indiscretion to the cardinal, which greatly delighted many courtiers when it was known. Pace has been thrown into prison, not that the king was very angry, but I hope by now he is at liberty.'[2] Brewer thought Wolsey never put Pace in the Tower, or in Sion, or anywhere save for care during his illness with the Bishop of Bangor.[3] The Tower was the prison for those charged with high treason and similar state offences.

There is doubt about the year of an important letter written to Wolsey by Thomas Skevington, Bishop of Bangor.[4] The month is certain enough—November ; and Brewer put it in 1528.[5] The letter refers to Wolsey's translation to the bishopric of Winchester and to the death of Sir William Compton, both of which occurred in 1528. It shows

[1] *L. and P.*, iv. 3944.   [2] Allen, *Opus Epist.*, vii. 455.
[3] J. S. Brewer, *Reign of Henry VIII*, ii. 388, footnote.
[4] Ellis, *Letters*, Series III, ii. 151.   [5] *L. and P.*, iv. 4927.

that Wolsey had entrusted Pace to the care of the bishop, who was also abbot of Beaulieu, in Hampshire ; so it looks as if he was not in the Tower for long, and that a great part of the first year of his detention was passed with the abbot, and that he was insane during the greater part of it.   This letter is not likely to have been written in November 1529, for then Wolsey was not worth writing to.   The letter is dated from Leysurles or Leisure-less, which may have been part of the abbey, and the abbot complains of ' so unaccustomed a charge ' as that put on him by the care of Pace.   ' Albeit for his comfort I have caused sundry persons, as physicians and others to see him, of whom some have promised to cure and help him, taking to that entent of me large money.'   But Pace was getting no better, and the abbot thought he was incurable ; or else that there was great default or lack of cunning in the physicians and others.   He gives a sad picture of Pace : ' for in his rage and distemperance, renting and tearing his clothes, no man can rule him, neither will keep him or serve him, like as this bringer can show unto your grace.   And he wastefully hath consumed and doth, such poor stuff as he occupieth and useth of mine.'   The abbot asked for fresh stuff and goods of Pace's own, to be sent by the ' bringer ' of his letter, a young man of the Inner Temple, who had been acting as Pace's keeper, and was a poor kinsman of the abbot's.   The abbot asked that as his reward the young man might continue as steward of the lands of the late Sir William Compton, in Hampshire, for the children were Wolsey's wards. This abbot was born with the name of Pace, and was now sheltering Richard, rather unwillingly, on the Southampton Water, and had set his young relation to nurse him.   It is pretty certain the abbot was related to Pace, and that Pace was related to the young templar.[1]   A Thomas Pace was steward to the lands of Sir William Compton in 1528.[2]   When the abbey of Beaulieu was dissolved a few years afterwards the manor of Holbury, which had been in the possession of the abbot, passed to a Thomas Pace, who was steward to Peter Compton, son of the Sir William here mentioned.   So the young templar was either Thomas Pace, or was succeeded by him in

[1] P. 3.   [2] L. and P., iv. 4442 (5), and Addenda, i. 614.

his stewardship. Pace went, or was sent, to the Southampton Water to be among relations, perhaps to be at his
birthplace.

Many things had happened since Pace was at Sion. His
old friend Cardinal Campeggio had come back to form with Wolsey
a court to hear the divorce case. Then the trial of the queen
was revoked to Rome, Wolsey fell, More, Pace's friend, became
chancellor, and the days of Parliament returned. On the 25th
October 1529 Chapuys, who had succeeded de Mendoça as
Spanish or imperial ambassador, reported to Charles on Wolsey's
fall and the appointment of Sir Thomas More to the chancellorship. He thought More ready to serve Catherine, and he referred to Mr. Richard Pace 'a good servant of your majesty,'
whom the cardinal had kept for the two last years in prison in the
Tower of London, or in a monastery. Pace had already been set
at liberty (Wolsey had given up the seals on 18th October)
and recalled to court, and it was thought—so wrote Chapuys—
that, unless his mind again became unsettled, he would rise into
greater favour and credit than ever, which would be a considerable advantage to Charles.[1]

Du Bellay thought the cardinal had trusted too much to
some of the men he had made, and that some of them had
betrayed him. He had made Pace, Gardiner, More, Brian Tuke,
Peter Vannes. Betray—as Mr. Bernard Shaw has pointed out—
is a word that may have different significations. Thomas
Cromwell would have regarded Pace as a traitor. But even if
he had been in good health there was then such general reluctance to be ruled by an ecclesiastic that he would hardly have
been appointed to a high office. Parliament said so much
against pluralities, non-resident clergy, the employment of
clergy in state affairs, that Henry could hardly have put him
into his old position even if he had sided against the queen.
More, the new chancellor, was known to side with her.
About the time Pace was set at liberty Pole, Lupset, and
many others left England in hopes of avoiding the divorce
controversy.

In 1529 Richard Pace, as Dean of St. Paul's, was summoned

[1] *L. and P.*, iv. 6026 ; *Cal. Span. St. Paps.*, iv. 304.

to Convocation of the Province of Canterbury. On 22nd March 1530 Erasmus wrote to him, expressing his pleasure at getting a letter written by him, and at hearing that he was restored to his old dignity after such great calamities ; he perceived the Deity was not asleep who rescues the innocent and casts down the proud (Wolsey). He sent good wishes to a Robert Feld, merely because he was dear to Pace.[1] But Pace was not as completely restored to usefulness as Erasmus had been informed. On re-entering the world he found the new and unpopular friendship between France and England at an end, through the Treaty of Cambrai between Charles and Francis. England's old enemy had become the ally of England's future enemy. Stephen Gardiner had been in Rome on the business of the divorce, and had come home to become Pace's successor as secretary, following Knight in June 1529, to be succeeded in turn by Thomas Cromwell. Foxe wrongly thought Gardiner was employed in Rome because Pace either would not or could not get Wolsey made pope.[2] Pace is usually thought to have retired to Stepney, though he was no longer vicar ; and at times he recovered his wits and would go back to his books for a while ' and reason and talk handsomely.' [3] His disease was, at all events for a time, not mere feebleness of mind but complete loss of reason.[4] Perhaps his servant, Thomas Clerke, was with him still, for he wrote to Cromwell as long afterwards as 1539, after Pace's death, making claims to rewards including service done in Switzerland, Rome, and other places with ' his old Master,' in the King's affairs. Perhaps Pace had a young relation or two to live with him.[5] There are references during these years to him as Dean of St. Paul's, and of Salisbury. In Thomas Cromwell's ' remembrances ' of 1534 is a reference to ' plate belonging to Mr. Pace,' as if it had passed to the King, or to the royal custody.[6] In February 1536 Cromwell made a decree, re-appointing Richard Sampson coadjutor to Richard

---

[1] *L. and P.*, iv. 6283.   [2] *Acts and Mon.*, iv. 599.
[3] Foxe, *Acts and Mon.*, iv. 599.
[4] H. Wharton, *Historia de Episcopis et Decanis Londinensibus*, etc., p. 239.
[5] See p. 4.   [6] *L. and P.*, vii. 923.

' Pacey,' Dean of St. Paul's, whose mental imbecility for many years past had interfered with the due government of the cathedral, as found by the visitors. On 8th May 1536, Peter Vannes, by then canon and prebendary of Salisbury, who had been the King's Latin secretary and an old colleague of Pace's in the government, was confirmed in his admission as coadjutor of Richard ' Pacey,' Dean of Salisbury, on account of the said dean's bodily and mental infirmities. The said Peter was to have full administration of the affairs of the deanery, except an annual ' prestation ' of £50 for the support of the said Richard.[1]

Finally, the 20th July 1536 is the date of a dispensation granted by Cranmer to Richard Sampson to hold the deanery of St. Paul's *in commendam, ' obeunte nunc Ricardo Paceo, nuper illius ecclesiae decano.'* [2] The Chapter elected Sampson, and reported that the vacancy had been caused by the natural death of Pace on 28th June.[3]

It was stated incorrectly that he died in 1532. His epitaph said so, and that he was then aged forty, which would have placed him at Padua University when he was only eight or nine. George Lily said he died ' paulo post Lupsetum,' who died at the end of 1530. If he had not entirely recovered his reason he may not have heard of the cruel deaths of Fisher and More. Margaret of Austria and Wolsey died in 1530, Warham in 1532, Peter Gilles in 1533, Clement and the Nun of Kent in 1534. Fisher, More, and a batch of Carthusian martyrs were executed in 1535 ; Queen Catherine, Anne Boleyn, and Erasmus died in the same year as Pace. The pope had become the emperor's tool, Cranmer had become Archbishop of Canterbury, Stokesley had become Bishop of London. Anne Boleyn had won and lost ; Princess Elizabeth had been born ; More had gone up and gone down; England had broken with Rome; the Pilgrims of the North, with their badges of the Wounds of Christ, were soon marching on London, hoping to overthrow Cromwell and restore the old order of things.

Pace was buried in the church of St. Dunstan, Stepney,

---

[1] *L. and P.*, x. 1015. [2] *Ibid.* xi. 125.
[3] Stokesley's Register, 1536, folio 98.

near the great altar [1]—Stowe says at the south side of the
chancel.   There was at first a monument and an epitaph ' in
tolerable good Latin verse ' which Weever gives :

> ' Richardus jacet hic venerabilis ille Decanus
> Qui fuit etatis doctus Apollo sue ;
> Eloquio, forma, ingenio, virtutibus, arte,
> Nobilis, eternum vivere dignus erat.
> Consilio bonus, ingenio fuit utilis acri,
> Facunda eloquii dexteritate potens.
> Non rigidus, non ore minax, affabilis omni
> Tempore ; seu puero, seu loquerere seni.
> Nulli unquam nocuit, multos adjuvit et omnes
> Officii studuit demeruisse bonos.
> Tantus hic et talis, ne non deleatur ademptus
> Flent Muse et laceris mesta Minerva comis.'

[1] Daniel Lysons, *The Environs of London* (1795), iii. 432.

INDEX

19

Clerk, John, in service of Cardinal
  Bainbridge, 9, 20, 51, 55, 56,
  61
Clerke, Thomas, 182, 188, 286
Clermont, 223
Cleves, 147
Clifton, John, 176
Coblenz, 151
Cochlaeus, 163
Colet, John, Dean of St. Paul's,
  47, 113, 116, 118, 137, 160–61,
  177
Cologne, 148, 154
Cologne, Cardinal-Archbishop of,
  143, 147–53
Colonna, Cardinal, 220–21
Colonna, Prosper, 54, 191, 213, 216
Commines, Philippe de, 255
Como, 250
Compton, Peter, 3, 284
Compton, Sir William, 3, 283, 284
Concordia, 27
Conegliano, 262
Constance, 74, 81–5, 105, 107, 110–
  113
Contarini, Gasparo, 8, 181, 192, 251
Cooper, Athenae Cantabrigienses, 4
Corchiero, Juanin, 279
Cordova, Gonsalvo de, 33
Cornaro, Giorgio, 205–6, 210, 212
Cornish, William, choirmaster,
  128–9
Cottian Alps, 248
Cotton, Thomas, 79, 87, 176, 188
Cranmer, Thomas, 275, 282, 287
Crema, 194
Cremona, 88, 216, 248, 250
Cromwell, Thomas, 1, 169, 273, 281,
  282, 285, 287
Croy, Adrian de, Seigneur de
  Beaurain, 227–45
Croy, Guillaume de, Seigneur de
  Chièvres, 166
Croy, de, Cardinal of Toledo, 166
Crucius, John, of Bergen-op-Zoom,
  276
Crusades, 125, 131–3, 192, 211
Crutched Friars, 123, 129

D

Darcy, Lady, 267
Darcy, Lord, 267
Dauphin. See Francis, Duke of
  Angoulême.
Da Vinci, Leonardo, 128
Devonshire, Earl of, 168
19*

Diest, 154
Dijon, 49, 74, 75, 82
Donatello, 7
Donato, Francesco, Captain of
  Padua, 194–5, 264
Doria, Andrea, 237
Dorset, Marquis of, 159, 166, 167
Dover, 165–6
Dowager Queen of France. See Mary
  Tudor
Draguignan, 238, 240, 241
Dudley, Edmund, 3
Durance, valley of the, 248
Düsseldorf, 147–8

E

Easthampstead, 121
Elizabeth, Queen, 79, 287
Elyot, Sir Thomas, 169
  The Gouernour, 169
Elys, Mr., 279
Enfield, 127
Ennius, Bishop of Veroli, 76, 209,
  225
Erasmus, 1, 2, 8, 10–13, 18, 20, 22,
  31, 41, 47, 69, 100, 107, 111,
  113, 115–20, 147, 154–5, 159–
  164, 167, 173, 175–6, 188, 263,
  267, 283, 286, 287
  Adages, 10, 11, 12, 119
  Antibarbari, 10, 12, 18, 115, 119,
  175
  Epistle to the Corinthians, Para-
  phrase of, 176
Esher, 121
Este, Alfonso d', third Duke of
  Ferrara, 12–14, 29, 33, 39, 73,
  128, 182, 191–4, 208–15, 219,
  254
Este, Beatrice d', 13
Este, Federico d', 23
Este, Hippolito d', Cardinal, 12, 13
Este, Isabella d', 13, 23, 27, 128,
  210
Este, Leonora d', Duchess of
  Urbino, 23, 262

F

Farnese, Cardinal, 220
Farnham, 121
Fayence, 240, 241
Feld, Robert, 286
Ferdinand, Archduke of Austria,
  203, 209–15, 217, 225, 252,
  253